EFFECTIVE PARENTING

PARENTING

FOR THE

HARD-TO-MANAGE

CHILD

EFFECTIVE PARENTING
FOR THE
HARD-TO-MANAGE
CHILD

A SKILLS-BASED BOOK

GEORGIA A. DEGANGI **AND** ANNE KENDALL

Routledge
Taylor & Francis Group
New York   London

Routledge
Taylor & Francis Group
270 Madison Avenue
New York, NY 10016

Routledge
Taylor & Francis Group
2 Park Square
Milton Park, Abingdon
Oxon OX14 4RN

© 2008 by Taylor & Francis Group, LLC
Routledge is an imprint of Taylor & Francis Group, an Informa business

Printed in the United States of America on acid-free paper
10 9 8 7 6 5 4 3 2

International Standard Book Number-13: 978-0-415-95546-1 (Softcover)

Library of Congress Cataloging-in-Publication Data

DeGangi, Georgia A.
   Effective parenting for the hard-to-manage child : a skills-based book / Georgia A. DeGangi and Anne Kendall ; illustrated by Ziza Craig.
      p. cm.
   Includes bibliographical references.
   ISBN 0-415-95542-4
   1. Problem children. 2. Child psychology. 3. Behavior disorders in children. 4. Child rearing. 5. Parenting. I. Kendall, Anne. II. Title.

HQ773.D43 2007
649'.154--dc22
                                              2007019089

Visit the Taylor & Francis Web site at
http://www.taylorandfrancis.com

and the Routledge Web site at
http://www.routledge.com

Contents

Acknowledgments

Many people have helped us in the writing of this book. First and foremost, we would like to thank the many children and families that we have worked with over the years. They have been our best teachers in discovering the most effective ways to help hard-to-manage children. Without them, this book would not have been possible.

Several superb mentors have been instrumental in helping us to discover new ways of working with and understanding young children. Dr. DeGangi was guided by Dr. Stanley Greenspan, child psychiatrist, who helped her in integrating sensorimotor, emotional, and developmental frame works into a holistic model of working with young children. Dr. Stephen Porges, developmental psychologist, collaborated with her in researching disorders of self-regulation in children and taught her the importance of linking theories and research with clinical approaches. Both Drs. Greenspan and Porges helped her to understand the profound effect that constitutional problems have on the child's developmental course and the parent-child relationship. Dr. DeGangi is indebted to Dr. Polly Craft who offered her the gift of discovering the special meaning that each child and parent have for one another. She was so fortunate to have worked with her in learning parent-infant psychotherapy. This book is dedicated to her memory. The work that is represented in this book is heavily influenced by the wonderful experiences she has had with these mentors. Dr. Kendall would like to acknowledge the insight, intellect, and support provided by Dr. Anne Wake during our 20-year collaboration. In addition, she would like to thank Marsha Linehan for her trail-blazing work in developing skills for helping individuals who have profound emotional dysregulation.

We have had the good fortune of working in a variety of settings that have allowed us to blossom as professionals. We would like to thank our colleagues at ITS for Children and Families, Inc. in Kensington, MD, the Kendall-Wake-Springer Group in Washington, D.C., and the Reginald S. Lourie Center for Infants and Children in Rockville, MD. They provided us with wonderful experiences that allowed us to blend knowledge of occupational therapy with clinical and developmental psychology and to blend different therapeutic perspectives including cognitive-behavioral therapy with psychodynamic approaches, exposure therapy and the power of mindfulness. It was at the Lourie Center that Dr. DeGangi learned the importance of fostering emotional health and development through the parent-child relationship and the value of early intervention and prevention in treating multi-problem families. In our current work, we are both very fortunate to be working with a sterling team of professionals at ITS for Children and Families, Inc. in Kensington, MD and the Wake-Kendall-Spring Group with whom we continue to collaborate on finding better ways to serve children and their families.

We are very grateful to T. Berry Brazelton, M.D., whose work we have greatly admired over the years. He very graciously agreed to endorse our book. Many thanks to Eliza Noyes Craig for the beautifully drawn illustrations in this book. We would also like to thank Antoine and Emily van Agtmael for their careful reading of this book from the point of view of concerned parents.

The case vignettes and examples that are described in this book are based on real clinical examples. The names and pertinent identifying information of children and their families have been disguised to protect their identities.

Last, but not least, Dr. DeGangi wishes to thank her loving husband, Robert Dickey, who endured many hours of listening to her as she formulated ideas for this book. She is so grateful for his unconditional support and encouragement for her professional endeavors. Dr. Kendall would like to thank the fabulously fit, erudite, and cute David Kendall for his thoughtful reading of this book as well as his ongoing humor and support. Her greatest happiness and pride comes from being the mother of her three children Mat, Elizabeth and Will. She wants to reassure them that they are not included in this book.

How to Use This Book

Who Should Read This Book?

We have written this book for **parents** of hard-to-manage children, and for the **teachers** and **therapists** who work with these families.

Do Parents Need Help?

The children described in this book are difficult for anyone to parent because they can be so intense and often uncooperative. This book will help you understand your child so that you can be caring and effective. Chapter 11, The Perils of Parenting, will give you an overall strategy for maintaining a close connection with your child and remind you that you only need to be a "**good enough**" parent.

Who Are the Hard-to-Manage Children?

The hard-to-manage children described in this book are all unique. However, they share in having an immature nervous system that responds to even minimal stress in an intensely reactive manner. This, in turn, makes these children vulnerable to a host of emotional, social, and learning problems. The children in this book struggle for self-control and find it hard to do what their parents and teachers ask. However, help is on the way! Our chapters describe different challenges that these children face and provide the tools you need to help them. **Do any of these behaviors describe your child?**

- Chapter 1: The Intense, Irritable Child
- Chapter 2: Coping with Different Kinds of Anxiety
- Chapter 3: Mealtime Battles, Picky Eaters and Kids Who Just Won't Eat
- Chapter 4: Up All Night, Crying and Fretful
- Chapter 5: The Dark Secret: The Mysteries of Obsessive Compulsive Disorder
- Chapter 6: He Won't Listen and Can't Finish a Thing: How to Help Your Child with ADHD
- Chapter 7: The Oppositional Child: You Are **Not** the Boss of Me!
- Chapter 8: Children with Sensory Overload
- Chapter 9: The Curious, Clueless, and Disorganized Child
- Chapter 10: Depression: Trying to Halt a Downward Slide

Why Do I Need a Tool Box with 25 Tools to Manage my Child?

Few people are trained for the most important job in life, raising a child. This job is made even more difficult when your child has a nervous system that suddenly gets him overexcited so he can't calm down, or that shuts down when faced with the smallest frustration. Here is a set of tools that have been shown to be effective in child rearing. You are probably doing some of these things already. **We want to expand your skills.** We have organized our tools into five categories and refer to them throughout the book with five visual icons. You will find this Toolbox at the back of the book.

Tools for Teaching Children to Calm Themselves Down

1. Self Soothing
2. Activities for Problems of Touch
3. Guidelines for Helping Children Move with Ease and Comfort
4. Teaching Your Child to be More Coordinated
5. Learning to Pay Attention
6. Distraction
7. Positive Self-Talk
8. Mindfulness: Stilling the Mind
9. Systematic Relaxation: Stilling the Body

Tools for Building Self-Esteem

10. Validation
11. Child-Centered Time
12. Having Fun

Tools for Managing Out-of-Control Behavior

13. Changing Behavior: Positive Reinforcement, Ignoring, Modeling, Shaping
14. Teaching Consequences and Repair
15. Observing Limits
16. Time Out
17. A Token Economy

Tools for Providing Structure

18. Food Rules
19. Being Content Alone
20. Managing Your Child at Night
21. Feeling Less Anxious at Nighttime
22. Providing Structure to the Day

Tools for Improving Interpersonal Skills

23. The Ice-Cream Sandwich
24. Having GREAT FUN Communicating
25. Teaching Responsibility and Cooperation

> **Tips:** are sprinkled throughout the book to provide useful information that parents should know.

Dip into this book and enjoy it.

If you learn **just one new technique** to help your child, writing this book will have been worthwhile!

1

The Intense, Irritable Child

Sam: A Fussy and Irritable Child

"I can't stand our child's crying another minute! Sam cries all the time and only stops when he eats. This has been going on since he was born. He's the baby from hell! My husband told me that if I didn't fix his crying, he was leaving home. I can't think of anything else that I can do to make him stop and nothing works for very long. We have tried car rides, swings, soft music, rocking in a chair, and entertaining him with new toys. He still cries no matter what I do. I can't even touch and hold him to comfort him because it seems that sets him off even more. You can't imagine what that does to me that I can't even hold my own child when he cries. We can't find any babysitters to take care of him because he is so irritable. I worry that someone else might abuse him because they wouldn't love him like I do. I feel like I'm a bad mom and I'm getting more and more depressed as the days go by. I'm exhausted and at my wit's end!"

These words, spoken by a parent with an irritable child, are depictive of the tremendous impact that a fussy and unregulated child can have on the child's development, the parent-child relationship, and family life. Parents become frantic in their attempts to console their child. When nothing works, parents often feel ineffective. They may worry why their child appears unhappy most of the time. For the child, it is an unsettling experience to be chronically unregulated when things like transitions to a new activity, getting dressed, or being bathed trigger a tantrum. Usually such children learn to depend on their parents to soothe them because they lack strategies for self-calming. And because they are irritable most of the time, they may not experience pleasurable interactions with others.

There are many reasons a child is irritable or has problems regulating his or her mood. It is helpful for parents to understand what might be setting off the irritability, as well as learn ways to help their child learn to stay calm when frustrated or distressed. Sam began his life as a very fussy baby. Throughout this chapter, we will revisit Sam's story and how his irritability played out over time. We will use Sam as our example to depict how irritability can impact the child's and family's life. In addition, we present concrete suggestions to help parents solve common problems related to mood regulation and high irritability.

Reasons Children Are Irritable

There are a number of reasons children are irritable. Sometimes there are medical problems like chronic ear infections, reflux, severe allergies, or urinary tract infections that may make your child uncomfortable and experience pain. A common problem frequently overlooked is milk intolerance. Children who rely on a diet heavy in gluten (wheat products) or sugar products can become crabby or have mood swings. Sam was a child who was an extremely picky eater. He ate only three foods for most of his life despite efforts to expand his food repertoire. He had an aversion to most food textures and resorted to eating only chicken, macaroni and cheese, and popcorn. Sometimes he went for long periods without eating, then became highly irritable. This was not the only cause of his irritability but was certainly a contributing factor.

Some children are born fussy and have a **difficult temperament.** Sam's mother described her baby as coming out crying from the moment he was born. Children with a difficult temperament are usually more intense, have a hard time tolerating change, and distress easily. It may be hard for them to sustain a happy, content mood for very long. These children tend to be less flexible or adaptable when changes are introduced. As a result, they often jockey for control of the situation, wishing that things be done exactly how they want them to be. Sam was this way. It was his way or the highway. Even with peers, he needed to control the situation, telling them that they had to play his way or not at all.

Perhaps the most common reason that children are irritable is because they become easily overstimulated in response to sensory stimulation. Basic experiences like face washing, dressing, noise on the playground, or a busy household can load their nervous system and create an internal state that can be overwhelming to the child. Sam was a hypersensitive child. If he got hurt, he overreacted strongly, screaming at his parents not to touch him. He showed signs of **tactile defensiveness,** such as hating haircuts, avoiding new food textures, and preferring long-sleeved garments and pants even in warm weather. When in a group of children, Sam tended to withdraw. He often over-reacted when someone might accidentally bump into him, a natural occurrence in a classroom environment. It became clear over time that Sam's nervous system would overload quickly with sensory input. When his threshold had been reached, a meltdown would occur.

An inflexible child is often an irritable child. Children who have problems with organization and planning often fall apart when they are required to come up with a new way of doing things. In addition to getting overstimulated easily, these irritable children often get dysregulated when they have to organize themselves to perform a complex task. This problem is commonly associated with attention deficit disorder, executive functioning problems, as well as motor planning issues.

Finally, it is important to determine whether your child has a **mood regulation** problem that makes it difficult for him to sustain a happy, content mood. Many parents worry about what this could mean for their child as he grows older. It is very difficult to diagnose a **mood disorder** in very young children, but irritability is a factor in many disorders such as anxiety, depression, ADHD, and oppositional defiant disorder. As your child grows older, you may notice other things that tip you off that there is an underlying mood problem that goes beyond a fussy, irritable temperament. When the mood problems are unresponsive to typical interventions like those provided in this book, a consultation with a developmental or behavioral pediatrician, a child psychologist or a child psychiatrist is important. They will help you to more fully understand your child's diagnosis and the proper course of treatment. However, an important principle for parents to keep in mind is that what the child needs most is to learn how to self-calm on his or her own and to tolerate distress and frustrations. This is a major focus of the strategies provided in this chapter.

Now and then a child will become irritable because of a lack of sufficient organization or structure in the environment or parenting. For example, suppose you are a person who does not like to set limits and you allow your child lots of latitude to do things when and where he or she pleases. This can lead to a child feeling overwhelmed when confronted with limits and structure, a sure thing that will occur once he goes to school. Inconsistent parenting can unravel a child. Suppose you and your partner have very different styles of setting limits and establishing daily routines. Your child may not know what plan is the one that he or she should follow or he might react by pitting one grown-up against the other. A chaotic or disorganized home setting can cause a child to become irritable as well. The child may feel that there is no good place to play, to be calm and quiet, or to engage in organized activities like homework.

What Makes Your Child Irritable?

Table 1.1 shows a summary of some of the things that contribute to irritability in children.

It is important not to overlook the impact that the parents' moods have on a child. It is not unusual for children with mood problems to have parents who also struggle with their mood.

Table 1.1 Common problems that contribute to irritability

Can't fall and stay asleep	Overstimulated by sensory stimulation	Mood highly irritable; distresses easily	Allergies, medical problems	Reflux, eating problems
Poor organization skills	Overwhelmed by limits and change	Inflexibility, can't adapt	Home life disorganized or chaotic	Parent angry, depressed or irritable

Often there is a genetic component. You may have a grandparent who had a diagnosis of bipolar disorder, an uncle with depression, or you yourself have struggled with anxiety or depression your whole life. If this is the case, it becomes even more important to consult with a mental health professional to understand if your child may have a mood disorder that makes him irritable. When children are exposed to a parent who is angry, upset, irritable, or depressed most of the time, they learn to respond to these strong emotions. Even if your child doesn't have a mood disorder, he can learn that this is how one behaves. The important thing is for parents to take good care of themselves and find ways to self-calm, feel organized, and be available for the difficult task of parenting.

What Happens to the Parent-Child Relationship When the Child Is Irritable?

> **Tip:** Remember—a difficult temperament doesn't mean that your child will remain unhappy and crabby his entire life. However, it is important for your child to learn how to regulate his irritability and find ways to self-calm when faced with frustrations, stress, or overwhelming events.

If you are around a fussy, irritable child for even a few minutes, you will notice a change in how you interact with this child. If your child is chronically fussy, there are changes in how the parents and child interact. The patterns can become well established over time. Here are some of the things that can happen.

Sometimes parents find that they are constantly walking on eggshells around their irritable child. They may be afraid to set a limit or impose a change of activity because they know their child is likely to fall apart and tantrum for hours. Some parents constantly structure every minute of the child's day to keep them organized. Something to pay attention to is whether you may do too many things to keep your child calm and organized. The trap is a tendency to overstimulate your child by talking too much to him or giving him one activity after the next in an attempt to guide or distract him. This can backfire and cause the child to become flooded with too much stimulation. We have found that most irritable children do better with the mantra, "Less is better!"

When children are irritable and have sensory issues that compound the problem, parents may find that they don't touch or move their child very much because it makes things worse. As a result, they may become more

comfortable talking to their child instead of using gestures or sensory experiences to organize them.

> **Tip:** Introduce one strategy at a time. Wait long enough for your child to process and respond to it before trying something else.

At school the smallest transition or change in routine might set Sam off. His typical response was to hit and kick whoever was in close range, throw books, upturn desks and destroy books and papers that were in immediate reach. All the while, Sam would scream, shout profanities, name call, clench his fists tightly, and turn beet red as his anger mounted. Sometimes when he fell apart, his response was to bolt from the room. He could be found hiding under the bleachers in the gymnasium. His mother lived in dread of these episodes, feeling that her entire life was on hold, awaiting her son's next meltdown. She often felt desperate, wondering what would help her son. Sometimes she felt completely depleted and unable to face another day when her son would unravel.

One can only imagine what Sam's school failure did to him and his family. At school he became known as violent and a "cry baby." Sam lamented that no one liked him. The other children steered clear of him, fearful of him. At home his younger brother and sister walked on eggshells around Sam, just as his parents did. Sam was quite aware that his chronic meltdowns were highly unsettling for himself and his family, but he also learned how much power he held. The whole family revolved their life around Sam's moods.

> **Tip:** As your child learns how to self-calm, direct him to use his self-calming strategies rather than doing it for him.

In our studies of children with regulatory problems, we found that irritable children communicate primarily through distress signals. They may kick, scream, bite, push, and yell to let you know how they feel. There may be very little calm discussion about things, or happy, content activity that fills their time. This chaos and intensity causes the parent-child interaction to go off the rails and the focus becomes negative rather than positive. Sometimes parents withdraw or disengage to avoid a negative interaction with their child. They may also let their child play alone when they are happy and content and miss the best time to interact with them.

How Does a Child Become Calm and Well-Regulated?

Every child has to learn how to become self-sufficient in handling his or her own distress. Initially the parents calm the child. As they read their child's cues and see what works, they come up with a set of soothing strategies that work for their child. The child begins to internalize these strategies and gradually takes over the task of self-calming. It is a key factor in how emotions become modulated. The process of becoming a well-regulated person depends on certain skills. The child also needs models in the environment for how to become a good self-calmer. Here are some of the tricks that help a child become well-regulated.

1. When babies cry and become inconsolable, it helps them to have a **responsive, caring, and sensitive parent** who helps them calm down. This gives the child the message that their basic needs can be met and that there are ways to handle distress. This step requires that the parent know how to read their child's signals and gestures, as well as have a host of calming strategies at their fingertips.

> **Tip:** Keeping a calm presence when faced with frustrations and distress will teach your child how to self-regulate.

2. As the child matures, he learns to *internalize strategies to self-calm.* Consistent use of good calming strategies helps the child learn which ones to call upon in different situations. The child also observes others solve similar problems and learns when and where to use which strategies.

One of the problems that Sam had was that he had a very limited repertoire of self-calming strategies. To help him stay calm in his early years, his parents relied heavily on the pacifier to calm him. When he reached four years of age, they convinced him that he should give up his pacifier because of its effect on his teeth. At the time, Sam was only using the pacifier at night to fall asleep. Because he had no other calming devices in place, Sam had extreme difficulty controlling his mood and became easily angry. He would often lash out verbally towards his parents, calling them names or being bossy..He wanted to be in control and to be the center of attention.

This example depicts the importance of finding calming devices that the child can use in several settings. It is important for parents to guide their child on three levels:

1. Things that the child can do for him- or herself to organize and calm when distressed.
2. Things that parents and teachers can do to focus the child when he is overwhelmed.
3. Things that can be done in the environment to support a calm and organized child.

Calming strategies and environmental modifications are most useful when one anticipates what could go wrong and have things in place for that moment when the child needs them. This leads to the importance of teaching the child to understand the precursors of irritability, to anticipate the onset of frustration and distress, and to utilize appropriate strategies that are available.

Self-calming depends on the ability to problem solve before, during, and after a distressing event. The child gradually learns a variety of ways to help himself organize and monitor his own actions and to tolerate various negative emotions. To help your child become a thinking child, it is useful to help your child step out of his emotions that he experiences and be thoughtful about the sequence of events that occurred. You can make this fun by having a "strategy session" at a nearby diner where you figure out a more effective strategy while you eat a banana split. Often the unregulated child needs time to figure out a better way of dealing with frustration. At your "strategy session" you might discuss alternatives, such as distracting himself from the distressing event. Appendix 2, Tool Sheet 6, Distraction, provides ideas for self-calming with body techniques such as squeezing a stress ball. **Tool Sheet 1, Self-Soothing,** provides other ideas.

Many parents lament, "I've told him a thousand times that when he falls apart, he needs to go to his bedroom and calm down, but he never does it. If I pick him up and put him there, he screams even more." The problem is that once the child reaches a distressed state, he may shut off his thinking brain and cannot enact the strategy that his parents are trying to teach him. For this reason, it is important to break the strategy down into steps so that the child learns a successful approximation of what may work. For example, instead of expecting the child to go directly to the bedroom, the parent may guide the child to go to a corner of the room and hug his body tightly while humming a calm-down song. The idea is to teach your child how to stop and think in the moment, then gradually move towards anticipating what could go wrong, remembering the strategy, and using it. It isn't until children have the capacity to remember past events and reflect on what has happened that they are able to internalize and recruit strategies that might work. This is when the child develops insight into his behavior.

Before Distress Happens	During the Tantrum	After the Blow-Up
Anticipate what may unravel your child. Think it through ahead of time. Make a plan!	Have soothing devices available and strategies at your fingertips for ready access.	Review how your child did—his successes at self-calming and what he should do next time it happens.

Self-calming requires the child to decrease the state of arousal he experiences related to distress. An adaptable child learns to recognize the internal state of distress and hyperarousal, then finds ways to inhibit the arousal through strategies such as closing his eyes. For example, an infant may avert his head when having his face washed instead of crying. A toddler may hold his hands together or put them in his pockets when told not to touch a fragile object, thus inhibiting himself in an adaptable way. An adult struggling to master a very difficult task may take a break to refresh himself mentally and physically, thus avoiding an adult-sized tantrum.

Over the years Sam needed an ongoing sensory diet to keep him feeling calm and organized. For example, it was essential that he had dimly lit enclosed spaces to which he could go when overwhelmed. He liked to sleep in a pup tent covered with a heavy blanket. When upset, he liked to bury himself under heavy weighted bean bags or blankets. At other times, he needed opportunities to be outside and move. At school, he would ask for a scheduled break to go out in the hallway and walk on a balance beam or to go to the occupational therapy room to swing on the suspended swing for five minutes. He also settled himself nicely when he could go to a room and sit in a nest of pillows. He could then return to the classroom in a more focused, calm state.

> **Tip:** Evaluate when your child needs to discharge his distress, blow off steam, and show you exactly how bad he feels. Validate his feelings ("you are really upset right now") and give him safe ways to explode. Provide opportunities for safety, security, and soothing that will help him settle down.

Another important way that we regulate emotions is by setting well-thought-out goals for ourselves and following through on them. What we hold in mind helps us to evaluate our success in accomplishing our goals and it motivates our activity. Internal goals may be immediate in nature and relate to security and basic bodily needs. For example, a person who is hungry will be preoccupied with their next meal. Another internal goal may be sharing interactions with others. For example, the young child may bring a toy to his father hoping that he will play a game with him. We also have internal goals for mastery and accomplishment of skills. While learning a new skill, a person may experience frustration and anger as they make mistakes. On the other hand, a person may feel a positive emotional state, such as joy and interest, while learning a new skill, which further motivates engagement in the activity. Take the young child who is learning how to crawl or walk and practices this skill over and over again. But if there is a block or an obstacle in the way that is too difficult to overcome, such as a gate blocking entry to the stairs, the infant may become distressed and angry. After a while, if the infant cannot overcome the obstacle or an adult does not respond to the baby's expression of distress, the infant may feel defeated, sad, and eventually withdraw from the situation. Pleasure and excitement motivate persistence in tasks. Distress and frustration make us want to quit and escape.

Tip: Plan ahead! Anticipate melt-down situations. Help your child to keep focused on a self-calming goal. Rehearse ahead of time what the strategy will be. "Just walk away and get a drink of water."

Self-regulation develops through synchronized, reciprocal, and well-modulated interactions between parents and their children. A task of the young infant is to be able to tolerate the intensity of arousal they feel while interacting with their mom or dad. An infant who is flooded with too much arousal during interactions will avoid them and shut down. For a child to gain pleasure from playing or interacting with his parent, he needs to find ways to avoid becoming overstimulated. The child has to find an optimal level of internal arousal to remain engaged in the interaction. The parent acts to help regulate the child's arousal by timing her responses, laughing at the right moment, touching her child periodically, encouraging him, and other behaviors that engage her child. If the parent is too active, doing more than what the child can process, the child will respond by backing away or becoming distressed. Research has shown that when the parent and child are out-of-sync, the child learns to withdraw from the overly arousing interaction. This can lead to a pattern of disengagement, with resulting insecurity in attachments.

> **Tip:** Less is better! Reduce stimulation, stay calm, and wait long enough for the self-calming strategy to work.

How do parents find the most optimal level of stimulation when they interact with their child? If the mother provides too much or too little stimulation, the child withdraws from the interaction. The optimal level varies considerably from one child to the next and depends upon the child's threshold for arousal, tolerance for stimulation, and ability to self-control arousal. The best way to know if you're on the right track is to watch your child's response. If you are offering an optimal level of stimulation, an interchange of smiling and gazing occurs. An increase in your child's attentiveness will usually relate to you becoming less active and more attentive to what your child is doing. Pay attention to what your child is seeking and needing from you. If you are too active and directive of your child, he is likely to become less focused and attentive.

Here is a summary of the skills that children need to be a good self-calmer.

SKILLS TO BECOME AN EFFECTIVE SELF-CALMER

Provide a model of what it looks and feels like to be calm.

Validate your child's level of distress. Respond to him gently through gestures and words. "I understand how distressed you feel right now."

Show your child how to calm down in many different situations.

Expand your child's repertoire of self-calming strategies so that when one fails, another one might work.

Help your child find activities that give him pleasure so that he can shift from a distressed feeling to a positive one.

Once your child is calm, help him think through what caused his distress and what he can do to make himself feel better next time it happens.

While he is distressed, help your child to decrease agitation in the moment. Use sensory calming strategies in addition to cognitive activities.

Help your child think of what the next step might be and remain focused on accomplishing that goal.

When Is My Child's Irritability More Than Just a Bad Mood?

A person's expression of emotion is usually fairly brief, perhaps only a few minutes in length. However, the emotion itself may last longer. Sometimes people store things up for quite some time, well after the emotion has been expressed. For example, when a person becomes very angry, he may feel "angry" after having expressed his anger. The longer an emotion is experienced, the stronger the person reports the feeling of a particular emotion. When angry feelings last for a long time, perhaps an hour or more, then it becomes a mood. A mother may say, "He's been in a foul mood all day long!"

In emotional disorders, duration of the mood becomes important. The person becomes prone to being flooded by a particular emotion—depression, anger, or anxiety. **Flooding** is the phenomenon in which almost any event will elicit the emotion. Sometimes the emotion will reappear without any particular stimulus. When this happens, the emotion is intense and interferes with everyday functioning (e.g., sleep patterns, eating, work tasks, social interactions). The person will also have difficulty suppressing the emotion and may not be able to shift to more positive, productive emotions.

We can impact our moods in a variety of ways. What we eat, being sick, being fatigued, or engaging in a stimulating sensory experience can produce different mood states. For example, if a person is tired, he may be more irritable. Or a child who rides on a series of carnival rides may become hyperexcitable and happy. If a particular emotion is elicited repeatedly over the course of a short period of time, it may produce a biochemical change that causes a mood state to prevail. If a person has experienced a series of maladies in a row, he may become angry and irritable over time.

Emotions can occur before an event happens simply by the anticipation of an exciting event, such as opening a birthday present, or the emotion may be anticipatory dread or fear, such as presenting a speech in front of a large audience. Feelings also occur while an emotion is being expressed. Often we hear people express these verbally while engaged in an activity. For example, we hear children exclaim, "This is fun!" Feelings may be elicited by memories of the event. Certain words, smells, or places often evoke strong feelings of past events. Sometimes children reared in institutional settings, such as an orphanage in Russia, remember things from their very early childhood based on certain sensations or smells.

Basic Guidelines to Teach Your Child How to Become a Good Self-Regulator

Help Your Child Adjust to Demanding Situations

When faced with a challenging situation, your child's reaction will be dictated by what he already knows about similar situations and memories of past experiences. This skill depends on the ability to read cues in the environment and to think through how to react to the current situation based on past knowledge. Children with developmental challenges such as a nonverbal learning disability or children on the autistic spectrum may have a difficult time processing past and current information about a situation. Their responses may be concrete and "in the moment" rather than based on prior knowledge from past experiences and integration of feedback offered to them by others.

Sam's Response to Change: To Attack!   Here's how Sam responded in demanding situations. When he was first going to school, he would frequently became irritable when there were transitions in activities, whenever his space was invaded by other children, or when the classroom noise level became loud. He felt that he wasn't ready to move on to the next activity when the children were expected to do so. Although he was a very competent child, he had trouble adjusting to change and would become distressed when expected to do certain tasks, such as share toys with other children or clean up his toys to get ready for snack. Usually after about two hours at school, Sam would begin to show his distress by hitting or biting other children or by withdrawing to a corner of the room or climbing under a table. His responses were very unpredictable, with some good days, followed by several days with multiple incidents. Each time he bit a child, he was sent home from school. Within a month, he was being sent home so frequently that his parents chose to keep him at home to give him a break from the stress of school. As his parents tried to work out a viable solution to the problem, such as getting a classroom aide, Sam began to make comments that he never wanted to go back to school again. In the next month that it took to find an aide, we saw Sam regress. With each day that he stayed home from school, he became increasingly more agitated, refusing to change his clothes, wanting to isolate himself in his bedroom, and screaming at his parents whenever they made the simplest of requests. As we reintroduced Sam into school, we had to change his thinking about school. We worked on getting him to say encouraging comments to himself such as, "I can do this! I like to see my teachers and my friends." See our **Tool Sheet 7, Positive Self-Talk** for more tips.

Here are some things that helped Sam at school that might work for your child.

1. **Lower the demands**: We began by giving Sam a shorter school day and a shortened week of school. He also had the option to come home early if he was overwhelmed in music class.
2. **Use positive reinforcement for accomplishing tasks**. We made a chart for Sam with simple expectations that he could accomplish. Immediate reinforcement was used at first (e.g., earn use of computer if he could play friendly with a calm child during free play).
3. **Give scheduled breaks** during the day when your child can reorganize himself. What worked well for Sam was sitting in a bean bag chair and looking at books, sucking on ice pops, or building a fort that he could go inside.

4. Reinforce behaviors at both school and home so that your child gets the message of **think before reacting**. The program for Sam included things like reinforcement for playing friendly (e.g., not biting other children), making transitions (e.g., cleaning up toys when it was time for snack), and self-calming when agitated (e.g., asking for time alone in the bean bag chair).

Within a few months Sam became much more compliant both at home and school and was beginning to make more **positive self-talk,** such as "I want to go to school"; "I like doing this"; instead of "I'm a bad boy"; "I'm angry."

Help Your Child Read and Give Good Social Cues

Some children with mood regulation problems have difficulty reading and understanding facial expressions of others. They seem to become overwhelmed by emotional expressions and may turn away to avoid eye contact. They may also misconstrue the meaning of different facial expressions. For example, some parents report that no matter how clear their signals are when setting limits, their child does not listen or he reacts by laughing at them. Suppose you present a picture of two children teasing another child to a six-year-old child who has problems reading social cues. The child may misread the picture and say that it is a picture of three children playing ring around the rosey. There are also some children who have perceptual problems in recognizing different people's faces and may react as if they had never seen the person before. Some children may be overwhelmed by anxiety or overstimulated by sensory input to the point that they cannot process the conversation while also reading the person's facial and gestural cues.

To best help your child, observe what your child thinks another person is expressing to him. Provide the right amount of stimulation so that he can take in feedback without becoming overwhelmed. For example, Sam had problems reading facial cues, but he enjoyed playing dress-ups. He particularly liked playing "Superman," putting on a gold cape and silver pants. Sam liked to play out disasters such as having airplanes crash, little animals getting stuck in crevices, or babies getting lost in the woods. It seemed that he liked seeing his mother express exaggerated expressions of alarm or surprise. He liked playing Superman who would come to the rescue of his mother in the burning block house. At first Sam needed his mother to do the same script each time so that he could predict and understand what facial expressions and gestures went with which scenarios, but after a while, Sam liked it when his mother made other things happen that might be silly or novel, such as having a stuffed animal purposely set the fire just so he could ride down Superman's fireman ladder. It was important to move from more animated emotions to more subtle ones and from predictable events to ones that were less predictable. The dress-ups and fantasy play were an ideal way of helping Sam to learn how to read social cues.

Help Your Child to Predict His Own Behavior and That of Others

Social situations provide many cues that assist the individual in understanding the people, the activity, the situation, and other meanings. When a situation is novel or the person lacks experience in interpreting meanings, the individual tends to rely heavily on feedback from other people, particularly those who are important to them (i.e., peers, parents) as well as cues about a situation.

The young child is more dependent upon facial cues of individuals experiencing the event, but as children grow older through the school-aged years, they rely more on situational cues. As children mature, they are also better able to integrate both facial and situational cues.

In order for an emotional signal to capture someone's attention, it should involve as many dimensions as possible. The toddler who sees his parent frown, point with his finger, and firmly state, "No!" knows that his parent means business. In contrast, parents who have difficulty setting limits may display weak or even discrepant signals that are difficult to read and are confusing to the toddler. An ambivalent parent may smile as they say, "Now, don't throw your food, honey!" Some toddlers may be confused by this mismatch of signals. Others may know what is expected of them, but continue on with their disruptive activity suspecting that there are no consequences to their actions.

The task of learning how to read body signals was a major intervention with nine-year-old Sam. He had a short fuse and would explode, screaming at his parents and throwing things whenever he experienced the slightest bit of frustration. His tantrums would go on for several hours, which resulted in the whole family being up all hours of the night trying to console him. At other times, he would shut down, hiding under a table or sitting inside his closet for hours on end. These mood changes would come on suddenly and once in an intense mood state, Sam had considerable difficulty coming out of them. Although he was a child who was helped by medications, through therapy Sam began to be able to recognize when he could feel his mood shifting to anger, frustration, or sadness. When he felt himself becoming upset by things, he could focus on what his body was telling him, then take steps to soothe himself before his mood state progressed too far. Doing things like jumping on a trampoline, kicking a soccer ball, or playing guitar helped him to self-calm. Sam also talked with me about his "Tantrum Warning Device," a concept that we used to help him predict what situations caused him to become upset. For instance, doing homework almost always caused his warning meter to go up to a "medium sizzle." Not getting to stay up late and play Nintendo would make him get "boiling mad." The object of the warning device was to recognize when his mood was moving from mild to mild-medium or medium anger and get it back down again by calming himself.

Read Your Child's Cues: Understand What the Irritability Means

It is often difficult to read an irritable child's cues to know what set him or her off, when the child's cry or irritability is changing, and to recognize when and how the child can self-soothe. It is not uncommon for parents of irritable babies to misconstrue normal babbling sounds as whining. Or the parents may view their child as constantly irritable when in fact they are not. Here is a simple thing that parents can do to look at what is really happening. Stop and listen to your child, watch them, and see if you can tell what your child is telling you right in that moment. By taking on a "watch, wait, and wonder" stance, the parent can step back from the experience to be better able to read the child's vocal and gestural signals. It may be possible then to distinguish between frustration, poor self-consoling, and expression of negative affects (e.g., aggression, discontent).

Treatment Ideas to Help Your Child

Before embarking on a treatment program to address your child's irritability, it is useful to think about when and where crying and irritability occur, and for how long, to determine the causes of the behavior. In some cases, a crying infant or irritable child may be responding to tensions that you are feeling which may cause you to handle your child briskly or to snap at them when they ask for something. All parents have bad days, but if this is a normal course of events for you, then what is irritating to you needs to be considered. Another reason for excessive crying may be related to emotional issues such as separation anxiety. For some children, irritability may occur whenever changes are introduced in the everyday routine or activity. Once it is more apparent what might be underlying the child's irritability, treatment ideas can be tried.

> **Tip:** Anyone trying to parent an unregulated child will have difficulty. Find two or three things that work to help your child self-soothe. Keep introducing these things until he learns to do them himself. Only change the strategies when it is clear that they don't work.

It is very hard to help intensely unregulated children to calm down. Sometimes parents say that once the tantrum begins, it has to run its course and may take several hours before things are better. An important aspect in helping your child is to develop a consistent plan in approaching different behaviors. The key principle to keep in mind is that we need to teach your child to calm himself down, to become a better problem solver, and to tolerate distress when he can't change a frustrating situation. As parents we need to keep calm, understand our own limits, and make a plan that will work. At the same time, it is important for you to understand your child's distress and feelings while learning how to set limits and redirect your child to purposeful activity. Below are listed a number of guidelines that can be used in helping your child become a happier child.

Rule Out Medical Problems

When an infant or child is inconsolable, it is important to determine if the child has any medical problem that may be the primary reason for the crying or chronic irritability. Common problems that occur include colic, chronic ear infections, reflux, severe allergies, and urinary tract infections. Milk intolerance or a diet heavy in gluten can sometimes contribute to irritability. A referral to a nutritionist is often helpful in managing diet.

Address Sensory Hypersensitivities That May Contribute to Irritability

Inconsolability may be related to hypersensitivities that the child has to environmental stimulation. These hypersensitivities may include wearing clothing that agitates the child, noises in the environment that overstimulate him, or too many activities in a room that create an overloading effect. The child's sensory hypersensitivities should be addressed whenever possible through play. Activities that provide deep pressure to the muscles and joints are useful, such as sitting in a bean bag chair with a weighted blanket on his lap or rolling up like a "hot dog" in a heavy comforter. If your child is hypersensitive to sounds, he should be encouraged to engage in activities that allow him to make sounds (e.g., banging objects on different surfaces to see what sound they make, learning a musical instrument). In addition, movement activities are very calming, particularly ones that provide linear movement (e.g., forward-back rocking, glider chair, trampoline).

Avoid Overstimulating Your Child

A common problem confronting the parent who is trying to console a crying child is a tendency to become frantic when consistent efforts do not seem to work. You may find yourself rocking your child vigorously in a forward and back motion for a few minutes, then swinging your child in the air when the crying resumes. Or if your child is older, you may hand him a book to look at, music to listen to, or beckon him to go outside on the porch for a change of scenery. When each of your ideas fails to work, you find yourself scanning the list in your mind to offer something else that might work. Whatever you do, it's a good idea to step back and think, "How many things did I just do to help my child calm down?" If it was more than two or three things in a short period of time, it probably is too many. The important thing is to try one thing long enough to see if it works. For example, you might give your child a pillow hug (e.g., taking the pillow, holding it against the child's back, then squeezing it firmly) and see if after a few minutes it starts to take effect. Or if your child is older, you might suggest that the two of you do 20 jumping jacks or push-ups to burn off some energy and focus the body. Another trick is to try to remain calm yourself, even if inside your head you are lamenting, "Here we go again! How long and how bad will this tantrum be?" Many parents feel that their tolerance for their child's fussy, irritable state is very low, especially when they are exhausted from dealing with it for so long.

> **Tip:** Reduce stimulation over the course of the day. Plan fewer activities and avoid over-scheduling.

One trick of the trade is to watch to see if there are certain situations, transitions in activities, or demands that consistently overwhelm your child. For example, some children are flooded by noisy, crowded environments. In this case, the problem is more sensory based. This kind of child needs to have smaller amounts of stimulation in his life. It may mean not going to certain places that are overstimulating (e.g., shopping malls, noisy playgrounds) or shortening exposure to noisy, bustling environments and even considering shortening a school day. It is helpful to teach your child to find healthy escapes when he is overwhelmed (e.g., take a break by walking to a calmer place). Other children cannot stand to have limits placed on them because of their inflexibility in tolerating change or their high need to control what happens to them. Once you figure out what might be contributing to the irritability, you might be able to help your child by prompting him when a limit or demand is on the horizon. An easy way to do this is to use a behavioral chart with clear pictures or symbols of upcoming events or tasks that need to be done. It is very organizing for children to know what's next on the agenda.

Soothe Yourself and Your Child

It is often necessary to find ways to help yourself and your child to feel soothed and calm. This is a basic task that we often forget. If a person overlooks doing their calming activities even for a few days, it contributes to feeling stressed and overloaded. Make a list of things that you find calming for yourself and think about when you can do these things regularly. It will provide a model to your child on how a person takes good care of herself to keep calm and collected. Now make a list of what you think might calm your child. Go through your house and think about where these things could happen. If you construct several calming areas that your child can go to, it will help him to have things in the environment that provide containment, holding, and soothing. For example, both you and your child can have a calming experience by sitting together inside a large inner tube or a pup tent filled with soft pillows while engaged in play together. Or you can put some soft pillows in a corner of the room with a few books to look at. Visit the reading corner with your child so that he learns to use it on his own. The idea is to have places in the environment where your child can go, activities that you do with that are calming, and for your child to see how soothing activities are part of everyday life. It is a powerful message of physical and emotional containment.

An important aspect of staying calm is to use our breath. Breathing exercises can be very helpful for both you and your child. If you are holding your child when he is upset, try to slow your own breathing down by breathing in for a count of three, then out for a count of three. As you slow down your own breathing, your child will feel the rise and fall of your chest and will start to slow his own breathing. Older children can be coached to do this same technique when they are in a calm moment. Then you can cue them, "Let's both breathe slowly. I'll count for the two of us."

Suppose you have reached your wit's end and can't take it anymore. This happens to a lot of parents. If you feel that you can't be available to calm and redirect your child, then take a break. Be sure your child is in a safe place and can't harm himself, then step outside onto the back porch and let the cool air blow on your face, or go to the bathroom and put a warm washcloth on your face. One parent told me that she would force herself to look in the mirror when she was screaming at her child to remind herself what her child saw. She said, "*I look like an evil witch. This is not who I want to be for my child.*" Find what works for you. If you are at a breaking point, then you need a more serious break. We'll talk more about getting relief in a bit.

Create Opportunities for Your Child to Learn How to Self-Calm

Parents of very young infants should calm their crying baby, but once a baby reaches six to nine months, the infant should be given the opportunity to self-calm and to learn to solve problems that are sources of frustration through support and encouragement from the parents. When crying persists beyond five or ten minutes even after you have encouraged your child to self-calm by giving him a pacifier, you should seek to calm your child by techniques like holding and rocking him or her, or other effective means. For older children, you may need to help your child to self-calm at first, then redirect him towards a calming activity that he can do on his own, such as solving a puzzle or looking at a book. Over time, you may direct him immediately towards the calm-down activity, gradually withdrawing the child's dependence on your body as a soothing device.

> **Tip:** Self-calming is learned by having you teach your child how to self-calm by himself. Structure in the environment and routines will help your child learn how to access these self-calming strategies on a regular basis.

An important step in this process is to help your child become proficient in the task of self-calming. Children who are fussy often depend on others to calm them rather than calming themselves. Self-calming should be introduced in two ways: through environmental modifications and through objects, interactions, and play that support self-calming. However, it is important to determine the best ways for a given child to soothe himself. For example, some children quiet when looking or listening to something novel. Others respond better when given opportunities to move. It is useful to think about what sensory channels (smell, taste, looking, listening, moving, and touching) help your child to be calm and which ones are stimulating. As you try to figure out what will calm your child, pay attention to what activities your child prefers when he is regulated and calm. See our **Tool Sheet 1, Self-Soothing** (Toolbox) for ideas.

Many children find it helpful to have a calming "den" or calm-down corner somewhere in your house. For example, you can simply place a table cloth over a card table and fill the space below with pillows. Or you can create a space between the back of the sofa and the wall where your child can retreat when overstimulated. In this space, there should be a box of calm-down materials that help your child (e.g., puzzles, books, flashlights, squeeze balls, or other calming materials). Because many children who are irritable fall apart during transitions, you may create several calm-down boxes that can be used for different situations (e.g., a box in the glove compartment of the car for car rides, a shoe box filled with squeeze balls and safe things to chew on).

Help Your Child to Learn How to Make Transitions

There are a number of tricks of the trade in helping children to learn how to make transitions in activities. Making transitions in activities requires the child to shift attention from one activity to the next, to anticipate and plan the next activity, and to make changes in activity, eventually without the help of a parent. Gaining a sense of autonomy and the capacity to tolerate separations from the parent help the child in making transitions. Therefore, objects need to be provided that help the child self-organize to transition from one activity to the next, but also represent the connection between you and your child.

You may carry a keychain with a picture of you and your child on it or a blanket, stuffed animal, or other symbol representing the connection between parent and child. When making transitions, you can signal your child, *"Don't forget your stuffed animal."* If your child is older and is discouraged from bringing personal toys to school, you can find something small for his pocket, a special wrist band or bracelet that might work equally well. This will allow him to fidget and will keep his hands occupied so that he is less likely to annoy other children. One boy was permitted to pack his stuffed animal in his back pack and leave it in a locker at school. At the age of 12, this boy felt calmed by the idea that his stuffed dog was in the school even though he knew he couldn't go to it during the school day.

Giving the child advance warning that a transition is about to occur is often helpful. The parent should help the child finish what he is doing, then give him an object to hold that represents the next activity. For example, you may say, "We're leaving for the store. Can you bring along your shopping list, too?" and give the child a pad of paper and crayons to scribble on while riding in the car. Some children respond well to photographs or picture cards that show the child doing the next activity. You will need to take photos of your child doing different activities, such as riding in the car, swinging on a swing at the park, getting dressed, etc., to implement this method.

Provide Clear Limits

It is very helpful to think through the steps of when things fall apart when you are setting limits. By dissecting what happens from start to finish, it is possible to think clearly about what might help to be more effective in setting limits that will work for your child. When your child challenges you with something that he shouldn't be doing, you should say "no" firmly, coupled with a gesture. If he still doesn't stop what he is doing, your child should be removed from the room or you should take away the object even if it results in a tantrum. Many parents fall into the trap of giving the limit in a calm voice at first, then when their child doesn't listen, they repeat what they said until the parents find themselves screaming. Not listening is a common problem of many irritable children. Be sure to get your child's attention when you say the first warning. This means going up to your child, touching him on the shoulder, giving the command in a firm voice, then waiting for the response. If your child still doesn't respond, make it clear how you will help him listen. Often parents tell the child what to do but don't couple the verbal aspect of the command with their physical presence or gestures to get the message across to their child. A clear idea of what will happen next and how you will help your child do it is very useful. Note that you should present to your child that you are **observing your own limits**. See **Tool Sheet 15, Observing Limits**.

> **Tip:** Cue your child what you expect him to do by showing him how to do it. As you do the actions, verbalize what you expect him to do. This gives your child a model of what it looks like. Make a chart with pictures of the sequence to reinforce it.

Many children do very well when these transitions are written down in a simple list or chart with pictures so that the sequence is predictable. Also, linking successful completion of the steps in the sequence with a behavioral reward is often necessary with young children. For example, you may start the day with the child earning TV time by compliant listening for certain tasks. Or you may say something like,  "If you get dressed now, you can have a few minutes to play before we leave." See **Tool Sheets 13, Changing Behavior**, and **17, A Token Economy**, for ideas on how to do this.

It is useful for you to validate the child's anger and frustration when a limit is set and she does not want to do what you have asked. *"Yes, I know that you are angry and don't want to do this right now."* Sometimes a child can be redirected to another activity before the crying escalates too far. If it is at the point where the child is inconsolable, the caregiver should move the child to a time out or calm-down corner, then as soon as the child has calmed, he should be redirected to a positive activity. It is helpful to think about how different situations might play out—a tantrum in a restaurant, when the parents are in a hurry, in a parking lot, etc.—and have a plan to handle a tantrum in public situations. Both caregivers should come up with a consistent way of handling the tantrum and enforce it. If possible, it is a good idea to keep visits short to public places such as the grocery store, a restaurant, or shopping mall so that the trip ends successfully rather than in a melt-down. When unanticipated tantrums occur, parents should avoid reinforcing the tantrum by buying a toy or giving the child a bottle or lollipop. It is usually better to remove the child from the situation and as soon as he or she is calm, then offer a calming toy or stuffed animal to hold while telling their child, *"I like how you calmed yourself down."*

> **Tip:** Catch your child when he does a self-calming strategy or is following through on what you want him to do. Praise his efforts and he'll do it again the next time.

Intense children often escalate when parents begin to curb their behavior. They become furious when they feel that they are being criticized. For this reason, we suggest that you observe your own limits and those of your child. This means that if you are in the grocery store and  your child throws himself screaming onto the floor, you might say, *"I need to get food for dinner and I cannot do that when you are lying on the floor. Help me so that we can go home and eat."* Here the parent is avoiding a direct criticism such as *"You are behaving badly."*

Parents should pick a few key behaviors that will be the ones they wish to work on with their child. For example, sitting at the table for eating, turning off the television when it's time to go to school, and getting dressed for bedtime may be the three targeted behaviors. Although it is difficult to do, other behaviors that don't fall into the targeted behaviors should be deemphasized. For example, if the child chooses to dress himself in odd clothing and it is not one of the top three or four target behaviors, the parents should leave it alone, letting the child do it his way. Compliance and good behavior should be reinforced with praise. Some families like using praise coupled with tangible reinforcers, such as stickers, checks on a chart, a cookie, or a visit to the "Mommy Treat Bag" at the end of the day. See the **Tool Sheet 17, Token Economy** for more ideas on this.

Help the Child Become More Self-Reliant

Many parents complain that their child is constantly whining and demanding their attention. To help build the child's capacity to organize himself and decrease reliance on the parent to entertain him, you should try playing with your child for about 10 to 15 minutes using the child's favorite toys. See our Chapter 11 for ideas on how to spend time with your child to make things better. After the child is playing well, you should encourage your child to keep playing while you do a small chore or activity in the same room. Every few minutes, you should check in, reassure, and praise your child, *"Good playing alone!"* Mom or dad may try to keep the connection between them and their child by singing a song from across the room while they work.

Whenever you are involved in a task such as cooking a meal, it is wise to offer your young child some pots and pans, plastic containers, and small objects to use in filling, dumping, stirring, etc., so that your child can play and imitate you while you cook. If your child complains, you should try to redirect him physically or verbally. You should be clear to your child about when it is time that you will pick them up or help them and when it isn't because you are busy. As soon as you are finished with your chore, you should reward them for playing alone or waiting by sitting with them to read a story or playing with them briefly. For young babies, they may be carried about in a sling or backpack while you do household chores so that he or she can see what you are doing.

With preschool and school-aged children, it is helpful to teach your child to label his or her emotions and to read bodily signals so that he or she can implement calm-down strategies on their own. Sometimes children respond to ideas like a traffic light or mood meter with red colors denoting "time to put on the brakes" or mad or angry feelings and green or blue colors for feeling calm and focused. Other children respond well to thinking about how their engine is running. A good resource book for therapists is the program developed by Williams and Shellenberger, *How Does Your Engine Run?* (Therapy Works, Inc., 1996).

Develop Tolerance for Frustration and a Sense of Mastery

Using child-centered play or floor time, parents can work with their child to develop the capacity to tolerate frustration. For example, suppose your child is trying to fit a toy into a container and is getting frustrated. You might reflect, *"Yes, it doesn't fit!"* rather than immediately help the child to solve the problem. Mom or dad might gently reposition the container for better success, but should avoid taking the object from the child and solving the problem for him. It is a good idea to wait for your child to look to you for help. In this way, the child learns to coordinate communication with others when frustrated.

> **Tip:** First reassure your child, *"You can do it, keep trying"* or *"What else might work?"* If this is not enough, you may help your child to solve the problem through physical or verbal guidance.

Developing a sense of mastery is important for the irritable child to feel that he can overcome frustrations and gain pleasure from his own accomplishments. This can be done by giving the child small "jobs" like turning the lights on and off when leaving or entering the room, closing the dishwasher, or pushing a drawer shut. If these things are done everyday, it will help the child feel that he contributes to the family and is a big help. Giving your child choices can be very empowering. The child should also be encouraged to do age appropriate activities that he can master, such as stirring with a spoon to make pudding. Young children should begin helping by using a small broom to sweep the kitchen floor and they should be encouraged to help put toys away. Remember, the goal is to do the task, but do not set the bar too high as to how well the task should be done.

Overcoming Feelings of Isolation and Getting Respite for Yourself

Parents of irritable children often feel very isolated because normal parenting experiences are often precluded. For example, many parents report that they cannot take their child to play groups, birthday parties, or other family gatherings because their child will fall apart. Parents often express the fear that other caregivers may abuse their overly distressed baby, thus resulting in the parents never leaving their child with other caregivers when respite is sorely needed. When parents must cope with an infant who cries in excess of two hours a day or a child who is highly irritable, respite should be explored to help parents restore their capacity to deal with their overly fussy infant or difficult child.

You should give yourself a break before you reach your boiling point and are going to explode at your child. Put your child in a safe play area, but avoid the crib or bedroom where he sleeps. Leave him for a few minutes so that he can calm down while you take a break for yourself as well. It is actually a disservice to your child to never leave him with another adult caregiver. Your child needs to learn that he or she can be safe with other adults. The child who is always with his parent may believe that he cannot function on his own. He will then be increasingly distraught at the idea of being left with someone else. Because of this, it is important to find caregivers whom you trust in the first months of your child's life before he develops stranger anxiety. If your child is older, set up opportunities for him to be with the babysitter while you are elsewhere in the house, then go out on short errands or take a nap.

Parent support groups and parent-to-parent networking are amazing resources for parents. They can help you feel support and know that eventually you will get through this difficult time in your life. If you are working with a therapist, ask him or her if he or she know other parents who have been through a similar journey and can offer advice to you. Many agencies offer parent support groups that provide helpful advice.

Explore What You Think Your Child's Behavior Means

It is very helpful to address the anxieties you may feel as to why your child is crying or is irritable so much of the time. For example, one set of parents believed that their young baby felt abandoned when she cried despite the fact that they were by her side almost constantly. As we explored this in therapy, it became apparent that both parents had issues around being emotionally neglected by their own parents. Once they learned ways of maintaining healthy connections with their child and became comfortable separating from their child, both parents and child became less anxious when together and apart. You may have experienced something in your past, perhaps with your own parents, that causes you to have certain feelings with your own child. Some of these feelings may be rational, others may not be. Whatever the root of the problem, it is helpful to know that you are reacting this way. Amazingly, children pick up on parents' anxieties and learn that their behavior is loaded for their parents. It may cause them to know that their behavior can unravel their parents and they learn to use it inadvertently.

It is often useful to become more attuned to your own reactions when your child is irritable. For example, if your child is anxious or angry, you may resonate to the child's emotion, becoming almost caught up in the same emotion. Instead of organizing or calming the child, your reactions may cause the child's emotions to escalate. Sometimes it is helpful to videotape your family interacting, the good and bad. Take a look at it and see if anything pops out at you about what is happening between you and your child. A mental health professional can also help you become more sensitive to what your contribution may be to the emotions that are stirred up in your household. Often it is difficult to observe oneself objectively until someone else helps to decipher the interactions between family members and what is helpful and not to emotional well-being.

Provide Forums for Your Child to Express What the Distress Means

Many children who have long histories of irritability begin to feel that there is something wrong with them. They notice that they unravel easily in comparison to other children. They need to understand why their nervous system functions this way. For example, it helped Sam to have opportunities to learn when his "engine" was running on overload and what it did to him emotionally to live in this state of internal chaos. Every irritable child experiences changes in his self-esteem and sense of identity as a result of living in a constant state of distress.

Over the years, play therapy was central to Sam's emotional growth. Because he felt anxious about his shortcomings, Sam played out that he was the master of the universe. In the face of his anxiety that he was vulnerable, nor perfect, and unable to cope with new situations or any kind of stress, Sam frequently expressed in play that he was the most powerful boy around, the smartest boy at school, or a secret service agent who fought evil forces and saved people. He struggled in the early years of treatment with strong feelings of isolation, that no one liked him, and that no one could help him. As he matured, his play depicted his high need to protect himself, usually with toy weapons, tools, and gadgets that gave him superpowers. He wanted me to play the less-able peer whom he trained to become skillful and competent in dangerous situations. He clearly wished for me to admire him and relished that I joined him in a range of emotional themes.

Summary of Strategies

Let's review the strategies that will help calm your irritable child.

SKILLS FOR CALMING THE IRRITABLE CHILD

Rule out medical problems that might be causing the irritability.

Provide sensory activities that inhibit overstimulation or hypersensitivities.

Avoid planning too many activities and overstimulating your child.

Provide a daily sensory diet of soothing activities for both you and your child.

Create opportunities for your child to learn how to self-calm on his own.

Help your child to learn how to transition from one activity to the next.

Provide clear structure, guidelines for expectation and limits.

Help your child tolerate frustration and distress in increments.

Encourage your child to become self-reliant and to enact the strategies he has learned on his own.

Help your child understand what his behavior means.

Encourage your child to talk about what his distress means to him.

Seek support from parents and professionals.

Summary

In this chapter, the different ways that irritability can be observed in young children were described. It is important for parents to take into account how emotion regulation develops and what their child needs to learn to become a happier, better regulated child. Some of the key components to a successful treatment program are to think about how the child models functions at home, school, and the community while focusing on helping the child develop the capacity to engage and self-regulate, to organize purposeful social communication and interactions with others, and to express emotional ideas and feelings. It is also important to help the child learn how to self-monitor and evaluate the appropriateness of his or her responses. Therapeutic approaches need to address the child and family functioning, environmental modifications that support self-calming and organization, as well as parent-child interactions.

2
Coping with Different Kinds of Anxiety

All children get anxious from time to time. They may be anxious about a test they have to take, or they may be anxious that their mother will discover the missing ice-cream sandwich from the freezer. A dash of anxiety is actually helpful in that it pushes the child to study or make sure that dessert has not disappeared before the meal begins. In this chapter, however, we are dealing with more extreme forms of anxiety that overtake a child and negatively affect that child's ability to function in the world.

Children who are overly anxious spend much of their time feeling upset, and frequently find it hard to do things that are effortless for other children. Some anxious children become so worried over performance that they spend an hour laboring over a task that should have taken only ten minutes to do. Other children do not want to leave their parents to go to school or visit with a friend. When children become anxious, activities that used to be comfortable make them fearful. This fear and agitation is infectious and parents can also become overwhelmed and worried.

In this chapter, we will consider different causes for anxiety in children, reflecting both the internal biochemistry of the child and the environmental stressors that can agitate children. We will look at children who are distressed at separating from their parents, children who refuse to talk, children who refuse to go to school, and children who become anxious as a result of personal trauma. In addition we will explore children who are anxious from birth, reflecting an intense biological vulnerability to anxiety. As we look at these different cases, we will study the strategies that different parents use to help their children. We hope that some of these tools will help you to help your anxious child.

As you consider whether or not your child has a significant degree of anxiety, consider the following behaviors that may be signs of anxiety in children:

- Sleep disturbance
- Aches and pains, such as stomachache, headache, nausea
- Being extremely agitated or shut down and withdrawn
- Difficulty with concentration
- Avoidance of something for no understandable reason
- Bad dreams, even in the daytime
- Panic attacks—rapid breathing, sweaty palms, rapid heartbeat, flushed face

Separation Anxiety

Foundations of Normal Development

An essential component of healthy development is the formation of a strong attachment between parent and child. Perhaps the most common source of anxiety in young children therefore results from the separation from the parent. As a new parent, you work hard to understand your baby and your baby works hard to understand you. As you read your baby's cues and respond when he is hungry or wet, your baby learns to trust you and recognize that you will help him. This sense of trust and dependability results in the baby becoming emotionally attached to the parent.

With this attachment comes a sense of security that the world is a safe place and his needs will be met. It is therefore not surprising that a separation from the parent can cause distress.

As part of normal development, children not only learn to attach to their parents but they also learn to trust people who are not family members. This does not always come easily. At approximately nine months of age, babies begin to distinguish the difference between familiar and unfamiliar faces. That stranger anxiety is why they may find it hard to leave their parent's arms to go to another adult. With time and exposure, however, children are able to become comfortable and trusting with a bigger community than the immediate family.

> **Tip:** Because of attachment issues and stranger anxiety, it is important to try to avoid leaving your child for a prolonged period during the first two years of his life.

Another developmental change occurs when the child nears two. Now, the child comes to learn that his parent is a separate being rather than a mere extension of himself. This raises the fear that if the parent goes away, he might stay away and not come back.

Children respond to this awareness in many ways. Some become intensely upset when their mother or father leaves the room or puts on a coat in preparation to going to work. Others may be upset for a few minutes and then calm down as they become engaged in a new activity. We are particularly interested in those children who feel separation most acutely.

Temperament

The difference in response between children who can or cannot tolerate separation reflects differences in personality traits and biochemistry. A classic study by Chess and Thomas (1969) identified nine variables of temperament that children displayed during their first weeks of life. Starting in 1956, Chess and Thomas followed a specific group of 136 children in a project that spanned many years. The results of this research showed that the individuals in the study retained similar temperamental traits from childhood through their teens and into their adult years. These variables are summarized as follows:

1. Activity level—the tempo or pace and frequency of movement activity.
2. Rhythmicity—regularity of daily biological functions, such as eating and sleep habits.
3. Approach or withdrawal—the child's initial reaction to any new stimulus.
4. Adaptability—ease or difficulty of modifying responses in a desired way.
5. Intensity of reaction—the energy of a response.
6. Threshold of responsiveness—what is needed to elicit a response in the person.
7. Quality of mood—amount of pleasant, joyful, friendly behavior as contrasted to unpleasant, crying, unfriendly behavior.
8. Distractibility—how effective extraneous variables are at capturing the child's attention.
9. Attention span and persistence—how long a child will pursue a particular activity and how long a child will maintain an activity when there are obstacles to its continuation.

Certain clusters of these temperamental traits can make your child predisposed to be anxious. Children who are anxious often show a wide range of moods, fluctuating from happy and joyful one minute to agitated, worried, or withdrawn the next. Anxious children also vary in terms of approach and withdrawal. They can be shy and hold back when faced with unfamiliar situations. Alternatively, they may be intense, outgoing, and extremely alert, jumping in before they have processed what is expected of them. In contrast, children with an easy-going, calm, and adaptable temperament have much less trouble with change and tolerate separation relatively well.

Temperament is one variable that can predispose a person towards anxiety although it doesn't automatically result in an anxious personality.

The Role of Parents in Separation

How parents respond to a child who has an anxious temperament is critical. Ideally, parents teach their children to tolerate separation from infancy by coming and going for brief periods throughout the day. Parents who are with their children at all times often create patterns of dependency that make it hard for the child to differentiate himself and believe that he can survive on his own. Similarly, parents who are away from their children for sustained periods may also create separation anxiety problems because the child cannot count on their presence. Both the over-involved parent and the under-involved parent can put their child at risk for an attachment disorder. Knowing that a parent or central caregiver can always be counted on is essential for healthy growth and development. Without healthy attachment and an emerging sense of individuation, children become anxious and do not take risks. This in turn restricts their ability to learn and develop a sense of confidence in themselves. We will look at a child with separation problems and then show how his parents successfully coped with this difficulty.

Albert: An Intense and Reactive Child

Albert is an example of an intense, outgoing, and alert child who found separation particularly hard. When his separation issues became most intense, he was a beautiful three-year-old whose chubby cheeks and curly blond hair gave him a deceptively angelic appearance. However, Albert's intensity was present from the time he was an infant.

Being a third child, his mother immediately noted that he had a completely different temperament from his older brothers. From the beginning he was demanding and became easily agitated. He never settled into an eating routine, rather he wanted to nurse frequently as a way of soothing himself. When he needed a diaper change, he would shriek in a piercing manner until his mother responded to his cries. The only time that he would calm down and stop crying was when his mother walked him and sang to him. When tended by another caretaker, he cried until he fell asleep.

As he grew older, Albert had more and more trouble with transitions and his mother worked hard to help him deal with his distress. From the beginning, she tried to teach him that he could handle being away from her. As a young child they played peek-a-boo, which made Albert roar with glee but also taught him that his mother could hide behind her hands and then pop back into view. She was not going to disappear forever. From the time that he was an infant, she had a babysitter come one morning a week so that Albert was familiar with his mother leaving for short periods. She also had a babysitter one evening a week so that he got used to his parents leaving and coming home.

As a toddler, Albert was captivated by his siblings, but he hated new situations. If his mother suggested they go visit another child, he would dissolve into tears. When he was almost two, his mother started a play group with three other families in an effort to get Albert comfortable with other children and different spaces. Initially Albert was overwhelmed by the other children, but from the vantage point of his mother's lap, he gradually became comfortable.

She never told him that he had to play with the other children, and if he wanted to sit on her lap for the whole hour and a half, that was fine with her. However, after a few meetings, that was not necessary. Albert became interested in the other toys and was fascinated watching the other children. These mornings became very important to the four mothers as well. As they talked about their children they gave each other support. As time went on, this cluster of four families would become the stable center of Albert's world.

Adjustment to School　Knowing that Albert would find it hard to leave her and go to nursery school, Albert's mother worked hard to prepare him for the transition. After she enrolled Albert in nursery school in the spring, she got a class list and arranged play dates with two of the other boys. This turned out to be effective because Albert liked the boys and when he went to school he was comfortable playing with them. Albert and his mother also went over to his future school on the weekends so that he could be comfortable playing on the playground. The week before the start of school, they arranged to visit the classroom when only the teacher was there. Albert and the teacher worked together setting up the sand tray.

There were important strategies that the school implemented to help avoid separation problems. First of all, his teachers came to the house to meet him before he even started school. They took a Polaroid picture of Albert with his favorite stuffed elephant and when he arrived for the first day of school, that picture was on the wall above his coat hook. The

first day, the parents accompanied their children to school. It was a short morning during which the teachers showed them around their classroom and let them play a while on the playground. However, after the first day, the teachers insisted that the children be dropped off at the curb where they were welcomed by the teachers.

Albert's mother talked with him about how they were going to say goodbye. She practiced during the summer saying "I love you," and then giving him a "thumbs up" signal as she left. He began giving her a "thumbs up" as well. Now they showed the "thumbs up" at the curb as he walked into school with the teacher.

Albert managed to get through the first days of school although he cried and was visibly pining for his mother. His teachers tried to engage him in projects as a way of distracting him (see Appendix 2, **Tool Sheet 6, Distraction**).

At circle time, the teacher let him sit in her lap. He was also allowed to bring his elephant from home. The elephant served as an important transitional object between home and school. The rule was that it stayed in his book bag, but he was able to occasionally give it a pat. It comforted Albert to know that his elephant was at school even if he was not allowed out of the bag.

Adjustment at Home　At home there was a marked change in Albert's behavior which reflected his stress at leaving his mother and going to school. He responded to this stress by becoming increasingly agitated and unhappy at home. He told his mother how much he missed her and that he didn't like the teachers. He also hated the other children and couldn't remember any of their names. The more he talked, the more agitated he became.

The most pronounced change was at bedtime. Going to sleep became a struggle because Albert did not want his mother to stop reading books and leave. As she bent over his bed to kiss him goodnight, he would grab her hair, pull it, and not let her go.

Although his mother understood the nature of the problem, she had to deal with his behavior. She used the strategy of giving consequences (**Tool Sheet 14, Teaching Consequences and Repair**) to deal with his clinginess and hair pulling. When Albert pulled her hair, she said "no" firmly and then removed his hands. She explained that if he did it again, she would leave the room. On one occasion she actually left the room for five minutes to give him a consequence for hair pulling. He never pulled her hair again. His mother then applied a structured system for getting Albert to sleep and keeping him asleep (**Tool Sheet 20, Managing Your Child at Night**).

His mother read Albert a series of stories and sang him a song. She left him in bed even though he was crying and wanted her to stay. She explained that he needed to go to sleep and she would check on him from time to time. His mother then left him to cry for five minutes. She returned to the room and reassured him in a quiet voice that he was fine and needed to get to sleep. She patted and soothed him, but she did not take him out of bed. She stayed for only two or three minutes and then left the room. This time she stayed away for seven minutes. She then returned and did the same thing.

On the first night that she set this limit, Albert was very unhappy and distraught. He cried so hard it sounded like hiccups. His mother stayed calm and reassuring, singing to him, patting him, and distracting him with his elephant. Ultimately Albert went to sleep on his own. The next evening was much better. After two nights Albert returned to his usual routine of listening to two stories and then lights out.

In summary, Albert is an example of a child with separation anxiety. In Albert's case, the symptoms of anxiety were characterized by extreme reactivity, clinginess to mom, and a predisposition to deal with stress by withdrawal and avoidance. His parents understood his anxiety and carefully gave him the time and support that he needed to adjust.

Anxiety Expressed by Refusal to Talk

Sometimes when children are stressed, they dig in and refuse to cooperate with others. The most dramatic example of this is when they refuse to talk. This is called *selective mutism* or *elective mutism*. The selectively mute child simply stops talking in certain situations, although he or she will continue to talk in other contexts. Children usually resort to this when they feel emotionally overwhelmed by a situation.

The following case history illustrates this extreme form of anxiety and demonstrates the techniques that adults may use to calm these children and help them cope.

Louise: Who Had to Cope With Severe Kidney Disease

Louise was a nine-year-old African girl, who was by nature warm and outgoing but who became intensely anxious when she was placed in a very stressful situation. Louise came to the United

States because of advanced kidney disease. She was a beauty, with large brown eyes, dark skin, and long brown hair. Because of her illness she was very small and looked more like a six-year-old than a nine-year-old. Louise was accompanied by an uncle who was childless and remarkably unsuited to dealing with a young girl in a crisis situation.

When they arrived in the United States, the family anticipated that Louise would need a kidney transplant, that a kidney would be available, and that a transplant would take place immediately. This was not the case. Although she did need a transplant, there would be a long wait until a suitable donor kidney was found.

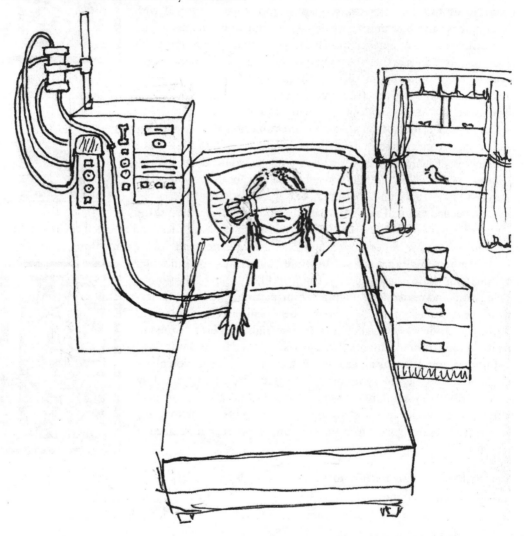

During this initial period of diagnosis, Louise was placed on a pediatric ward and gradually began to interact with the other children and staff. She was bright and rapidly learned English. In order to treat her illness, she had dialysis several times a week, which required her to be attached to a machine that cleaned her blood. This procedure required that she have a permanent tube or shunt placed in her abdomen so that the machine could be connected directly to her blood stream and her blood could be cleaned. Each treatment took several hours. Louise was horrified to have this permanent tube attached to her body. She felt disfigured and damaged. In addition, the machine itself was frightening to her.

Slowly it became clear to Louise that the transplant would not be immediate. She learned that finding a donor could take months if not years. Furthermore, after the initial assessment, Louise was moved to another hospital in another city. She had been away from her family for two months at this point and she was overcome with homesickness and dread. Therefore, she did the one thing that she could control and stopped talking. She spoke only to her uncle, but he came to the hospital infrequently. She refused to speak to anyone else. During the four months that followed, Louise began to withdraw more and more. The hospital contacted the family and tried to get her mother or father to join her. However, her mother had had another child, a son, and could not travel.

In the hospital, the nurses were warm and cheerful. They established a predictable routine for Louise (**Tool Sheet 22, Providing Structure to the Day**), which was important as it kept her busy. She went to school with the other children when she was not on dialysis. She particularly liked doing math workbooks, which the nurses welcomed as a distraction that usually engaged and calmed her (**Tool Sheet 6, Distraction**).

However, Louise remained silent and increasingly withdrew into herself. They also tried to distract her during dialysis by setting up a TV for her to watch cartoon videos. Another intervention that seemed helpful was art therapy. Here Louise drew powerful pictures of small children and giant needles and machines. Her therapist worked with Louise to prepare her for her transplant surgery by showing her a doll that opened up to show its organs. The therapist could then role play all the steps that she would go through as she prepared for surgery, had the transplant, recovered in the recovery room, and took medicine to protect the new kidney. Louise was very attentive to this doll play, but never asked a question.

Eventually a kidney was found for Louise, and the surgery was successful. However, in order to prevent the body from rejecting the new organ, Louise was put on powerful medication that caused her face to become swollen and distorted. At this point, Louise's mother arrived with her baby boy for her first visit in six months. She was shocked at the change in her daughter's appearance and this disappointment immediately registered with Louise. With her mother's arrival, Louise began speaking. By now her English was fluent and she was articulate in expressing herself; however, she was strangely deflated. She had worked so hard to be compliant with her doctors to get her new kidney, but she perceived that somehow she had failed her mother because she was not the same pretty little girl who had left home six months before.

With time the situation became much better as the hospital worked with Louise's mother so that she could understand what Louise had been through. Eventually Louise went off the medication to prevent the rejection of the transplant. She finally returned home almost a year after she had started on this difficult journey.

Selective mutism is an extreme form of self-control that develops in response to acute anxiety. It is similar to anorexia in that the child is seeking to control the one thing that she has power over, herself. In these difficult circumstances, parents need to keep validating their child (see **Tool Sheet 10, Validation**) and observing their limits (**Tool Sheet 15, Observing Limits**).

Do not end up enabling your child. If your child refuses to speak, do not interpret his gestures. Make him ask for what he wants. In general, as a parent your job is to encourage your child to do what he fears. This is called exposure and is discussed in detail in Chapter 6, The Dark Secret.

School Anxiety

It is not surprising that many children have anxiety connected to school because environmental factors can create distress in an otherwise well-balanced child. In some children, anxiety develops when children have trouble learning and then worry that they are not being as successful as their classmates. In other children, anxiety develops because they are not interested in school and their parents are disappointed that they are not performing at the level of their ability, or the level of their sibling's performance. Children also develop performance anxiety as a response to the high expectations that they impose on themselves and their relentless drive to meet those expectations. We will look at a child who developed a high degree of anxiety in response to the demands of school and see what actions her parents took to help her.

April: A Child Who Could Not Count Dice and Hated School

April was a third grader who was having trouble with learning. Reading was slow and hard for her and she never read for pleasure. However, her major trouble was that she could not understand the concept of number. She was slow to learn to count to 10 and did not count reliably to 20 until she was eight and a half. She simply could not remember the numbers and their order. Her trouble with the concept of number was seen when she played games with dice. No matter how long she played, she never could recognize the five and each time had to count the dots one by one. Addition was hard for April, but subtraction was almost impossible because she had trouble conceptualizing taking numbers away from other numbers.

At school, April felt perpetually confused and inadequate. Every morning she delayed getting ready so that she and her brother were always late. Once at school, she struggled through the day. She spent an hour each morning with the learning specialist, a welcome respite from the classroom. When she returned to her class, she was clearly uncomfortable. She tried to compensate by laughing too loudly at jokes that her classmates made or leaning out of her seat until her head touched the floor. At lunch time, she sat alone in the cafeteria. She refused to invite anyone over for a play date. She reported that the other children thought that she was weird.

Parent Strategies   April's parents were very sensitive to her anxieties about school. They thought that if she were more comfortable socially, she might feel better. They therefore developed a networking strategy. Their plan was to start having barbecues with other families who had children April's age. Because of this, April became comfortable with one other child and had a weekly play date with her. She described this other child as being "weird" like her.

In addition to helping April interact with children, her parents also arranged for a tutor to work with April outside of school. Tutoring involved hours of work with materials that could be manipulated, such as rods, blocks, and coins until April finally understood the concept of "five" or "ten."

Even though she was making progress, she still wasn't happy at school because the other students were so far ahead of her. The family therefore decided to put her in a special school program that catered to children with learning disabilities. This program was not in her home school, which was a relief to her because she was able to start anew with another group of children. April was relieved by the change and gradually she relaxed. In the new setting she reported that, "*There are other children who have trouble like I do.*" She made a friend for the first time and actually had play dates with this girl on the weekends. The girls shared a wonderful imagination and made up elaborate fantasy stories about space travel and aliens. Now that she was comfortable, April no longer tried to avoid going to school and actually began to make progress in math.

> **Tip:** Placement can be an important intervention for an anxious child. Children with anxiety need teachers who understand this problem and can reduce stress in the classroom. For children with learning disabilities, special programs can be important.

Anxiety Caused by Personal Trauma

It is normal to develop anxiety in response to an environmental catastrophe. In Washington, D.C., many children showed anxiety following the 9/11 attacks on the World Trade Center and the Pentagon. Two years later, Washington was again traumatized for several months when two snipers repeatedly attacked innocent strangers as they stopped at a shopping center or put gas into their cars. One of these victims was a middle school boy going to school in the morning. Area schools responded to this threat of violence by eliminating all outdoor activities. Nursery school children could not play on the playground and high school children were not allowed to do their fall sports schedule.

Following both of these tragedies, school counselors saw an increase in anxiety in children. They did workshops in classrooms and reassured the children about what was being done to protect them. In both of these situations, the children had the comfort of knowing that everyone was in the same boat. As time passed and the snipers were arrested, many children found their lives return to normal. However, for some sensitive and reactive children, the fear would not go away. Years later, some children still tell their parents that they are afraid to be near a window because they fear that a bad guy with a gun will shoot them. Many adults also remain anxious and have restricted their children's activities so that they are always under close supervision. These restrictions in themselves often enhance the anxiety in children.

We will look at a child who experienced trauma in a much more private manner. In this case the trauma was caused by his parents.

Eric: Trauma From Living in the War Zone of His Parents' Hostility

Personal traumas can be particularly devastating to children because they often involve secrets that the child feels unable to share outside the family. These events may be hard to understand and impossible to control. When this happens, it is very difficult to stop being anxious. Some traumas are dramatic, such as the case of rape or personal violence. Other traumas are not so dramatic, but they are nonetheless profoundly disturbing.

Eric was a seven-year-old boy who faced an intractable problem. His parents had come to hate each other and in the process Eric became a weapon in their war. Although they were deeply alienated, neither parent wanted to leave the house because they felt this would weaken their rights to the family assets and child custody. Every night when his father got home, there would be a continuous verbal battle between the parents, often involving the children. If the mother wanted Eric to do soccer, the father wanted him to do football. If the mother felt that he needed a reading tutor, the father protested that they could not afford tutoring and he would tutor Eric himself. The parents' differences of opinion even extended to reading matter. On her nights to put Eric to bed, his mother read him C. S. Lewis's *Narnia* books; however, on the father's nights, the choice was E. M. Forrester's *Horatio Hornblower*.

Poor Eric was consumed with anxiety as he tried to keep the peace in this traumatic situation. He initially was referred for treatment because he was encopretic. This meant that Eric was frequently constipated, but then inadvertently soiled himself. Constipation often has a psychological component related to holding things in. In Eric's case, he was holding in a lot of strong feelings, including fear for his family and himself.

Because of his agitation, Eric had trouble concentrating and was frequently tuned out at school. At home, homework was a battleground because his father insisted on tutoring Eric but became angry when his son did not understand the work. Eric found it calming at night to sleep in the same bed as his mother. This situation persisted for two years until his parents' divorce was settled. By this time Eric was a marginal student and in the lowest reading and math groups. His self-esteem was shattered. He was both anxious and depressed and he had withdrawn from many activities.

Eric worked with a therapist around his anxiety. Initially he was soft spoken and worried about speaking up about his problems. He was so emotionally closed off by the family trauma that he simply had no idea what he felt. What made this situation particularly hard was that for years his family appeared normal on the outside. His parents went to school functions together and drove carpools. Only Eric knew the state of warfare that existed within the family and he felt a need to keep this secret, adding to his anxiety. In this case, therapy was an important intervention because Eric needed a neutral place to reveal the secrets that were dragging him down.

Learning to Cope With Divorce Gradually Eric began to feel comfortable with the therapist and was able to express thoughts and feelings that he had never told anyone before. He talked about how angry he was at his father for shouting at him when they did homework and for making him feel stupid. He was also angry at his mother because she always said negative things about his father. He felt that he could not be loyal to one parent without being disloyal to the other one. Eric came to perceive therapy as a safe haven where he could talk about his anger and sadness toward both parents. As he gained more strength, he brought more energy to therapy and began seeking strategies that would help him deal with his situation.

> **Tip:** Parents can induce clinical anxiety and school failure when they maintain a hostile relationship with the other parent and criticize that parent to the child. The child is literally ripped apart by his inability to be loyal to both parents. Surely one parent is lying; they cannot both be right. Whom to believe?

After the divorce, Eric's life improved slowly. The family home was sold and both parents moved to smaller houses. Eric spent alternate weeks with his parents, with the transitions between households taking place on school days at school. This is often an important part of a visitation plan. The idea is to minimize the periods in the week when the child is in the presence of two warring parents. Visitation schedules differ, but making the exchange at school means that one parent drops off the child and then the other parent picks up the child. Both parents take responsibility for having the clothes and toiletries that the child needs at their house. Another critical component of a successful visitation plan is to have the same calendar at both houses so that the child can check to make sure he knows what house he will be in when. Here structure (**Tool Sheet 22, Providing Structure to the Day**) is critical so that there is one schedule of school and extracurricular events that both parents promise to maintain. A predictable schedule that is supported by both parents will go a long way toward reducing anxiety.

Eric was discouraged by his school work. Because of his internal turmoil, he was finding it hard to concentrate and school seemed very hard. His mother found a high school student to help him with his homework when he was at her house. Eric found comfort in the tutor because they took breaks every 30 minutes and threw a football together. Tutoring can be an important therapeutic tool. If the child can be helped to feel that he is competent in school, his anxiety will decrease.

Eric had spent so long trying not to rock the boat that he had trouble figuring out what he wanted to have happen for himself. In therapy he talked about his fear that whatever he said would offend one parent or the other. Gradually, with the therapist's help, he was able to voice what he wanted.

His therapist taught him a communication skill called Great Fun (see **Tool Sheet 24, Having Great Fun Communicating**). Here are the steps:

G—What is the goal of your communication?
R—Review the situation.
E—Express what you are feeling.
A—Ask for what you want.
T—Think why someone might want to do it your way.

After learning these steps, Eric screwed up his courage and made the following Great Fun communication to his mother:

G—His goal was to get his mother to give him permission to play football.
R—He reviewed the situation to his mother. "Mom, I know that you think that football is violent and you don't want me to play."

E—He expressed how he felt: "I have always wanted to play football. My dream is to be a wide receiver like Santana Moss, my favorite player."

A—He asked for what he wanted: "I really want you to let me sign up."

T—He thought about how to get her to agree: "Being a wide receiver is not a very danger-ous position and I will be very careful. If I could play football, I would be with my friends and you could come and watch the games. We would all have fun and I really need to have more fun in my life."

Here is *how* he made the GREAT communication. He used FUN:

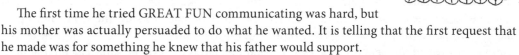

F—He knew that he had to be fair. He had to respect her views even as he tried to prevail.

U—He was understanding and showed that he knew what she was thinking.

N—He was prepared to negotiate if he needed to. If she insisted, he would offer to do football next year.

The first time he tried GREAT FUN communicating was hard, but his mother was actually persuaded to do what he wanted. It is telling that the first request that he made was for something he knew that his father would support.

In Eric's case, his parents finally were divorced, which lessened his trauma, but because the tension persisted between his parents, his anxiety continued.

Parents' Response to Trauma

Our children are exposed to many, many frightening things. They see scary things in movies, pictures, newspapers, and on television, and all of these can induce anxiety. Who can ever forget the trauma of September 11, 2001, with many of our children watching as airplanes flew into the twin towers? There are many kinds of trauma but there are things that parents can do to protect their children or weaken the impact of the trauma. Here are a few suggestions.

Actions Parents Can Take to Minimize Trauma

1. In the case of a national threat, such as a terrorist attack or war, parents should limit the information that reaches the child. Most young children cannot handle exposure to television news shows because the graphic visual coverage of violence is scary.

2. If parents are agitated, their children will become agitated. Try to be calm with your child and do not talk about your fears in front of him. Even if you are talking on the telephone, you will transmit anxiety to your child. Watch what you say if the child is in the house.

3. In cases of personal trauma, the child needs to know that horrible, unfair things hap-pen; however, he is not to blame for these events.

4. Parents should reassure their child that he will be fine and that his parents and others in authority are doing everything in their power to keep him safe.

5. In cases of domestic conflict, parents must try to keep the child out of the parental dis-agreement. Arguing with the other parent either in person or on the phone is destructive because the child will often misinterpret what is said and remember vividly the emotional tone in which the parents were speaking. All too often there is a "he said," "she said" sce-nario where children do not know whom to believe. Is my mother or father really a bad person? One person must be right, which one is telling me the truth? It is imperative that parents not say negative things about the other parent. Even if you profoundly feel that the other parent has treated you badly, it will do serious damage to your child to tell them that. Children need two parents whom they can love and whom they perceive love them.

6. In a domestic conflict if separation or divorce is the result, this should be explained to the child in a way that does not make a villain out of either parent. The child should be assured and reassured that he is not to blame and that being apart will make both parents happier.

7. In a divorce, it is important to convey to your child that together his parents have a plan for his future and they are united in doing what is best for him. Meet with your child together and clarify when the child will see each parent by giving him a calendar that shows where he will be each night.

8. When your child has had a traumatic experience, it is important to get professional mental health help for the child as quickly as possible. The child needs to talk about what has frightened and overwhelmed him so that the event does not go underground and become a secret negative force within him. The more your child can talk and process what has happened, the more he can get control of the event rather than have the event control him.

Anxious From the Beginning: Children Wired to Be Anxious

In many of the cases that we have explored, children are responding to outside events that cause anxiety. There are other children who show signs of anxiety from their first years of life. They are born with a nervous system that is intense and becomes agitated or shuts down easily. Often there is a family history of parents, uncles, aunts, and grandparents who have all struggled with anxiety. These children can be on edge and irritable, worried by any number of things. These worries can be reasonable or they can be fantastic, it does not matter. Because sleep can be a problem, anxious children are often tired and have trouble concentrating. Occasionally, these children have panic attacks, in which they respond to something frightening by manifesting physical symptoms such as chest pain, stomachaches, or rapid breathing. We will look at a child, Indira, who was born with a propensity for anxiety. Here an environmental stress triggered the anxiety. However, her parents developed skills to help Indira deal with her stress and not let it immobilize her.

Indira: Intense Anxiety in Response to Every Demand in Her Life

Indira's parents reported that there was a history of anxiety in the mother's family, including a brilliant aunt who had not been able to leave home to go to college and has been unable to work. Indira was a slight child with dark eyes and short black hair. At three she was smart, artistic, funny—and anxious. Loud sounds made her particularly distressed. At her nursery school, she could not tolerate the other children singing. She also did not like dramatic play because there were too many surprises. When she was acting the role of a pig in the *Three Little Pigs* story, the child playing the wolf unexpectedly hissed at her. She screamed hysterically and demanded to go home from school. She remained at home for a week.

Indira was an only child of older parents who doted on her. At three she had never slept through the night and awakened frequently feeling frightened and wanting her parents. Occasionally Indira had night terrors where she would suddenly sit upright in bed screaming. She appeared to be awake, but she was unable to tell her parents what she had dreamed. When Indira cried at night, her mother could not tolerate her distress and became anxious herself. She therefore simply climbed into Indira's bed, which comforted Indira and resulted in them both ultimately getting some sleep.

The summer Indira turned four was particularly hard. She refused to be separated from her mother for any reason. Summers in general can be disorganizing for intense children because their schedules change and there is often less structure in their lives. As the summer progressed,

she demanded increasingly that they stay at home. She would not go on play dates, although she liked other children coming to her house. On the few occasions when she went shopping, she feared that she would lose her mother in the store. In the fall, she returned to preschool but she was frequently upset both at home and at school.

The summer Indira turned five was tense as she faced the hurdle of a new school and kindergarten. She started her new school with some crying as she separated from her mother at the bus stop, but little crying at school. She made a gradual adjustment, although the one thing that she could not tolerate was school assembly. She had to sit on her teacher's lap and she was agitated throughout the gathering. By first grade, her worries were shifting to friends. Fortunately academics were easy for her; however, she started obsessing about other children and worrying about whether or not they liked her.

In elementary school, Indira continued to have sleep problems and had never been left with a babysitter. The only break that her parents had was when Indira's grandmother came to visit, the one person with whom she would happily stay. These visits were the only time that her parents were able to go out alone to a movie or dinner.

Indira is an example of a child with a biochemical disorder that results in ongoing anxiety. She was intense and reactive as an infant, and that intensity continued throughout elementary school. Indira experienced all the anxieties typical of children: separation anxiety, night terrors, fear of school, and panic attacks. She was constantly ricocheting from one anxious thought to another. As Indira continued to worry, her parents' lives were shrinking.

> **Tip:** When a child is frightened, most parents respond by wanting to provide support and be with the child. However, it is important for the parents to have time on their own, away from their child. This helps the parents keep their perspective and remain calm, and it helps the child know that he can be safe with another caring adult. Parents need time off and children need to know that adults other than their parents are trustworthy.

It is hard for a parent to deal with a child's anxiety, because it unleashes a huge desire to protect the child from whatever makes him frightened. For Indira's parents, it was intolerable to have her cry in the night, knowing that their presence would comfort her. Similarly, it was easier for them to arrange a life at home rather than take her places that made her uncomfortable. After all, they had waited a long time to have children and they were willing to make sacrifices to benefit their daughter. However, in the long term accommodating her anxiety to such a degree was not the best strategy for helping Indira. We will look at a variety of effective parenting strategies that ultimately helped Indira become more outgoing and able to cope with her world.

Summary of Parental Strategies for an Extremely Anxious Child

There are a number of actions a parent can take to help his anxious child. Some we have already mentioned. We hope that as you read in this book about different children and the tools their parents have used, you will find some strategies that are useful in your own situation.

1. Validation: Telling Your Child That You Understand What He Is Feeling Perhaps the most important strategy in this book is the concept of validation (**Tool Sheet 10, Validation**). When we validate a child, we are telling that child that we understand and appreciate him or her. Validation is more than telling that we see the good things that he is doing. We are also joining with him to tell him that we understand and are on his side. This is an essential point to understand. What he is feeling is real, even if it is not rational to feel the way he does. For instance, your child may not want to go to another floor in the house because he is afraid that there are monsters there. You know that there is nothing to be afraid of. However, if your child is afraid, tell him that you understand how he is feeling. Do *not* tell your child that he is silly to be anxious. Instead, say you understand that he does not want to go upstairs because he is  afraid. If he can wait until you have finished what you are doing, you will be happy to go with him. Remind him that there will be a time when he is no longer afraid to be upstairs by himself.

Once your child understands that you "get it" that he is anxious, you can then work together to figure out which anxieties are working in his favor and which anxieties are hurting him. With his permission, you will work together to change the anxieties that are not rational and are not helpful. To give an example, in Indira's case it was helpful to be worried about whether or not the cake was going to burn, but it was not helpful to worry about having a babysitter. Her mother appreciated being told to check on the cake. However, they were going to work together to get her comfortable with a babysitter because her parents needed to have some private time for themselves.

2. Child-Centered Time For the preschool and early elementary school child, dealing with anxiety often involves helping him or her child feel grounded, safe, and in control. Child-centered time, described in **Tool Sheet 11**, is an excellent way to deal with this. This concept is explained in detail in Chapter 11. In brief, the parent's goal is to give the child blocks of undivided attention during which there are no interruptions such as phone calls or interactions with other siblings. The parent is fully present with the child as he engages in an activity such as building with blocks or playing with stuffed animals. The child is in control and the parent does what he is told (within reason). If the child asks him to build a tower, the parent might ask exactly how high the tower should go. If the child starts making a vehicle out of Legos, the parent might comment that it looks like he is making some kind of van or truck. In general, the parent does not make suggestions about the play unless the child does the same thing for a very long time and the parent feels that he needs to expand the play in a new direction. It is helpful

for the parent to describe aloud what the child is doing, thereby providing a verbal mirror for the child. This works because it helps an anxious child like Indira feel seen and in control. When much of life is scary and unpredictable, this sense of control is deeply reassuring. By building in child-centered time with each child, 10 to 20 minutes a day, you are providing exactly what the anxious child needs, at a time and place that works for you.

3. Exposure A central principle to bear in mind when dealing with anxiety is that the child will often overcome his anxiety when he has lots of practice doing the thing that is frightening. This is called exposure. Indira's parents initially thought that they were protecting their anxious child by staying at home with her and never getting a babysitter. They did not think that anyone would be able to get her to be comfortable and they could not bear thinking that she was at home, crying, while they were out. As a result, the only time that they went out was when Indira's grandmother visited, about twice a year. The parents' view of protection was actually preventing Indira from having the experiences that would help her gain self-confidence and understand that she could cope. Exposure is the technique whereby one has to experience what one fears in order to learn that it is not fearful.

An important first step in the process of exposure is to set an appropriate goal. In Indira's case, a goal might be to get her to tolerate a babysitter. The next step is to preview for the child what is going to happen. Indira would need to be told that she is going to have a babysitter, that the babysitter is going to come over on Saturdays, and the parents are going to go out and leave Indira with the babysitter. Indira became upset when this was initially presented to her. She said that she could not do it because her babysitter would leave her alone and would not understand that she was afraid of being by herself. Indira's mother *role played* with her how to tell the babysitter what she needed. The mom first played Indira. She *modeled* asking the babysitter to stay in the room with her. Then Indira tried it. Indira then explained that she was afraid that at bedtime the babysitter would go downstairs to watch television. Together Mom and Indira worked out a solution that made Indira feel comfortable. As a special treat, Indira could watch her favorite video and stay up 30 minutes longer than usual. Then she would stay in the family room and look at books until she felt sleepy. She would not have to go upstairs to her room and the babysitter would read quietly on the couch with the lights on. If Indira stayed up late that was fine; she could sleep in later the next morning.

The previewing and role playing were helpful in getting Indira used to the idea of having a babysitter. Indira also was encouraged to use her good problem-solving skills to troubleshoot what was frightening to her. Now it was time to actually practice these skills in real life, what psychologists call *in vivo*. Only when you do the real thing can you fully get over the anxiety that you are feeling. Usually the pleasure of getting a positive response, as well as the feeling of success at having done something difficult, is very reinforcing. However, often hesitation returns. Here is where the parents' resolve and patience are critical.

This is what actually happened. Initially the babysitter came on a Saturday and the mother did not go out but left Indira and the babysitter to play a game together. The next week the babysitter came at the same time and the parents went out for a short while. Indira learned that she would be fine. The third week the parents actually went out to a movie. Each time she stayed with the babysitter, Indira gained more confidence that the babysitter would not let anything frightening happen. Gradually, the parents were able to have time together and even see their adult friends. Indira learned she could cope.

A further discussion of exposure is found in Chapter 6, The Dark Secret, which deals with obsessive compulsive disorder. In this chapter we describe a formal exposure technique that deals with trying to eradicate obsessive thoughts. This is a good example of **Tool Sheet 13, Changing Behavior**.

4. Play Therapy Sometimes children who are constitutionally anxious benefit from working with a mental health professional. In Indira's case, her anxiety was so pronounced that she worked with a therapist. The idea underlying play therapy is that the child expresses what is worrying him through play. He may not be able to tell you exactly what the problem is, but the themes of the play reveal issues of concern and his coping strategies. Often children work through an issue simply by playing it out over and over again.

Indira is a good example of how this works. The therapist allowed her to do whatever she wanted during their sessions. Throughout her last months of preschool, Indira chose to tell a story she called "Day Care." Every week she gravitated to the dollhouse. She would start with the beginning of the day, getting the children ready to go to day care. They then walked next door to the day care center, where they found two teachers who welcomed the children warmly. However, each day terrible things happened. One child dove into a pool and seriously hurt her head. Another time, the child fell from the second story of a house and broke a leg. This play continued for six months with only a few alterations.

During this time Indira finished preschool and went through the summer with greater success than the preceding year. Her parents this time did not let her stay home. Instead she attended the summer camp at her nursery school. When asked about what she was going to do in the fall, she named her new school happily. However, back in the therapy room, the disastrous "Day Care" play continued with children facing near death experiences.

In October, the therapy play changed abruptly. No longer were we playing "Day Care." Now the story was called "Assembly." This new drama described a little girl in a large room with many obnoxious children and animals that were doing outlandish things. However, this new play theme only lasted a month. Indira had now learned that she could handle the challenges of her new school with the help of the teachers she had grown to trust. Play therapy was concluded at this point.

5. Changing Behavior Sometimes children do unproductive things when they are anxious, such as refusing to go to school or pulling their mother's hair when she wants to say good-night. Each parent needs to have some strategies for changing these trying behaviors.

- *Validate* how the child is feeling.
- *Set a goal*, what you want to happen. Which of Indira's many difficult behaviors should her parents target first? It is usually best to work on one thing at a time, rather than attempt to make the child perfect in one fell swoop.
- Try to get your child's *commitment* to work on this goal.
- Use *positive reinforcement* to encourage the good behavior.
- *Ignore* behavior that is not productive.
- *Shape* the desired behavior by encouraging successive approximations of the desired behavior.

Here is an example of how this works. Indira was happy to see children at her own house, but she absolutely refused to go to a friend's house. Her mother told her that she totally understood that she felt uncomfortable at other people's houses, an example of validation (**Tool Sheet 10**). However, this did not seem to be working because her friends did not think it was fair that Indira would not come to their homes. Her mother's goal was that she go to her friend Nancy's house for a play date. Indira finally agreed that she wanted to see more of Nancy, and because she would not come over, Indira would go to her. We now have commitment to change. Her mother would now use positive reinforcement, ignoring, and shaping to achieve the goal, all skills related to changing behavior (see **Tool Sheet 13**). The plan was that every time Indira went to Nancy's house, she earned a trip to the ice-cream parlor with her mom. This is an example of reinforcement. When you are trying to get a child to do a difficult thing, giving them  something concrete is a good idea. Once you are over the hump and the behavior is part of the general repertoire, praise may be enough. However, occasionally there is backsliding. Indeed, after the first visit Indira decided to back out and refused to go again. Her mother ignored her protests and reminded her that they had a deal. This is an example of ignoring. On two occasions mom accompanied Indira and stayed during the entire play date. The next time she stayed for 30 minutes, and then came back an hour later to pick her up. The fourth time she stayed for only five minutes. This is an example of shaping behavior. You reward an easy behavior, but gradually you change your system and give rewards for increasingly difficult behavior. This process continued until Indira had no trouble going to the houses of her three school friends.

6. Observing Limits Because anxiety is so infectious, parents often find it easier to give into their child than have a battle. Indira's parents were extraordinarily good at figuring out how to accommodate her worries even if it meant that they rarely had a night alone in their own bed and never went out as a couple. It became increasingly clear why she was an only child! Although giving into your child may seem like a battle prevented, you will ultimately lose the war. Each parent needs to figure out *where he or she is drawing the line*. The important point is that a line is drawn, not where that particular line is! We like to refer to this as the parents observing their limits (**Tool Sheet 15**). If you don't get sleep and develop cabin fever, your child will ultimately suffer. Here is how it works.

- Have your *goal* clearly in mind. In this case the goal is for Indira to stay in her own bed at night.
- Explain your goal in terms of *your own limits*. What you need rather than what she needs. "We need to have sleep so that we can have a busy day and feel rested. Getting

up at night makes it hard to go back to sleep and then mom and dad don't get the rest we need."

- *Preview* what is going to happen: "I will say good night to you. I will come back frequently to check that you are ok, but I will not get into bed with you. I will stay upstairs and be in my room reading. You may not get out of bed after we have said good night."
- Gradually *shape* the behavior; for example, the first time you leave the room for two minutes and then check back in, then leave for five minutes. If the child is upset, you rub her back a minute and then leave, saying that you will be back. You keep checking in every five minutes until the child is asleep.
- *Reinforce* your child for doing it your way: "I know that you are uncomfortable when I leave the room, but you are doing a good job of handling this. If you stay in the bed all night, I will give you a prize." Give a concrete reward the next morning in terms of a grab bag prize or a poker chip for a token reinforcement system. (see **Tool Sheet 17, A Token Economy**)

7. Consequences   Sometimes your anxious child becomes so distressed that he is out of control. You can validate him by explaining that you know how hard the situation is for him, but ultimately you need to explain that there are consequences if he does not do what you expect him to do. For instance, one parent had a young child who refused to sit in his car seat. Mother and son had drag out fights as the mother tried to strap him into the car. Both were getting upset, with shouts, screams, and threats.

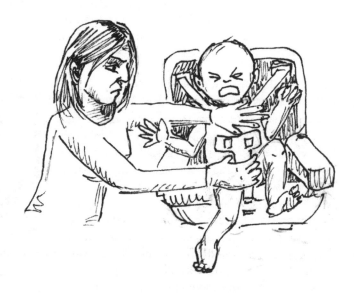

However, the mother then changed her strategy. She explained to her son that if he did not get into the car calmly and allow himself to be buckled into his car seat, he could not go in the car. Instead his mother would have to leave him with their friend, the next door neighbor. The first morning of this new regime the mother arranged with her neighbor to be ready. She previewed the plan with her son, who went through his normal distressed crying and struggling. The mother then did what she had said and left the boy with the neighbor. No one was happy, but the next morning the child was much more compliant. Children need to know that their actions have consequences. You are not being heartless by enforcing a consequence. You are instead helping your child manage his anxiety and learn to cope effectively with things that make him uncomfortable.

> **Tip:** Make sure you spell out consequences in advance so that the child understands the cause and effect relationship you are trying to teach. Be clear, calm, and consistent.

8. Positive Self-Talk Changing the way that a child thinks about a problem is an important strategy for reducing anxiety. Here, what you are trying to do is to identify unproductive thinking and then alter it to productive thinking. This is not easy. In Indira's case, her parents noticed that when she was upset, she said that Nancy's house was scary. Her parents kept reinforcing that in fact she loved playing with Nancy's dolls. Gradually they were trying to get her to say, "*I have a good time at Nancy's house.*" **Tool Sheet 7,**

Positive Self-Talk, is helpful in outlining how to change negative cognitions to positive ones. However, sometimes the fears were more all encompassing. Indira would talk about monsters in her room at night and at times she worried about her parents dying. Her parents had the following plan to help her cope with these free-wheeling anxieties:

- First, try to distract the child from what is bothering him. Using **Tool Sheet 6, Distraction** is a good way to turn his mind from something upsetting to something that is centering. In the case of Indira, this usually meant reading a story about an American Girl doll. As she grew older, her parents suggested that she try to distract herself by doing something soothing such as rereading an old and much-loved story.
- Next, dispute the fear and get a cognitive plan for dealing with the things that are worrisome. Indira's parents talked about all the ways in which it would be impossible for a monster to get into her room. They then set up a dream-catcher in her room that would catch the monsters and hold them so that they would not bother Indira. This helped. When Indira suddenly started worrying about electricity shocking her in her bed, her parents got a Richard Scary book that described electricity and how it worked. They then rewired a light with Indira. After she gained this knowledge, she stopped being anxious about the electricity.
- Try calming the child with gentle support. When she was in bed and worrying about monsters, her parents came in turned on the lights to check for monsters, patted her, and left the room. They returned later at infrequent intervals to check on her and assure her no monster would get her. Her father also found that it was soothing when he sang camp songs to Indira.

- Teach self-soothing strategies (**Tool Sheet 1**). If Indira got upset about going to Nancy's house, her mother suggested that she calm herself down by combing their dog. This worked to soothe her and allowed her to get more emotionally regulated. At night she loved listening to *The Secret Garden* tape that she had listened to many times before. The familiar story was also soothing to her.

- Reassure the child that the worries will go away. For parents it is important to remind yourself and your child that *these strong and difficult feelings will pass.* The analogy of a wave is useful. You cannot stop a wave from coming, but you can learn how to cope with the wave so that it does not throw you off your feet and grind your face into the sand. You can learn to dive under the wave in order to survive it.

- Mindfulness. Indira's parents taught her some mindfulness techniques to help her calm down. They told her to take three or four deep breaths as a way of getting through the difficult moment. This strategy, described in **Tool Sheet 8**, is a useful tool for both parents and child. Practice it with your child when he is not upset. Encourage your child to breathe in for a count of three and out for a count of three. There is no prescribed speed, simply breathe at the speed that feels comfortable. Usually as your child calms down, the breathing will get slower. Encourage your child to think only about the breathing and push the worries out of his head.

- Explain why positive self-talk is better than negative self-thought. As your child grows into the elementary school years, you can begin to help him understand the extent to which what people think and say to themselves determines how they feel. If you keep saying, *"I'm stupid and I am going to fail the test,"* you probably will. But if you say, *"I am going to study 20 minutes a night for the test each day this week,"* you will probably do just fine.

- Problems have a solution. You can help your child become a good *problem solver.* No one can think well when he or she overcome by emotion, which is why you first have to calm down. Then you are free to think up alternative ways of solving the problem, like Indira did in regard to monsters. Remind your child that if one plan does not work, he can always think up another plan. At this point, the parent is shifting from being the person who comforts the child when he is anxious, to a consultant who listens to the child in order to figure out how to deal with things that are hard.

Summary

All children will experience anxiety in their lives. Usually the episodes are short-lived and calm support helps your child to get through them. However, in this chapter, we have discussed children with extreme cases of anxiety that result in significant emotional upset. Here the normal parenting techniques may not work. Unfortunately, if this intense anxiety is not addressed, it can lead to major emotional difficulties in the future. As we have discussed, separation anxiety is a normal part of growing up, but if separation fears are ignored they can lead to problems with attachment. If school fears are not addressed, children will feel unsuccessful and try to leave school as quickly as possible, thus forgoing advanced education. If trauma is not treated at the time, it can resurface later as post-traumatic stress disorder and take years of therapy to uncover and deal with the consequences. If you ignore the fact that your child is wired to be anxious, you will place unreasonable demands on your child that can lead to a profound sense of inadequacy. Yet we know that when children feel understood and accepted by their parents, they can cope with extraordinary adversity. We hope that in this chapter you have learned that the causes of anxiety can occur from outside stressors in the environment or from the inside as a result of specific biochemistry. We also hope that some of the tools that other parents have tried will be helpful to you.

3

Mealtime Battles, Picky Eaters, and Kids Who Just Won't Eat

Jamie: The Very Picky Eater

"I thought that I had problems with Jamie and his eating, but I'm counting my lucky stars after what I just heard in your waiting room. The other mothers were talking about their children's eating problems. One mom said that her four-year-old child refuses all solid foods and is still on bottles. Everything that goes in his mouth has to be liquid. The other mother was talking about how her child gags on any food with texture, then throws up most meals when she is finished. I don't think I should complain that Jamie eats only three foods after hearing that!"

The words of this parent reflect the frustration that many parents feel who have a child with eating problems.

Eating problems in children can be very overwhelming to parents who struggle with children whose behavior can make mealtimes a nightmare. Parents often worry that their child won't be nourished properly if they eat a limited diet. The child may have problems sucking, chewing, and swallowing, making the process of eating difficult and exasperating for both parent and child. Some children are so hypersensitive to touch on their faces and in their mouths that certain food textures are aversive. There are also children who simply refuse to eat, hate sitting at the table, or have no desire for food. As you can see, there is a range of eating problems, all of which require different approaches. This chapter will give an overview of how children become good eaters, the different kinds of eating problems, how the parent–child relationship is impacted, and what parents can do to help.

Why Is Good Eating Important?

When children are good eaters and can feed themselves properly, they are showing that they can be organized, self-regulated, and able to control their bodies. They demonstrate adaptability and responsiveness to demands, such as being called to the table or told to stay seated. The child develops a healthy response to being nurtured by others and learns to nurture himself. Just as in sleeping, many variations exist in how families feed their children, what types of foods they eat, expectations to self-feed, and what the family mealtime looks like depending on the family's customs and culture. Nevertheless, there are certain developmental tasks that all children need to learn to become good self-feeders.

Skills for Healthy Eating

Sequencing: Children learn about food preparation, coming to the table, feeding themselves, and setting and clearing the table. These skills require motor, cognitive, and social planning.

Rules: They learn about mealtime rules, such as "sit in your chair while eating" and "don't throw your food."

Attention: They learn to sit for a short period of time, pay attention to the mealtime experience, and contain their activity level for the duration of the meal.

Motor skills: They learn to use utensils and tolerate a variety of tastes, smells, and tactile sensations to the mouth and hands.

Interaction and communication: These skills are major aspects of mealtime. Children learn to listen, take turns, and keep up a conversation in a group while eating.

Autonomy: They learn to assert their autonomy by making food choices, deciding how much food is eaten, and how they will eat the food (i.e., fingers or use of utensils).

Flexibility: They learn to make the transition from whatever they were doing to come to the table and to tolerate changes in the mealtime or feeding routine. For example, they may need to eat a new food, eat elsewhere than home, and sit in an unaccustomed seat.

Satisfaction: They also experience satisfaction from learning how to feed themselves and fixing food that appeals to them, and to enjoy eating with others.

What Can Go Wrong With Eating?

There are many aspects of self-feeding, and many ways that it can go off the rails. Some children are born with problems that cause them difficulties with eating. For example, a young baby may have difficulty with the mechanics of suck and swallow. Some infants experience *reflux*, which often causes eating to be painful. *Tactile hypersensitivities* may be present in the mouth, face, or body, causing the infant to pull away from the nipple, reject food textures, gag when presented with certain foods, or have difficulty being held and fed. Eating problems may also develop because of emotional difficulties in learning how to self-regulate, become attached to caregivers, or be in control and autonomous. These difficulties may be manifested by refusal to eat, rejection of the breast or foods, or other behavioral problems such as screaming when exposed to certain foods.

Refusal to Eat

Some children have such severe feeding problems that they fail to gain weight and grow, a condition termed "failure to thrive." There are a number of reasons for this condition. Some children have medical problems that affect absorption of food, such as a malformation of the esophagus or gastroesophageal reflux (severe acid indigestion) which contribute to the growth disturbance. Other children have developmental difficulties that alter their ability to chew and swallow properly. The most puzzling children are those who have no developmental or medical reasons for their failure to thrive. These children tend to have more underlying sensory and emotional problems. Regardless of the reason for the failure to thrive, it seems that most children in this category who struggle with the task of eating eventually develop some emotional difficulties with this process. Feeding takes place in the context of the relationship between the child and his or her caregiver. When struggles exist in the eating process, it is easy for the parent and/or child to enter a battle over how it is done.

> **Tip:** Avoid making mealtimes a battleground. Kids like to eat when they feel calm, nurtured, and hungry for a good meal.

Overeating

The origins of overeating can be multiple. Some children with an under-aroused nervous system overeat to load their stomachs, which enables them to better feel bodily stimuli. Some children who overeat have limited interests and resort to what's easy—like watching television and eating. There are children who overeat because they can't tell when they are full, packing their stomachs until they are sated. Overeating can arise when a child uses food to soothe herself when she is distressed, anxious, or depressed, or perhaps has a wish to "get back" at mom or dad. Metabolic problems and certain medications can also induce overeating. Likewise, a family's tendency to have frequent meals or snacks and consume high-calorie foods can create weight problems. Whatever the reasons, overweight children are often subjected to teasing and criticism from others because of the way they look. Poor body image and low self-esteem often result.

Helping children to eat should be tailored to the specific needs of the parent and child. In this next section, we talk about what can go awry with feeding and what emotional needs typically accompany the eating problem.

Types of Eating Problems

Many infants and children with feeding problems cannot tell when they are hungry or full. Some children may confuse being hungry or full with the need to eliminate. Problems of this type are common in children who have poor processing of the sensory receptors in the gut and colon. Here are some examples of common eating problems.

Amy: A Child with No Appetite Drive

Five-year-old Amy did not know when she was hungry and could go all day without food unless reminded by her parents that it was time to eat. She often had no appetite, which worried her mom and dad because she was so tiny for her age. When she did finally start to eat a little, she could not tell when she was hungry or full and needed her parents to teach her ways to read her body signals. A worried mother whose baby is not gaining weight may try to repeatedly feed the baby every hour or two in hopes that she will eat. Often the baby senses the parent's anxiety and becomes increasingly resistant to eating. Regularly scheduled meals and snacks helped Amy to anticipate her bodily needs and prevented her parents from becoming desperate.

Colin: A Child Who Ate to Settle His Irritability

Colin would scream almost nonstop, regardless of whether he was hungry or not. At age two, he had no words and used screaming to express anything he needed, as well as when he was unhappy or distressed. The only discriminating scream came when he was thirsty for juice—he screamed in front of the refrigerator—and when he was hungry for Cheerios, which happened to be the only food he ate, he screamed in front of the cupboard. Eventually he began to seek food as a source of comfort because he had so few calming devices in his repertoire.

> **Tip:** Children learn appetite cues when meals are provided on a set schedule and when parents talk about feeling hungry before the meal and feeling full when finished eating.

Samantha: A Child Who Ate to Nurture Herself

Because feeding is a nurturing experience, the impact of "being fed" is very powerful, as demonstrated by 8-year-old Samantha, who was stealing food from friends at school. At home, she had developed a pattern of eating anything in sight. Her slightly older sister, Corinne, had physical challenges and needed help with the basics of eating, dressing, and day-to-day activities. As a result of these needs, Corinne was always fed first; Samantha had to wait. Samantha had been a very placid baby, which led her parents to believe that it was okay to have her wait while they first cared for her sister. The key to helping Samantha was focusing on ways for her to feel nurtured—to have special time alone with her mom or dad—and to provide her with experiences that made her feel wanted, deserving, and cared for. As she began to feel nurtured, she was able to move past her need to steal food and overeat.

> **Tip:** Nurture your child in many ways: through loving gestures, play, hugs, reading to them, pleasurable activities, food, and messages of safety.

Many children who struggle with self-regulation also have problems integrating sensory information. A very common problem is hypersensitivity to touch around the mouth, which may cause the child to reject the nipple or new food textures. Likewise, infants who cannot tolerate being held during feeding may arch their backs and struggle out of the parent's arms. They may cry because the contact is aversive or because the position of their body is uncomfortable due to problems with their ability to process movement or with muscle tone.

Oral tactile hypersensitivities can greatly interfere with early feeding. Some babies react to the nipple touching their lips as if it were an electric shock. Latching on and sustaining a suck may be difficult because of problems maintaining skin-to-skin contact. The baby with this problem often pulls away from the breast or bottle and screams in distress. Some babies clutch at their hair or body and flail their arms and legs about in obvious distress. Mothers feeding a tactually defensive baby become extremely anxious and often depressed as the mere act of holding and feeding their baby evokes such a severe reaction.

Stephen: A Child with Severe Sensitivities to Touch

Stephen, at 6 months, was rapidly losing weight and showed severe defensiveness to touch around the mouth. He had a weak suck and was slow in developing his motor milestones. Stephen was hypersensitive to sounds and tended to shut down and sleep whenever the room was filled with people talking or laughing loudly. By chance, his mother discovered that he would take a good-sized bottle while he was asleep and soon she began to use this method to feed him. Addressing his sensory hypersensitivities was the first step in helping Stephen to overcome his eating problem. We began by helping him to tolerate touch in the mouth using Nuk toothbrushes and his mother's finger massaging his gums and cheeks. We worked to help him tolerate sounds through cause–effect toys that made music or interesting noises. At the same time, we provided him with a calm environment at home, with a little stimulation at a time to decrease his tendency to shut down when overstimulated. These ideas, combined with oral–motor activities to improve his suck and swallow, helped to launch Stephen's ability to be fed and to feed himself.

A common problem arising from oral tactile hypersensitivities is rejection of different food textures. This usually emerges around 9 months of age when table foods are offered. Some infants develop a preference for food with a firm, smooth texture, such as crackers or crunchy cereal. When this occurs, the infant is usually seeking deep pressure to the mouth by selecting foods that allow him to bite. Foods with uneven textures, such as applesauce with sliced bananas, are often rejected.

> **Tip:** If your child rejects food textures, start with firm, smooth textures like a piece of cheese or chicken or steamed vegetable. When he accepts a range of foods of this texture quality, add in another texture, for example, smooth and soft like applesauce.

Some babies are distressed by eating in a semireclining feeding position. Usually these babies dislike being placed in face-up or prone positions and prefer to be upright. Often the mother abandons breastfeeding for the bottle because she finds that the only way she can feed her baby is by placing her upright in the infant seat or high chair.

At times a baby will have such severe sensory hypersensitivities and motor planning problems that he cannot handle the complex tasks of simultaneously coordinating suck and swallow, feeding, maintaining tactile contact with the nipple, and looking at the mother's face. When this occurs, the mother may observe her baby looking away from her face or arching away from her body. Sometimes the mother finds that feeding is more successful when the baby is in a sitting position facing away from her body. As a result, the intimacy of the feeding experience is replaced by a mechanical quality. Jeremy's mother had to feed him a bottle in a sitting position facing away from her and she felt cheated of the experience of breastfeeding her baby. As Jeremy grew older, he continued to avoid social contact at meals. The only time he enjoyed mealtimes was when he could watch videos or be in a restaurant with ceiling fans that he could watch. As a result of his sensitivities and his early experience, Jeremy had learned to detach himself from his parents and the eating process.

Impact of the Child's Feeding Problems on Parents

When parents have a child with poor feeding, it is not uncommon for them to become depressed and anxious. Often they feel inadequate because they cannot feed and nurture their child. When opportunities for nurturing are disrupted, parents may feel at a loss as to how to connect with their child. Most parents in this situation feel rejected by their baby. As the parents become more agitated about getting their baby to eat, both parents and child develop high anxiety around feeding. There develops a confusion in reading signals between mother and child.

A Mother's Story: How Her Eating Problem Impacted Her Child

One mother revealed that she, too, had been a fussy baby and a picky eater growing up. As a teenager she was very thin, with little appetite, often needing to be reminded to eat. When pregnant with her first baby, Josh, she was anxious that her baby wouldn't eat. She feared that Josh would reject her breast or be a fussy eater. In the first few days of life, the mother was puzzled by her own reaction when the nurse brought Josh to be fed. She felt that her baby was overly demanding and bothersome to her. She felt "sucked dry by this little creature" instead of welcoming her baby's normal desire for feeding. The baby developed a significant problem in expressing hunger and satiety, often going for long periods without eating. In this situation, the baby had become as anxious about feeding as his mother, but demanded that his mother was the only one who could feed him.

> **Tip:** Helping your child read his body signals of fatigue, hunger, or discomforts like being too hot, too cold, or too wet will help him begin to meet his own needs. Remember—you can't eat or sleep for your child. You teach him how to read his body cues and learn how to maintain a good daily schedule. Your child's job is to take charge of these important tasks of body regulation.

Relationship Problems and Impact on Feeding

Picture the very young infant who gazes up at his mother, smiles, and reaches for her face, then cuddles or molds toward her breast while feeding. It is a wonderful intimacy between mother and child that emerges while the baby suckles. There is a strong sense of oneness between mother and child during this early feeding experience. Very soon the mother and child develop a reciprocal relationship, vocalizing back and forth, gazing at one another, and enjoying interchanges of smiling and cuddling. The feeding experience is very important in building the attachment bond.

Problems of Attachment

Infants and children with poor attachment avoid gaze or eye contact with other people, even to people who are important to them. The child may appear listless and apathetic. He might seem hypervigilant, looking around the environment but avoiding eye contact when approached by someone. They do not cuddle when held. Sometimes they lack the motivation and drive to explore the environment.

When attachment problems affect feeding, the child shows a lack of pleasure in feeding and does not enjoy playing with his caregiver. Usually the child has little appetite. This may be an indication of underlying depression, a lack of signal reading and giving between mother and child, or a low motivation to feed.

Children Growing Up in Orphanages: Emotional and Sensory Deprivation

The scenario of a secure and loving attachment between mother and child that is fostered by the feeding relationship does not always happen for all children. Children adopted from foreign orphanages often had a poor attachment with the caregivers at the orphanage, and some of them developed serious problems with feeding. Some of the children had their hands held down while being fed so that they could be fed more quickly. Many were exposed to a limited range of foods and would gag when introduced to new textures. Some had to wait long periods before they were fed. Often children with this history have had little nurturing and they accommodate by refusing to eat. Other children with this same history respond differently. They develop a pattern of constantly asking for food in hopes of connecting with a caregiver. Sometimes the child indiscriminately seeks attention from any adults with whom they come in contact.

> **Tip:** Build your child's attachment to you in many ways—by sharing pleasurable moments during play, care giving, and nurturing experiences.

Fostering Independence and Self-Control

It is not long in a child's development before he starts to want to do things by himself. By the time a baby is 7 to 9 months old, he already is interested in finger foods, using utensils to self-feed, and trying new food textures. The baby progresses from a stage of total dependence on his parents for feeding to wanting to control the feeding experience. For success in accomplishing the task of self-feeding, the baby needs to feel comfortable separating from his parents. He develops competence that he can nurture himself and that he is in charge of what goes into his own body.

As the child enters his second year of life, he learns to assert himself through feeding and play.

Some infants refuse certain foods, even favorite ones, but it is usually a temporary phenomenon. If the child is denied opportunities for autonomy, he might choose to keep food refusal in his behavioral repertoire.

The child learns to become separate and distinct from his parents in many ways. It may begin when the baby tries biting on his mother's nipple as he feeds. The infant gives clearer signals when he is distressed, full, hungry, or tired. If his mother is responsive to these cues, he feels secure that he is understood and listened to.

> **Tip:** Mealtime should be a time for the family to socialize. As the child develops gestures and words, he enjoys being the center of attention, wishing to be admired, and laughing whenever anyone laughs to be part of the group. The preschool child learns the give-and-take of offering food to family members and taking turns in conversations at mealtimes.

As children begin to self-feed, it becomes quite a sensory experience. Most babies enjoy dipping their hands in food and smearing their faces with food. This tactile experimentation with food may or may not be met with pleasure depending upon the child's tactile system. Likewise, parents who are uncomfortable with messes may struggle with how messy their baby gets when trying to self-feed. As the infant develops the motor control to manage the spoon, cup, and finger foods, the parents need to be comfortable in allowing their baby to take charge of the task of self-feeding.

Sometimes children don't develop the capacity to exert their autonomy. If parents insist on feeding their child past the point that the child wants to be fed, he may resist by pursing his lips and turning away from the spoon. Or he may bang his head, arch out of the high chair, or throw cups, bowls, and food off the food tray to express dissatisfaction in being controlled. Other children who are fed by their parents develop passivity about eating, and develop a dependence on their parents' doing things for them. The child's refusal to eat may be a way to get the mother's attention or to express anger at her. At the dinner table, the child may throw food, have a tantrum, or show extreme food preferences (with random refusal of preferred foods). Some parents resort to feeding their child as he walks about the house because he is difficult to feed in the high chair. Children with low weight may be forced to eat past the point of satiation, which can result in vomiting the meal. The parent usually becomes angry and more forceful about the child's eating, often introducing another meal within an hour or two. The child may begin to feel that he is held hostage in the high chair with no way to assert control except by compressing his lips and turning his head away.

> **Tip:** Never force-feed your child. Keep a regular schedule for three meals and two snacks. Most children will begin to feel hungry and anticipate the mealtime schedule. If he doesn't eat at one meal, he'll be good and hungry for the next one.

Eating problems at this stage are characterized by refusal to eat or extreme food selectivity. Overeating can also occur. For refusal to eat, the feeding problem seems rooted in the infant's bid for autonomy whereby the mother and child become immersed in a control battle around eating. The parents have usually tried everything to get the child to eat—distracting (one parent plays circus clown or entertainment committee while the other parent feeds the child), bargaining ("eat the peas to get a toy"), force-feeding, and coaxing. Instead of allowing the child's own body to regulate what and how he eats, the focus becomes the emotions that occur around eating—anger and control, parent's intrusiveness, and no natural back-and-forth exchanges between parent and child. The parent frequently experiences feelings of anger, sadness, and frustration and feels completely demoralized that she cannot feed her own baby. The parent

may worry excessively about the baby's growth and feel insecure in the role of parent. Because of anxiety about her child's eating, the parent may become flooded by emotions and unable to read her child's cues.

Getting an Evaluation

Whenever a child has an eating disorder affecting physical growth, there may be low body energy and delays in development. Often there is a lag in motor skills development because the child has decreased muscle mass and weak muscle strength. Social and emotional problems are usually present because of the disruption in the nurturing that normally occurs between parent and child. If your child has failure to thrive, it is important to find out whether the problem has a medical origin. You will need to rule out medical problems that interfere with eating and normal digestion and/or oral-motor problems such as drooling, or uncoordinated suck and swallow. Once you have determined this, find out what emotional issues may have developed. What might be getting in the way of nurturing your child? Did you experience deprivation growing up? Are there control battles between you and your child? Does your child reject your attempts to nurture him? A sensitive therapist can help to investigate these things with you. It is useful to have an occupational therapist determine if the child has sensory or motor problems such as oral tactile hypersensitivities that result in rejection of food or a limited diet. Lastly, the evaluative process may involve a nutritionist. It is reassuring to know that there are certain food supplements or vitamins that can balance your child's intake for healthy eating habits.

Because assessing and treating the child with an eating disorder is complex, a multidisciplinary team is often needed that may consist of a physician, a mental health professional, such as a child psychiatrist, clinical psychologist, or social worker, a speech and language therapist, nutritionist or pediatric nurse, and an occupational therapist. Children should receive a comprehensive set of assessments in order to delineate the nature of the child's feeding disorder. Close collaboration among members of the team is integral in order to assure that the evaluation and treatment process does not become fragmented or further disrupt a family under extreme stress. A pediatrician must be involved to monitor weight gain or loss and address any medical complications that may arise.

Suggested Assessment Process for Eating Problems

1. See a mental health professional to talk about your concerns. Provide her with a complete medical and family history. She can help identify any emotional underpinnings to the eating disorder.
2. A pediatrician should evaluate your child's health, measure his weight, height, and head circumference. A food intake history should be completed.
3. A developmental assessment, sensory, oral-motor and feeding observation is essential to determine your child's strengths and needs.
4. Observation of a family mealtime by your mental health professional helps to assess family dynamics in how meals are structured and how your child eats. Sometimes videotaping several meals and sharing these with her helps her to understand the problem.

Strategies to Help Your Child Eat

In this next section, specific strategies are discussed for common eating problems.

Medical Management

It is very important to consult with your pediatrician to rule out any medical problems such as reflux that might be contributing to your child's eating problems. At the very least, your child's weight and dietary needs should be closely monitored. Often it is useful to complete a three- day food record to look at food intake, food preferences and cravings, and frequency of intake. Sometimes children eat large amounts of a certain type of food such as dairy products only to find out later that they have a milk intolerance or allergy that causes poor sleep and irritability. A nutritionist or pediatrician can guide you on food supplements that can increase appetite for healthier foods. This is especially important with children who crave sugar or a high-carbohydrate diet. There are many children who seek "white foods" such as pasta, bread, popcorn, and Cheerios. Sometimes chicken is accepted because it is fairly bland in taste and an easy texture to tolerate in the mouth. High dairy intake is common as well. These children usually resist eating fruits and vegetables.

When children have low weight or poor growth, it is important to monitor the weight gain to be sure that your child is gaining weight, particularly as you begin any eating program. Ask the pediatrician what the "weight window" is. This means, how much weight your child can afford to lose before it is dangerous for his health. This may sound daunting, but when a child has issues around refusal to eat, resistance to eating new foods, etc., he will dig his heels in at first. For a few days, the child may not eat much of anything until he realizes that you mean business. It is critical to stick with the program that your therapist outlines for you so that your child learns what is expected of him. The first few days or weeks of the program are the most difficult for parents. They worry that their child might lose even more weight and they might feel the urge to feed their child on the sly to avoid further weight loss. Take comfort that your pediatrician and therapist are helping you through this. They will make sure that your child remains healthy through the process until he overcomes the physical, sensory, and emotional barricades that prevent healthy eating. Sometimes children do lose too much weight as they begin a program of self-feeding and then need serious medical interventions such as insertion of a nasogastric tube or gastrostomy tube. This should not be construed as a failure. It will help your child get the nutrition he needs as he learns the ropes of self-feeding and appropriate eating habits. In most cases, the tube is used for only a short while (i.e., up to 6 months), then is removed once the child has learned to eat well during his or her waking hours.

Tactile Problems of the Mouth, Face, and Hands

Many children refuse to eat because they have tactile hyper- or hyposensitivities in the mouth, face, or hands. When the child is hypersensitive to touch in the mouth, he may purse his lips vigorously to avoid being spoon or bottle fed. The contact of the spoon or nipple on the lips can be perceived as if it were an electric shock to the mouth when the child's problem is extreme. Food within the mouth can feel unpleasant, depending upon the texture and temperature. When this occurs, children frequently end up developing strong food aversions or eating only a small variety of foods. They can be very picky, preferring foods with a firm or even food texture. When the child is under-sensitive to touch in the mouth, the child usually has low muscle tone in the mouth, causing an open mouth posture and lazy tongue.

If there are tactile hypersensitivies on the hands, the child is apt to resist touching foods, particularly ones that are slimy, wet, or lumpy. Often the tactile problems in the hands go along with those in the face and mouth. Sometimes the mere sight of a food creates a sensory defensive reaction and the child gags and pulls his hands away. The tactile problem soon becomes one of aversion not only to touch, but to the visual presentation of the food and the idea of putting the food in the mouth. Often this evolves into an anxiety about certain foods.

Get the Face, Mouth, and Hands Ready for Food: Tactile Wake-Up

1. Address tactile problems at a time other than mealtimes unless your child has problems with muscle tone and needs a "muscle wake-up" to ready him for feeding.
2. Pat the cheeks gently with a firm touch, using either your hands or a soft wash cloth. Don't wipe the skin. This may be interpreted as aversive. Dab rather than swipe the face to clean.
3. With younger children, play fun games with the lips. For instance, you can lay your finger horizontally over your child's lips and wiggle them up and down as your child vocalizes or you can pat your child's rounded lips as he makes an "ahh" sound. Older children enjoy vibrating their lips with toy horns, harmonicas, or other interesting blow toys.
4. To work inside the mouth, begin by rubbing the gums with a plastic Nuk toothbrush with bristles on the tip. Some children like the feeling of terry cloth on their gums. Rub the child's gums three or four times back and forth in each quadrant of the mouth.
5. Older children often enjoy and respond well to an electric toothbrush or water pik. As with any tactile experience, the more the child can do him- or herself, the better the touch is received within the mouth.

Sometimes children with tactile hypersensitivities need sensory experiences that help desensitize them to touch that occurs during mealtime. For example, such a child may flinch every time he sees his mother come toward him to wipe his face.

Kayla: A Child with Food Aversions

Often children who are hypersensitive to touch gag at the sight of certain foods. Thirteen-year-old Kayla could not stand the sight of wet foods with lumps in them. She would literally gag if she saw ice cream with cookies chopped in them, applesauce with chunks, or granola on top of yogurt. Her problem got so bad that she ate alone in the school lunchroom to avoid looking at other children who were eating these foods. She engaged in a combination of treatments that included desensitizing her mouth to touch and developing a hierarchy of foods that she could stand to watch others eat, eventually introducing texture into wet foods.

Improving Utensil Use

Difficulties using utensils are common among children with incoordination or problems with motor planning. Children with these difficulties often resort to using their fingers to self-feed. One often sees the 9-month-old holding a spoon while his mother feeds him with another spoon. By 15 to 18 months, the toddler self-feeds with a spoon, with some spillage. When a child experiences low muscle tone in the hands, it affects his ability to maintain a proper grasp of the utensil and affects how the hand brings food to the mouth.

Strategies to Improve Utensil Use

Begin with tasks that require a hand-to-face or a hand-to-mouth movement without the extra requirement of carrying food on the utensil. For example, bubble blowing, putting goofy hats or sunglasses on the head, and face painting develop this skill.

Use a Nuk toothbrush or breadstick as a spoon. It is easier to grasp and requires less wrist rotation.

Use foods that stick easily to the spoon, such as melted cheese on peas or mashed potatoes.

Just like learning to walk and talk, there is a magic window when children learn certain skills. If the child remains at an earlier skill level too long, it is difficult to launch into the next-level skill.

Matthew: A Child with Motor and Sensory Problems Who Resisted Eating

Four-year-old Matthew fed himself solely with his fingers. He wanted to feed himself and resisted his parents using utensils to feed him, yet he didn't have the motor control to use a spoon or fork proficiently. If his parents insisted that he use the spoon, he would shriek and throw the food. His finger feeding was extremely messy, with food spread all over his hands and face as well as the table surface. To help him with this problem, we determined which foods he loved to eat. We used breadsticks for the utensil and began the meal encouraging him to dip the breadstick in a favorite food (i.e., chocolate pudding). If he could do three dips with the breadstick or use the spoon, then he earned another favorite food that was acceptable to eat with his fingers (e.g., piece of peanut butter sandwich). It took some time to help Matthew develop new eating habits, but eventually he had expanded his food repertoire and learned to eat in more acceptable ways.

Improving Appetite Drive

It is common for children with eating problems to have difficulties distinguishing when they are hungry or full. Some can hold out for many hours without eating until reminded that it is time for a meal, and even then, may become annoyed if interrupted by their parents to come eat. Children who don't eat often experience low blood sugar and emotional dysregulation.

Joseph: An Irritable Child Who Rarely Ate

Eight-year-old Joseph became extraordinarily irritable when he hadn't eaten for a while, as many children do. It was a major breakthrough in managing his foul moods when he internalized that eating at regular times would help him feel better, both physically and emotionally. Despite the fact that a child may resist eating at regular times because he or she feels absolutely no urge to eat, it is important to maintain a regular eating schedule. Parents should label being hungry and full before and after meals to help the child recognize these states. If a family member is dieting, it is wise not to bring this up in front of the child, otherwise he learns to refuse eating certain foods because it might make them "fat."

Helping the Picky Eater

Children who develop the habit of eating only a few foods and resist trying new foods usually have hypersensitivities to touch and smell coupled with an emotional response of aversion to trying new foods. Sometimes the child develops a visual hypersensitivity as well, choosing not to eat foods with certain colors or that look a certain way. The most common picky eating problem is the child who eats only "white" foods—macaroni and cheese, Cheerios, rice, chicken, and milk products.

Strategies to Help the Picky Eater

Use treatment techniques described above to desensitize the mouth.

Desensitize the child to one food at a time so as not to overwhelm him. If he eats only "white" foods, introduce a new white food such as rice cakes.

If there is an aversion to smell, put a competing, pleasant smell in the environment to override the smell aversion of the food. For example, burn a pleasant smelling cinnamon- or peach-scented candle during meals.

Begin with firm food textures like crackers, steamed vegetables, or a piece of turkey.

Expand the food repertoire, beginning with smooth, soft textures like yogurts and applesauce before introducing uneven textures (banana chunks in yogurt).

Mimi: A Child with Aversions to Food Textures

Nine-year-old Mimi had an extreme aversion to food textures and made a decision that she would only eat popcorn, white rice, Cheerios, and macaroni and cheese. She was adamant that there were no other foods on her list and strongly resisted even discussions about her diet. Mimi had dark circles under her eyes and a pallid skin tone despite the fact that she slept enough. It seemed that poor nutrition impacted her ability to focus and attend at school. Because we had worked on sensory problems that might influence her food aversions, I approached her resistance through a cognitive technique, appealing to her intelligence. I asked Mimi to draw a rainbow in colors on a piece of paper. We then discussed that in order for our brains to grow and learn properly, we need to eat foods from all the colors of the rainbow. Our conversation went something like this.

Therapist: "What color foods do you like to eat?"

Mimi: "I guess that they're all yellow or white."

Therapist: "Do you think that you could pick one or two of these other colors and think of a few foods you might consider trying this week?"

Mimi: "I suppose I could try an apple. That's red. And I would consider trying carrots. They're orange."

We developed a behavioral contract that she had to try one or the other food each day that week, with a reward at the end of the week if she could take five bites of the new food per day. It was a start for her. It took nearly six months before we had accomplished a better eating regime. In the meantime, her parents consulted a nutritionist to add supplements to her diet to ensure healthy nutrition.

The Problem of Overeating

When children eat constantly, they are packing the gut and overstretching the stomach to the point that the stomach no longer signals that it is full. Usually the child eats frequently, quickly, and prefers heavy or starchy foods. Here are some suggestions for this problem.

Addressing Problems of Overeating

1. Do not use food as a reward for good behavior.
2. Set up an eating schedule and focus on portion control (i.e., eat a portion of pasta no bigger than your fist; fill only half of a small plate).
3. Encourage your child to select foods from the food pyramid. As your child eats foods from each category, he marks or colors in that he has eaten something from it. When a column is full, he looks to other food groups to be sure the diet is balanced.
4. Apply grandma's rule—"Eat your peas to get the French fry."
5. Encourage the child to take two or three bites of a food he doesn't like to earn eating the preferred one.
6. Develop other activities your child likes besides eating, preferably more physically active ones that burn up calories or that foster creativity.
7. Improve sensory feedback to the gut by applying deep pressure to the abdomen. Use a weighted blanket or squishy pillow, pressing it into the abdomen to give pressure to the gut.
8. Stimulate the airway and abdomen by playing with blow toys (blowing up a balloon, playing the horn or harmonica).

Addressing Anxieties Accompanying Reflux

Reflux is sometimes not properly diagnosed, particularly in children who have less severe forms of reflux. This is a problem that causes the child to have indigestion that leads to regurgitation of food in the esophagus, vomiting, or heartburn types of symptoms.

Sophie: A Child with Anxiety About Swallowing Certain Foods

Thirteen-year-old Sophie had this problem and developed anxiety around swallowing certain foods, particularly wet foods with lumps in it. She would hold ice cream in her mouth until it was completely melted before swallowing. If she tried to eat something the consistency of a hot dog, she would chew it for minutes before swallowing for fear that a piece of it would get stuck in her throat. Whenever she was stressed she would feel like she was going to vomit or choke, but in actuality, her problem originally began with reflux then became associated with anxiety around swallowing. In addition to helping Sophie get medicine for her reflux, we worked with her on tolerating different textures in her mouth, swallowing different kinds of foods that were aversive to her, and addressing the anxiety that she felt just thinking about eating these foods. Visual imagery was especially helpful to her. For example, Sophie could imagine a warm, gold light in her throat. She breathed slowly and deeply and imagined opening her throat in her mind to allow the gold light and breath to enter her body. Once relaxed, we talked about what would be the worst thing that could happen to her if she swallowed something that was too big in her mind. A small pellet-sized piece of food could elicit a choking feeling in her throat. We did some "science experiments," dropping raisins and beads into clear plastic tubing to show how impossible it would be to block the airway with something that small. She was coached on what to do if she did swallow something and it felt like it was getting hung up on her throat. For example, tucking her neck forward slows down the swallowing process so that she has more control. Eating slowly helps reduce reflux and promotes digestion, therefore it is a good idea to remain upright, in a sitting or semireclining position after eating. It is also a good idea to chew gum after a meal to help promote digestion. In babies, we encourage them to suck on a pacifier after eating for the same reason.

Helping Your Child to Come and Sit for Meals

Many parents lament that getting their child to the table is a major endeavor. Parents with an energetic toddler may find their child resists being strapped into a high chair and finally they give up, feeding him wherever they can—the car, the bath tub, or in the stroller. Older kids sometimes get on the computer or video games and don't want to shift gears for a meal. Some children prefer to have a meal in front of the television and might eat a meal only if they are duly occupied. Children with a short attention spans may be up and down out of their chair throughout the meal or sit only briefly before asking to leave the table. Getting the child to the table and enticing him to sit for a meal can be very difficult.

Strategies to Help Your Child Come and Sit for a Meal

- Provide a relaxed, unrushed atmosphere for mealtimes. If you can't do this for every meal, try to do this at least once a week as a start.
- Find something that makes your child want to come to the table. For example, some children like being in charge of serving the food, cutting the food into interesting shapes like a sandwich triangle, setting the table in an interesting way, or picking the "lucky" centerpiece.
- Engage in a ritual of hand washing, setting the table, and clean-up before and after the mealtime.
- Sing a song or play music that signals the transition.
- Create ambiance by lighting candles and putting on soothing music.
- Set out a "talking ball" for the children to use. Whoever has the talking ball is the one who speaks; the other people must listen. Encourage "one at a time talking" and asking a question of the speaker.
- Rotate the job of who gets to put out the lucky centerpiece for the day. That person selects something he or she likes or wants to share with the family. It can be anything from an art project to a found object.
- Reward good sitting at the table with a dessert, an extra story at bedtime, or getting to watch television. You may set a timer and gradually lengthen the sitting time to 15 to 20 minutes.
- Having jobs for the children can be fun. For example, you can have the "caterer" help to serve the food; the "mealtime planner" asks family members for suggestions for a special meal; the "story teller" tells a joke, an interesting story, or relates something about the news.

Guidelines to Improve Eating Behaviors

In this section we provide a number of guidelines that are useful for the range of eating problems. **Tool Sheet 18, Food Rules,** provides guidelines to help children to know what is expected of them during the mealtime experience. Being consistent is essential.

1. Set up a mealtime schedule, including scheduled snacks. The best schedule is one with three main meals, and two small snacks, one mid-morning and the other mid-afternoon. If the therapist advises one before bedtime, then add a snack. Do not give the child a middle-of-the-night bottle feeding. This sabotages the program. We want your child to be actively engaged in his or her eating program. Also, avoid feeding your child little snacks while going about your daily activities. This encourages grazing and results in the

stomach never achieving a full then empty state. If you have a busy life and cannot manage one of the snacks at the table, you can give your child a small manageable snack in the car seat while driving. The important thing about the schedule is that it encourages your child to anticipate the routine and develop an appetite for eating, thereby increasing motivation to eat.

2. Establish food rules during mealtime (i.e., no throwing of food or utensils, no standing in the high chair; one warning for inappropriate behavior, then remove food). Refer to **Tool Sheet 18**. Many parents find it difficult to stand firm on these rules. It is important that your child learns that he cannot manipulate the mealtime into a play time, or expect you to fix another meal if he doesn't like what you have provided.

3. Put on the plate only what the child can reasonably eat. Avoid putting out too much food (i.e., a whole buffet) because this will overwhelm the child.

4. Oral-motor needs related to sucking, swallowing, and chewing should be practiced at a time other than mealtime, if possible. Stimulation of the mouth can be done during tooth brushing or playtime focusing on oral-motor games. Work on oral-motor control at mealtime only if your child cannot eat without this stimulation.

5. Avoid using food as a reward for doing other behaviors.

6. Provide opportunities for your child to play about nurturing, feeding, separation, control, or other emotional themes that might underlie his eating problem. Refer to our **Tool Sheet 11, Child-Centered Time**.

7. Seek support from other parents who have been through the same problem. It is very helpful to acknowledge the feelings of rejection and depression that come up from not being able to nurture and feed your own child.

8. Explore the meaning of food and eating with your therapist to see if there are "emotional triggers" that are set off when you work on your child's eating problem. For example, if one or both parents had problems around eating in the past, such as a history of anorexia, bulimia, poor appetite, or overeating, your own emotional responses to eating, being nurtured by others, control, and body image might get stirred up.

9. Socialize the mealtime experience so that it is a fun time for the family. While you are eating, talk about the day and enjoy one another during the mealtime. Sometimes children need help in how to do this. You might set up a structured "share" time whereby you pass around a pretty candle or funny-looking salt shaker that symbolizes who has the spotlight. You can encourage your children to share their accomplishments, interesting events, future plans, a favorite book, toy, or movie, things they have done with friends, and problems that have come up in their day. Television should be eliminated during mealtimes so that maximal interactions can be stimulated.

10. Everyone should eat at the mealtime to model eating. If you are not hungry or are dieting, then try to have a small healthy snack. Sometimes parents like to be able to eat a nice meal without the children. This is fine to plan once or twice a week, but the children need the experience of a family meal with everyone eating together as much as possible to learn good eating habits. Similarly if the children need to eat before a

parent is home, have them join their parents at dinner time, perhaps saving dessert for that time.

11. Avoid making more than one meal at a time if your child doesn't like what is served. If your child doesn't like what you have served for the meal, have a simple back-up option like a bowl of Cheerios. This way your child learns that he can't manipulate you into fixing something else for him.

12. Go places where people are eating and having fun. Take your child to places like McDonald's or mall eateries where he can see other children eating and having fun. It's a great experience for him to learn how to order and pay for food as well.

13. Talk with your spouse about what you would like mealtimes to be like at your house. Iron out any differences of opinion and try to find ways to integrate your religious or cultural perspectives into the experience. It's a great way to pass on your family heritage and to instill values.

14. Mealtime is family time. As children grow and progress through school, mealtime may be the only time that the family gathers each day. As they get older, mealtime enables family members to talk about national news events and local community happenings. Family dinners have been shown to correlate with higher academic performance of the children because of these kinds of discussions.

Summary

The best way to help your child become a better eater is to help him learn to feel states of hunger and satiety, become a proficient self-feeder, and develop emotionally healthy patterns that support autonomous feeding. An important aspect of the treatment is to support your child's sensory needs to help him become comfortable with the eating experience. A successful treatment program not only embraces the emotional underpinnings of the eating problem but provides your child with structure and guidelines as to what is expected.

4
Up All Night, Crying, and Fretful
How to Help Your Child Fall and Stay Asleep

Evan: Ten Years Old and Still Not Sleeping

"Ever since our child was a young baby, he hasn't slept. It is a huge problem when he doesn't sleep. We are up all night and all of us are completely sleep deprived. Nothing has ever worked! When Evan was young, we tried ignoring the crying, rocking him back to sleep, and riding in the car for hours on end. One time I even put him in the laundry basket on top of the dryer, hoping that the vibration would soothe him. We discovered by accident that the vacuum cleaner sound helped to put Evan to sleep, so we would turn it on, leaving it on for hours at a time to help him fall asleep. We even burned out the engine on the vacuum cleaner. When he was 18 months, we had a brief period when he actually slept. Then the night terrors began. Now he's 10 years old and he sleeps in a sleeping bag with his head sticking in our bedroom door. That's not so bad, but he won't fall asleep until we've done this enormously long bedtime ritual. We're exhausted, at our wit's end, and nobody is functioning in the house."

These could be the words of many families who have struggled with a sleepless child. For many parents, solving the child's sleep problems is extremely challenging.

Sleep plays an important role in restoring the body. When a person sleeps, nutrients are absorbed into tissues and the brain. Children grow when they sleep. When a person doesn't sleep, everyday functioning and learning are seriously challenged. A person who is not sleeping enough or has interrupted sleep is often inattentive, has trouble remembering things and thinking clearly, and can be very irritable. When sensory hypersensitivities are present, they are worsened. The child is more apt to be bothered by touch, noise, and sensory stimulation.

Skills for Good Sleep Habits

Here is a list of skills that children need to have good sleep habits.
Regulating sleep-wake cycles
Anticipating and following daily routines and schedules
Transitioning from active and quiet alert states of arousal to falling asleep
Screening out noise from the environment when falling asleep
Self-calming when distressed or when awakened in the night
Use of a calming device or transitional object (i.e., stuffed animal) to self-calm
Feeling attached to the caregiver while feeling secure enough to separate at bedtime to fall
    asleep

Parents help to support sleep-wake cycles by establishing set times for naps and bedtime and by enacting bedtime rituals (e.g., bath, story). When a child has a soothing device to use in the bed or crib, it helps him in falling asleep and when reawakening occurs. Parents also help their child by avoiding overstimulation, which may include noise stimulation such as the television. Finally, it is important that parents provide experiences that support both attachment and separateness. Parents foster attachment by having defined periods of the day when they engage in intimate, shared activities that give pleasure to parent and child. Separateness is developed when parents and children engage in activities independent one of each another. When the child is alone and separate from his caregiver, he feels secure yet can hold in mind his parent's presence. Later in this chapter we will elaborate more on how this is developed.

For some children, falling and staying asleep may become problematic in the second year of life even when it wasn't an issue before.

Developmental Tasks that Support Sleep in Toddlers and Older Children

Calming down after a stimulating day of activities

Engaging in a balanced sensory diet of movement stimulation (i.e., playground activities, sports, rough house play) and calming activities (i.e., reading books, doing puzzles or art projects)

Screening out noise from the environment when falling asleep

Negotiating fears of dark places, "monsters" in the closet, and of being alone

Tolerating limits set by caregivers around bedtime rituals

Feeling attached to the caregiver while feeling secure enough to separate for sleep

Developing autonomy or independence in being secure with aloneness

It is important for caregivers to help the child negotiate different levels of sensory stimulation through the day without becoming overstimulated. For some children this means not getting so hyped up by an activity that they can't calm down. For others, it's a matter of processing different kinds of sensory experiences over time and not letting the cumulative effect overwhelm them. For example, some children can do one after-school activity, but a play date and an outing to the store may be far too much stimulation for them. Another challenge that confronts the child is listening to his parents' rules about bedtime while reserving the right to say "No!" and asserting his own autonomy.

As children grow older, these same needs continue; however, worries or anxieties creep in. For example, at bedtime a school-aged child may worry about conflicts with peers or a sick pet. Seven-year-old Sandra was such a child. She worried that a fox from the woods would sneak into

the house by the chimney and attack her at night. Or she worried that a bad man would climb the tree outside her window and steal her away. For a child prone to anxiety, media reporting of bad events in the world will fuel that anxiety. A child who previously slept well can suddenly have problems with sleep for this reason.

Sleep Problems in Children: Birth through School Age

Sleep problems are common in children who have difficulties regulating their mood and activity level and in children with sensory integration disorders. Sleep problems often peak in babies around 10 to 12 months when separation anxiety first emerges. By 19 to 24 months, many young children who are irritable and highly sensitive to sensory stimulation can fall asleep on their own, but they may continue to awaken frequently in the night. Between 2 and 3 years of age, children start having fears (e.g., "monster" in the closet, thunderstorms) and may develop night terrors that awaken them regularly. As children grow into the school years, anxieties can keep them awake at night, causing them to toss and turn until they eventually fall asleep.

Here are some of the symptoms that are apt to occur at different ages when sleep problems are present.

Infants

At 7 to 9 months, sleep problems may occur because the baby has a high need for *movement stimulation*. Caregivers often report that the only way to help their baby fall asleep is to bounce or rock their baby for long periods of time. Some parents place their infant in an infant swing or drive them around in the car for an hour or so, allowing the movement to help the baby fall asleep. Other infants are calmed by white noise, such as an oscillating fan in the bedroom.

At 10 to 12 months, *separation anxiety* seems to compound the sleep disturbance. Parents often report that their baby is very clingy and can only fall asleep when held in their arms. Some mothers find that nursing their baby to sleep works, then they have problems when they withdraw the nipple from the baby's mouth. One mother stated that she slept with her baby latched onto her breast the whole night. It took many months to break this pattern. Distress upon awakening in the night may have been accompanied by anxiety that the child is alone in the crib rather than in the parent's arms. If the baby falls asleep in the parent's arms, when he awakens he may panic, not knowing what happened to his mom or dad who had helped him fall asleep.

> **Tip:** Fostering a secure attachment between you and your child and helping him to separate from you in the daytime will help him to fall asleep on his own.

Toddlers

By 13 to 18 months, many children with sleep problems show a higher need for movement stimulation. The child's high need for movement seems to increase his arousal, making it more difficult for him to fall asleep. This problem may be exacerbated in children who become conditioned to rough house play. For example, often fathers come home from work in the evening and the child expects some fun time with dad, jumping on the sofa cushions or being tossed in the air. Distress at sounds in the environment such as the vacuum cleaner, dryer running, or television is often present and seems to begin around 13 to 18 months. Many parents state that their child only falls asleep if they help to screen environmental sounds by using white noise such as an oscillating fan or white noise audiotapes. Severe separation anxiety may also be a contributing factor at this age.

By 19 to 24 months, falling asleep may be less of an issue; however, waking in the night usually persists. Many children who continue to awaken through the night crave movement and appear restless throughout the night. A common pitfall for parents is falling into the trap of taking their child out of the crib and allowing him to play or move around. This helps to condition the child that night time is also play time rather than a time for sleep.

Preschool and School-Aged Children Sleep problems in older children are usually long-standing. Problems with sensory hypersensitivities, particularly to touch and sound, can cause the child to have difficulty settling in the bed. Many school-aged children become overstimulated by movement activities. However, it is common for children to develop sleep problems when they are on the computer or playing video games in the evening hours. The visual stimulation of these modalities heightens arousal and makes sleep more difficult. Likewise, the inactivity of sitting in front of a computer or TV screen for long hours results in a body that has not had the opportunity to burn off physical energy.

School-aged children develop increasing anxieties that may make sleep very difficult as they thrash in bed, worrying about these issues. Conflicts with friends, world news, family problems, watching a frightening movie, past fears, and worries about upcoming performances load the deck. Without adequate ways of dealing with these day-to-day anxieties, the child is apt to develop agitation at bedtime and have difficulty getting much needed sleep.

Other Factors that Influence Sleep

Sleep problems may be attributed to a number of other factors. Some studies have found that mothers who experience a high degree of stress or feel anxious or depressed are likely to pass their tension on to their child. The tension can be as simple as a mother who feels guilty leaving her child all day long while she is at work, feeling that the only time she has with her child is at bedtime. A chaotic, disorganized family life can fuel a sleep problem. It is especially unraveling for a child to sleep in a disheveled bedroom with clothes and books strewn on the floor, toys everywhere, and barely room to lie down on the bed.

Sleep interruption can also occur in children with gastroesophageal reflux, ear infections, sleep apnea, allergies and problems breathing, and in some cases, neurological problems. Your pediatrician should help rule these things out for you.

Children with a fussy or difficult temperament and who are more emotionally reactive are also more likely to have sleep disturbances. They have a higher need to be soothed by their parents and often struggle with how to use soothing techniques on their own.

> **Tip:** When parents are lax and inconsistent in adhering to sleep routines, the sleep problem in the child will become worse. Because there are multiple causes for sleep problems, it is important to be systematic and thoughtful about what might be contributing to the problem.

Impact of Sleep Problems on Development

Many young infants who experience sleep problems often resolve this problem on their own by 9 months of age. However, when sleep problems persist, there may be developmental and/or emotional problems that accompany the sleep disturbance. Children with muscle tone disturbances have difficulty getting comfortable in the bed. Frequently children with autism spectrum disorders have unusual sleep cycles and may awaken thinking that it is time to play or they awaken and become agitated or disruptive. Children who are hypersensitive to sensory stimulation commonly struggle with sleep because of their hyper-aroused nervous systems. Anxiety disorders, especially involving separation anxiety and problems being alone, are common among children with sleep disorders. Finally, children with attention deficit disorder with increased activity level, poor attention, hyperactivity, and impulsivity often struggle with sleep.

Developing Good Sleep-Wake Cycles

As children grow older, changes occur not only in the duration of sleep but also in the quality of sleep (e.g., REM vs. non-REM sleep) and the number of times that a child awakens in the night. A newborn's sleep has about 50% REM (rapid eye movement) sleep, in contrast to 20% REM sleep in the adult. As the child matures, there is a decrease in REM sleep. Newborns have a 50-minute sleep cycle in contrast to the adult's 90-minute sleep cycle. We need REM sleep to feel emotional well-being because that is when the brain's unconscious reworks what we think about during the day and integrates events in life for emotional adaptation. Poor sleep patterns or insufficient sleep can lead to crankiness, inattention, and increased emotional and sensory hyperreactivity.

Table 4.1 provides guidelines for you so that you can know how long your child should be sleeping.

Table 4.1
Normal Trends in Sleep Patterns

Age of Child	Sleep Patterns in the Typically Developing Child
Newborn	Sleep 16.5 hours/day
2–3 months	Sleep 3 to 4 hours continuously then awaken for feeding
4 months	Sleep for longer periods at night with shorter naps during the day
6 months	Sleep 14.25 hours/day
	Awaken 1–2 times in a 5- to 6-hour sleep cycle
10 months	90% of children sleep through the night
12 months	Sleep 13.75 hours/day
2 years	Sleep 13 hours/day
3–5 years	Sleep 10–12 hours/day
6–12 years	Sleep 9–10 hours/day

Self-Soothing and Why it Is Important for Sleep

Evan's Nighttime Ritual Ten-year-old Evan, the boy in the example at the beginning of this chapter, lamented that he couldn't fall asleep unless his parents engaged in a long ritual of back rubs, play time, hot showers, and listening to stories and music on tape. If his parents were not there during these activities, he simply couldn't fall asleep. What was missing for Evan was that he had never learned to soothe on his own. He depended on his parents to do the soothing for him.

What we see in children who learn to sleep on their own is that they develop the skill of self-soothing. Infants and children who signal their parents by waking and crying are typically put in their crib already asleep and don't have a "sleep aid," such as a pacifier, stuffed doll, or special blanket. Many times the parent lies down next to the child to help him or her fall asleep. This can backfire on the parent when she is so exhausted that she falls asleep while the child lies there awake. The key for the child to become a self-soother is to be put in her bed awake and have some sort of sleep aid. Then when she awakens, she can snuggle with her stuffed animal to help her fall back to sleep instead of relying on her parents to do this for her. It is helpful to know that all children awaken between two and four times per night. The difference between a good and poor sleeper is that the poor sleeper signals his parents on each awakening by crying or going to  the parent. In our modern society, parents are highly attuned to their child's awakenings because of the use of sound monitors in the child's room. Parents often find that they need to resist going into their child's bedroom upon the slightest rustling, whimper, or sound. See our **Tool Sheet 1** on self-soothing.

> **Tip:** Children who use soothing devices to fall asleep on their own also use these soothing objects or activities should they awaken in the night. Help your child develop a soothing object that he holds or uses during both his waking and sleeping hours.

Making the Bedroom Environment Conducive to Sleep

Emma: Trying to Sleep in a Chaotic Bedroom When I asked 9-year-old Emma to take a picture of her bedroom so that I could see what it looked like, she reacted in horror. I inquired, "What would I see if I appeared at your home today to take a peek at your bedroom?" She replied, "You don't even want to know!" Apparently it is impossible to find the bedroom floor. There were papers, clothes, toys, stuffed animals, trash bags, and food wrappers strewn everywhere. Forget about doing homework or any focused work in a bedroom like that. When it came time to fall asleep, she could barely find the bed. In essence, it is like trying to sleep in a trash dumpster. No one can rest in that environment.

An important aspect of sleep is where the child sleeps and what the child's sleep environment is like. Sleeping alone in a bed or sleeping in the family bed are very different experiences. Consider how old your child is and whether sleeping with you interferes with his development and learning. For example, it is very common for parents to have their young infant sleeping in a bassinet in their bedroom until the baby reaches 3 or 4 months of age. Unless the parents support the family bed philosophy, a child may seek to sleep with his parents or the parents may use this as a solution when frequent nighttime awakenings occur that disrupt the family's sleep. Children often enjoy the closeness of sleeping with their parents and quickly become used to a family sleeping arrangement. Once a child reaches 7 months and is beginning to negotiate issues related to trust, separation, and attachment, it is useful for the child to sleep in his own space except in special circumstances. The issue of sleeping alone becomes particularly important as the child nears the second year of life.

> **Tip:** Sleeping alone provides the child an opportunity to feel secure with his own separateness, thus paving the way for good self-esteem and self-reliance.

Some children have difficulty settling for sleep because of problems such as hyperactivity or sensory hypersensitivities that make it hard for the child to self-calm, to become physically comfortable in the bed, or to screen noises from the environment. When this occurs, the child may need certain props in the bedroom to help him sleep. For example, William found that he was able to fall asleep if his bed was covered with a pup tent and he lay beneath a heavy comforter. This helped him relax and quiet his body for sleep.

A home environment that is noisy and stimulating with few established routines will be less conducive to sleep than one that provides balanced levels of stimulation and calming, regularity in routines, an organized bedtime ritual, and a sleep environment that helps the child feel secure and calm. If the bedroom is very stimulating or cluttered with toys strewn around the floor, the child will be less able to get ready for sleep. The child will be stimulated by a busy or noisy home. For example, there may be other children sharing the bedroom and making noise, the television may be on after the child has tried to go to sleep, or adults in the house have different sleep schedules because of their work life.

When children sleep with their parents, the preschool or school-aged child may become aroused by the physical contact but not know how to handle these sexual impulses. Some children become aggressive towards their parents, siblings, or peers during the daytime as a way of trying to discharge these urges. The child may have difficulty accepting limits, complying with requests, and tolerating distress because of the lack of boundaries at nighttime. In addition, the child may witness sexual activity between the parents that they do not know how to handle emotionally. Usually the child misconstrues the sexual activity as aggressive. Addressing the sleep problem becomes more than simply one of working on separation and individuation, but one that is tied up in physical and emotional boundaries.

The parent's schedule may inadvertently affect the child in adverse ways. If the child is picked up at day care or after-school care at 6:00 p.m., then there is the drive home for half an hour. Dinner time may not happen until 7:00 to 7:30 p.m. There is a mad rush to finish homework, get ready for the next day, take a bath, and have story time or debriefing from the day. There is little time for relaxation or soothing activities. Getting to bed at a reasonable and consistent hour is next to impossible. The child is likely to get less than 9 hours of sleep, which is well below the amount of sleep he needs.

> **Tip:** A regular, consistent schedule and a balance between calming and stimulating activities during the day will help your child develop cycles of both alertness and a state of calmness. Your child needs to experience both during his waking hours to help him ready himself for sleep.

Types of Sleep Problems in Children

There are different types of sleep problems, some more common at different ages. The most common sleep problem is insomnia when the child has trouble falling and staying asleep. Occasionally one sees children who sleep many hours of the day and night. As children develop, they may develop unusual sleep behaviors, such as recurring night terrors or nightmares. The child may have an unusual sleep cycle, sleeping for a few hours at a time then fully awakening. Of course, whenever sleep problems are present, it is important to rule out medical problems, including sleep apnea, painful conditions such as reflux, or severe ear infections or allergies (e.g., milk intolerance) that may contribute to the sleep problem. In this next section, the most common sleep problems will be discussed.

The Hypersensitive Child

Children with sensory integrative dysfunction who are hypersensitive to touch and sound may experience sleep problems because they are easily hyperaroused and find it difficult to get comfortable and settle for sleep. A child with this problem may become agitated with the bed sheets lying on his body or fuss with the way his pajamas feel. Sometimes the tactually defensive child falls asleep more easily if he has the body contact of a parent lying next to him, which in turn reinforces the child needing a parent next to him to fall asleep.

Sam: A Child Who Needed a Protracted Bedroom Ritual to Fall Asleep   Four-year-old Sam had this problem. Since he was an infant, he insisted that his parents go through a series of bedtime rituals. First he wanted his mother to give him a 15-minute massage before getting dressed, but only after he changed his night clothes several times before finding just the right one. This was followed by three bedtime stories with Dad. Mrs. N would return to the bedroom and lay down next to Sam. He would fall asleep while twirling his mother's hair in tight knots for almost 30 minutes. This routine took about 2 hours each night. Sam often reawakened in the night and wanted parts of the routine to settle him back to sleep, particularly twirling his mother's silky hair.

To help solve Sam's sleep problems, we took one set of behaviors at a time and worked on just that problem. For example, finding a silky stuffed animal to stroke helped as a replacement for mom's hair. We set up a chart showing which parent would help Sam fall asleep on a given night. The other parent had the "night off." We kept the 15-minute massage and three short stories as part of the routine because Sam clearly needed these, but we eliminated all other parts of the ritual. Teaching Mr. and Mrs. N to *observe their limits* (**Tool Sheet 15**) was important, while at the same time we helped Sam to feel more emotionally secure to separate during his waking hours.

Hypersensitivities to sound may result in the child having difficulty screening out noises in the environment to allow for sleep. The slightest noise agitates him or causes him to reawaken. The problem is aggravated when the household tends to be very noisy and active, with several children in close quarters and the television on constantly.

Amy: A Child with Extreme Sound Sensitivities   Five-year-old Amy was so hypersensitive to sounds that she often ran screeching from the room if her mother turned on the food processor, vacuum cleaner, or almost any household appliance. At school the fire alarm would send her into total disarray and toilets flushing were overwhelming as well. A noisy playground environment and echoing lunch rooms or auditoriums were too much for Amy to bear. By the end of the day, Amy was so overloaded by sounds that she was high wired and unable to fall asleep. Children like Amy who are hypersensitive to sound often do well when provided with white noise when they try to fall asleep. However, this was not enough for her and she needed to wear heavy ear phones that blocked out certain sounds. She also needed to shorten her exposure to noisy environments and limit the sounds she heard during the day. It wasn't until we had come up with a sensory diet of how much sound she could tolerate that she began to sleep better.

In rare instances, the child who is extremely hypersensitive may shut down and sleep for long periods of time because they are overwhelmed by stimulation. Some parents misconstrue the child's need for sleep as simply a high need for rest. Ian, at 12 months, slept about 18 hours each day. He basically woke up to eat, play a little, then went back to sleep. Ian was the youngest of four children living in close quarters in a very active, busy family. By decreasing the level of stimulation at home and keeping a calm environment for him, he became more interested in participating in activities and accommodated fairly quickly to a normal sleep-wake schedule.

> **Tip:** Decrease stimulation in the household and reduce the number of activities that your child experiences over the course of the day to help balance cycles of alertness. A child with an overwhelmed nervous system has trouble calming for sleep.

Courtney: A Child Who Shut Down and Slept Because of an Overwhelmed Nervous System   In another instance, 3-year-old Courtney came home after 6 hours in day care and would take a 3-hour nap, then wish to go to sleep by 7:00 p.m., sleeping through to 6:00 a.m. She, too, was hypersensitive to touch and was not only shutting down when she came home, but was becoming aggressive at day care, biting and hitting other children who came near her. Problems with sleep patterns and aggression both improved with a program that included sensory integration activities to address her tactile defensiveness, calm-down areas at day care and home, and decreasing the number of demands at day care to participate in so many activities.

The Child Who Craves Movement Stimulation

Another type of sensory integration problem that may affect sleep is found in the child who craves vestibular stimulation but becomes hyperaroused by the movement. Young infants with this problem love to be bounced vigorously, wish to be held and carried constantly, like to ride in the infant swing, and may fall asleep only if they ride in the car for long periods of time. Some young babies with this need for movement also like vibration. For example, one 9-month-old would only fall asleep if he was placed in a laundry basket on the clothes dryer (with the heat turned off, of course). Many parents report how their child is gleeful when father comes home from work and can rough house or wrestle with them on the floor after dinner. Although the child needs vestibular stimulation, he becomes overstimulated by the movement and finds the task of settling for sleep very difficult.

> **Tip:** Many times children who crave movement stimulation also like heavy deep pressure on their body or vigorous activities that engage their muscles, such as climbing, pushing heavy objects, or wrestling with a sibling.

Joshua: A Child Who Craved Movement But Became Overstimulated By it   At 7 years, Joshua was a hyperactive boy who constantly moved and sought movement activities. If he wasn't directed to do focused movement activities such as riding his bicycle to get milk from the grocery store after school or playing soccer with his friends, he would become aimless, running up and down the stairs and whirling around the house, crashing into furniture and people. At nighttime he was at his worst. After the bedtime routine, his parents would put him into bed, then after a few minutes, he would escape from the bedroom, run up and down the hallway, jump on his parent's bed, and laugh loudly. Limit setting at bedtime was unsuccessful until it was coupled with a program of helping Joshua to get enough movement stimulation in the afternoon. He engaged in a program of soccer, basketball, games using weights, and running around a track. After dinner, he engaged in slow movement and deep pressure activities consisting of sitting in a glider rocker chair with a weighted blanket on his lap.

Problems with Attachment and Separation

Some children struggle with falling and staying asleep because of problems related to *attachment*. Problems separating from the caregiver can occur for several reasons. The child with an insecure or disorganized attachment will become anxious whenever there are separations from the parent during the day or night. If you suspect that your child has this problem, it is important to explore the origins of the insecure or disorganized attachment to properly address its impact on sleep. The parent may experience conflicts around leaving her child, projecting fears that relate to her own past.

Danielle: An Anxious Child Who Couldn't Fall Asleep   A good example of a child who had separation and attachment difficulties is seen in the case of Danielle. Her parents had tried to use the Ferber method (this will be described later in the chapter) with their baby but could not stand the crying and felt compelled to rush in immediately to console their child. They found the crying so intolerable that soon the child was sleeping in their bed. This lasted for the next 4 years. In treatment, the parents revealed that each felt that they were abandoning their child, but for different reasons. When the mother was 8 years old, she had a sister who died from leukemia. The ghost of the sister seemed to loom over her parenting, affecting how she parented Danielle and her ability to allow her daughter space to leave her side and explore the world. She constantly hovered over Danielle, creating the feeling that there were constant dangers in the world around her. For example, she would not allow her to play at other children's houses or go to birthday parties without her being present and within sight. The father was anxious about being left alone and needed to be surrounded by people and activity all day long. He was less open to exploring what it was about being alone that troubled him. By the time Danielle was 4 years old, she appeared to be a highly anxious, hyperactive child who needed to be occupied by her parents all of the time, unable to organize even a single play activity by herself.

When Danielle was 5 years old and had been in therapy for about 6 months, her parents were finally able to allow her to sleep in her own bedroom. At first her parents needed to constantly check on her to be sure that she was safe. Mr. P took to sleeping in a sleeping bag in the hallway for a while until he felt assured that Danielle was secure. Despite their anxieties about leaving her alone, they did not know how to play with Danielle and needed help in allowing Danielle to self-organize her play. It was difficult for Mr. and Mrs. P not to constantly teach her or provide structured activities all day long.

Emphasis in the treatment was on helping Mr. and Mrs. P to understand the developmental task of being and sleeping alone, the importance of gaining a sense of self and separateness from others, and in learning how to negotiate normal boundaries of intimacy with others. Learning how to have fun and engage in child-centered time (**Tool Sheet 11**) was very important to helping both parents and child to resolve the emotional entanglements that kept them stuck in a bad pattern.

Sometimes parents who need to leave their children at a babysitter's or day care during the day feel ambivalent about leaving them to sleep alone at night, perhaps feeling guilty about leaving them for many hours during the day while they work. Other parents have strong unmet needs for intimacy that are fulfilled by their children. This problem was depicted by Ms. S and her 18 month-old, Lisa.

> **Tip:** Some children use the sleep situation as a means of controlling their parents, getting them to give them attention that they may not get during the daytime hours. When exploring sleep problems, it is useful to think about how you and your child spend your waking hours together and the quality of engagement with one another..

Devon: A Child Who Controlled His Parents at Bedtime   By 9 months of age Devon had learned to control his mother both during the day and at night. When his mother sought the advice of a psychologist, she described her child as "the devil himself." An eating problem first developed when 6-month-old Devon would refuse to eat in the presence of his mother, compressing his lips and turning his face away from her. He ate well for the nanny, which caused his mother to feel rejected by her baby. By 9 months, Devon began to fight off sleep, sleeping only 20 to 30 minutes at a time for a total of 6 hours per day. When he awakened, he would scream at the top of his lungs until his mother would come and hold him. He would gasp and hyperventilate so badly that his mother would take him out of the crib and hold him. Father could not stand the screaming and would go in and yell at Devon. His attempts to comfort his son made no difference. Devon would shake his head "no," then he would lunge his body around in the crib, sometimes catapulting over the crib's edge. In the end, the parents concluded that what he wanted was mother to go in to be with him. The parents had tried everything with Devon, including the Ferber technique, and had finally resorted to using medications, starting with Benadryl and later Valium, all with a physician's oversight. There was no beneficial effect from any of these medication trials.

In working with Devon and his mother, several things became apparent. Devon was an extremely bright and competent child who was on the verge of walking and talking at 9 months. He was highly vigilant, constantly looking around the room and extremely wary if approached by a stranger. Mrs. P could play with Devon for short periods of time in a highly engaging way, but after about 10 minutes, she would need a break from playing with him, finding the intensity of the interaction overwhelming to her. Mrs. P revealed that she had had several miscarriages before having Devon and was enormously disappointed that she had a baby that was so demanding after trying so hard to conceive a child. Marital issues were an overriding factor, with mother feeling little support from her husband, who tended to work long hours to avoid being around Devon's screaming and controlling behavior.

Tip: Reinforce your child for getting attention in positive ways. Help him learn how to engage in pleasurable interactions with you in many different ways. Balance your child's need for control in positive ways, such as letting him pick out what your family will eat for dinner one night each week, pick out the clothes he'll wear, and choose what he wants to play with you.

The case examples provided in this section demonstrate the wide variety of problems that can occur when sleep is an issue. Our **Tool Sheet 20, Managing Your Child at Night**, includes suggestions to help your child fall asleep as well as strategies for managing night-time awakenings. If you are not making any progress after a month or two, then it may be useful to work with a mental health professional, nurse practitioner, or a developmental pediatrician who can guide you further. They can help you to explore what developmental needs your child might have, what might be going on in your relationship with your child, and other things like past history or marital issues that may affect your child's sleep.

Helping Your Child Be Alone

In **Tool Sheet 20**, we discuss methods for getting your child to settle down and go to sleep. One central concern here is helping your child to tolerate time on his own. Many children play easily on their own, but children with self-regulatory problems crave the presence of others. They use others to structure their time because they have trouble structuring time themselves. They also use others to help them calm down when they are agitated because it takes a long time to learn how to calm themselves. As a parent, you can be very helpful in encouraging your child to be comfortable by himself. If you work on these skills in the daytime, it will help your child tolerate the sense of being on his own at night.

Helping Your Child Cope with Sleep Anxiety

One of the major reasons that your child cannot sleep is that he is anxious. He gets easily worried by the sounds of the house creaking, which may suggest the threat of thieves, or shadows flickering on the walls, which suggest monsters. In **Tool Sheet 21, Feeling Less Anxious at Nighttime**, suggestions are made to help your child reduce his fears and regulate his body. These techniques will also help you calm your child when he is experiencing daytime anxiety.

Summary

This chapter provides an overview of common sleep problems in children. The suggestions provided in the chapter should be useful for infants, preschoolers, and school-aged children but could easily be modified for older children as well. Sleep difficulties can develop into problems related to attachment. It is therefore important to help your child feel close but also to help your child learn how to tolerate aloneness and separateness. The nighttime routine requires your child to learn how to accept limits and structure. When children have sensory, attentional, mood, or other developmental problems that impact sleep, these need to be considered, especially as they affect your child's ability to self-calm, be less over-aroused, and better able to modulate different amounts of sensory stimulation. The ideal treatment program for sleep should incorporate playing with your child to shore up any worries your child might experience around being alone, losing you, or dealing with other fears or anxieties, and separation issues. You should provide clear structure around the bedtime ritual and nighttime awakenings, as well as activities that are organizing for your child's sensory and emotional development.

5
The Dark Secret
The Mysteries of Obsessive Compulsive Disorder

Grier: A Girl with Frightening Thoughts That Would Not Go Away

How Grier Appeared to the World

Grier was an exceptional child. She was attractive, with a sturdy build, pony tail, and a big grin. She was verbal from an early age, which commanded attention from others. At six, Grier was a natural raconteur. She told her friends about her inner tubing trip to Philadelphia where she had gone with her brother and a close friend. She described how the inner tube flipped over, throwing her under water and she couldn't breathe. Her friend was frightened but Grier said that she had not been worried. Then there was the time that her family went to South Africa, where her father ate bugs and worms. This didn't upset her. She thought that the lions were cute but they were so far away that they had not scared her.

She was finishing up first grade and her parent teacher conference was a song of praise. Academically, Grier was making great progress in reading, writing, and math. Her teacher commented on her wonderful memory and how curious Grier was. She also noted that Grier was one of the most popular girls in the class. The teacher's only complaint was that Grier was a perfectionist when it came to handwriting, and she kept erasing her work because it did not look quite right. The teacher also was somewhat concerned that Grier would not go to the bathroom alone.

Grier on the Inside

Although on the outside Grier was in great shape, on the inside she was wrestling with powerful thoughts and feelings. These thoughts were obsessive and she often felt scared. She also was developing compulsive behaviors that were very difficult to control. However, unlike most children who experience these uncontrollable thoughts and are afraid to talk about them, Grier, the raconteur, was able to tell her parents what she was thinking, feeling, and needing to do.

Many of Grier's thoughts were scary. She described bad dreams that spilled over into daytime. These bad thoughts focused on monsters who were everywhere. However, the most frightening of these monsters lived in the basement of her house. In one dream she described the monster chasing her but eating her mother instead and turning her mother into juice. Grier avoided the basement, especially on dark days, and tried to be quiet in the house so that the monsters would not know where she was. The monsters also inhabited the bathroom, where they lived in the toilet. She was afraid that someone might call to them and make them come out. The monsters took different shapes. She said in one dream there were vines all over the room, but that the vines were in fact snakes that were very long and coming after her.

Grier's drawings of a snake coming after her and a monster.

Grier's drawing of a girl worried that an airplane will crash.

As she got older, Grier's worries expanded into her daytime activities in addition to bad dreams. Grier started worrying about germs. Germs were everywhere. When she swam in a pool and accidentally got water in her mouth, she worried that bugs were growing in her stomach and she felt sick. The fear of germs was so strong that she would not touch her underwear. When she touched a railing at the Metro by mistake, she became extremely agitated because she was afraid she was infected by the Metro germs. She also worried intensely about flying because she was afraid that the airplane would crash.

The Impact of These Fears

Grier's fears had an impact on her life. In school she had obsessive thoughts that she was not neat enough. She kept erasing and rewriting, trying to be perfect. She would not go to the bathroom on her own because she had a fear that there would be a fire in the bathroom. At home, she was so worried about germs that she washed her hands repeatedly. In a further effort to deal with these scary feelings, Grier began to pray. She initially was taught to say grace before meals. Now she wrote out the grace on a file card and said it every time she ate anything. If she was at the zoo and wanted to have popcorn, she would pull out the file card and say grace. When she forgot the card but needed it, she would cry inconsolably. She also said prayers to apologize for all the bad things that she had done and to ask God to take away her bad thoughts.

Grier was seen initially for play therapy to get a better understanding of her hidden world. At one point she was asked to create a scene in the sand tray using any toys that she wanted. Grier's scene was rich with frightening details. In the upper left-hand corner of the rectangular tray, she had a trapped girl half buried in sand, watched by a ghost. All around her were army figures but they were clearly the enemy rather than friends. Nearby, an ugly serpent was burrowing in the sand surrounded by menacing spiders. In the center of the tray at the bottom was another girl, this one guarded by a dragon. She was trapped in a haunted house. Above her was "a guy with no head who haunts houses." Nearby, spiders were lurking so that anybody walking there would have "to watch where they stepped." On the right side of the box, a giant ant was eating a dead horse. A snake was buried deep in the sand, ready to attack. Finally at the bottom right was an airplane. Grier explained, "There is one chance to get away on the plane." Her sand tray shows the vividness of her fears. It also suggests how trapped she felt in this scary internal world.

How this Illness Developed

Grier's parents reported that Grier had been an irritable baby, who struggled with colic. By age two she was talking in sentences and would tell her parents that certain things scared her. However, her obsessive bad dreams and frightening thoughts started in earnest after the age of four. Her parents explained that this was a stressful time for the family because Grier's grandfather died suddenly and her parents were very upset. It is possible that the distress of her parents was a catalyst that tipped Grier into becoming overwhelmed by her scary thoughts. As her dreams and worries grew, Grier, being Grier, was able to tell her parents what she was thinking. It is important to remember that many children are unable to do this and so it is harder to learn that they have hidden compulsions and obsessive fears.

What Is Obsessive Compulsive Disorder?

Obsessive compulsive disorder (OCD) is a serious illness that affects over 4 million people in the United States. This disorder has been studied for the last 30 years by researchers at the National Institute of Medicine. This research is presented in the book *The Boy Who Couldn't Stop Washing* by Judith Rapoport (1989). Obsessive compulsive disorder occurs suddenly, often affecting children. This is a disease that affects one's ability to control thoughts and behaviors because of irrational fears. We think and do ineffective things because we are afraid that if we don't do them, something even worse will happen.

The thoughts are repetitive obsessions. They stick to the brain and keep recurring in an effort to keep danger at bay. In one case, a boy must check seven or eight times that he has delivered the newspapers to every house on his paper route. In the case of Grier, her obsessive worries focused on monsters coming out of the toilet, germs growing bugs in her stomach, and God being mad at her. She could not get these worries out of her mind. As you can see, the thoughts are often very irrational but pervade the child's belief system and ultimately impact her concept of self.

In addition to these intense recurring thoughts, there are often rituals that one must follow to ward off peril. These rituals may not at first be apparent to other people. One girl had a compulsive need to order her belongings in a particular way. She could not go to bed unless her shirts were all folded and organized by color and her shoes were lined up beside her bed with the laces crossed in a certain manner. In another case, a boy had to touch a mirror three times before he brushed his teeth. One preteen had to pick up trash whenever he saw it and then keep it. In Grier's case, her needs to wash her hands and say prayers are typical compulsive behaviors. The majority of compulsive behaviors in children involve checking that something is right (delivering papers), counting in a prescribed manner (touching the mirror), ordering things in a particular manner (stacking shirts in terms of color), hoarding (the boy picking up trash), or repeating a certain pattern of behaviors in a prescribed manner, such as twisting string in a special way at certain times. As children with this disorder reach adolescence, 85% of them develop a washing or other grooming ritual (Rapoport, 1989).

> **Tip:** Be alert to any behavior that is odd. Is it repetitive? What emotion is the child showing?

Many children who experience this strong internal coercion to think or act in a certain manner know that what they are thinking or doing appears weird. They therefore go to great lengths to hide what they are doing. They don't want other people to think that they are different because that would be embarrassing. Grier explained this in the following way:

> Kids don't want to share it (their compulsions) because they are afraid and embarrassed. A girl might have to do things that she might not want to do. I think she might be scared and lonely.

Because of this sense of embarrassment, children often don't tell their parents what is going on in their heads. They suffer in silence and may not get the help that they need to cope with their frightening internal set of demands. It is therefore important for parents and school officials to be on the lookout for the subtle signs of the disorder. Rapoport's research estimates that 1 in every 250 children has some of the symptoms of obsessive compulsive disorder. This is true cross-culturally. It is important to treat OCD early. The longer it is untreated, the more generalized the symptoms become and the more they take over a child's life.

Are All Rituals Signs of Obsessive Compulsive Disorder?

No. Rituals can be a normal part of childhood development. Between the ages of two and eight, it is normal for children to try to control their environment by means of regular and repetitive behaviors. This is very clear at bedtime, as we have shown in Chapter 4. Children often insist on following elaborate rituals before they can go to sleep, such as saying good night in a specific manner, arranging toys or animals in an exact way, or kissing their parent a specific number of times. As children grow older, similar behaviors are common. Children often have elaborate collections that resemble hoarding. Between the ages of 7 and 11 children are naturally very rule bound. They may insist on following convoluted procedures in their games and their imaginary play. Often these rituals are in the service of deepening social interactions and may also help the children deal with separation anxiety. As they get older, these rituals disappear and children become more flexible about rules.

In children with OCD, these rituals and rules begin to interfere increasingly with their overall ability to function. Rather than being socially useful, the obsessions and compulsions come to weigh the child down and take over an increasing part of the day. Rather than adding interest and color to their lives, the rituals of children with OCD reflect huge anxiety. They do not go away when they are no longer interesting. Rather they often intensify as one grows to adolescence and adulthood.

Here is a list of symptoms typical of the child with obsessive-compulsive disorder:

- Being overly concerned with dirt and germs
- Doing certain behaviors to avoid punishment from God
- Hoarding objects for no reason
- Picking up trash

- Frequent hand washing or grooming
- Long and frequent trips to the bathroom
- Avoidance of touching unclean things
- Counting things in a prescribed manner
- Having to check several times that the lights are out, the stove is off, or the door is locked
- Excessive concern about harm to self or others
- Doing odd rituals, such as going through doorways in an eccentric manner, taking a specific number of steps to move from room to room, touching things a specified number of times
- Checking school work over and over again
- Rereading and rewriting, or repetitively erasing
- Repetitive "bad dreams" at night and recurring during the day

What Causes Obsessive Compulsive Disorder?

When researchers at the National Institute of Mental Health (NIMH) started to study OCD in the early 70s, they were perplexed as to the cause. Initially they thought that it might be the result of different styles of parenting. However, they learned that the symptoms of OCD developed in children regardless of whether they were raised in very strict or very permissive houses. The researchers therefore had to look further.

Research in Sweden was showing that a drug called Anafranil was helping to diminish the obsessive thoughts in adults. This pointed to a biochemical cause to the disorder. Research at NIMH and other research institutions has since documented that the neurotransmitter serotonin is at abnormal levels in the OCD population. Serotonin is a chemical that transmits information from cell to cell. The failure to have enough serotonin can lead to problems with mood, aggression, and impulsive control. It is now known that various antidepressant medications that work on increasing serotonin levels can be effective for children with OCD. In some cases the medication makes the coercive thoughts go away entirely. More often the medication helps to reduce the intensity of the thoughts. One might still have unusual ideas cross the mind, but they are like other thoughts that come and go. They are no longer screaming at you and demanding immediate attention and action.

Further research has revealed some structural abnormalities in the brains of people with OCD. These abnormalities are located in several areas. One area of difference is in the left frontal lobe, the area above the left eye. This area is called the orbital cortex. It is where thoughts and emotions combine. This area of the brain serves as an early warning system, signaling us when something is wrong and needs to be dealt with. There are also differences in the most primitive part of the brain, the basal ganglia. This area controls the filtering of thoughts. Sensory information is sorted there, with the result that unnecessary information is discarded. In the case of people with OCD, some primitive behavior patterns are activated that are normally filtered out. Another difference is found in the center of the brain. This area is called the cingulate gyrus, a part of the limbic system. It directs you to shift from one thought or behavior to another in order to respond to the most important demand facing you. In the case of people with OCD, the frontal lobe is warning that danger is present. The cingulate gyrus responds to this and prioritizes their thoughts and actions. When it is overactive, the person gets stuck in certain behaviors or thoughts. Judith Rapoport points out that these specific areas of the brain are also the location of other brain illnesses, such as epilepsy and Tourette syndrome, which cause tics in the body. Rapoport describes OCD as a "tic of the mind."

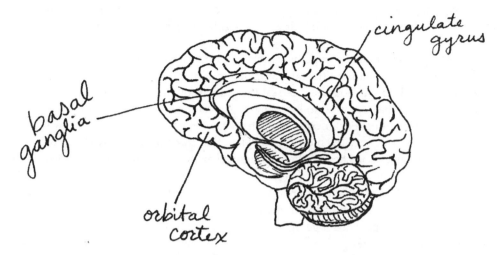

In addition to atypical brain chemistry and structural abnormalities, there is a clear genetic predisposition in OCD. Different research studies have shown that 20% to 40% of those with OCD symptoms have blood relatives who share the disorder. This is particularly true when there is a childhood onset of the disease.

Recent research has linked childhood onset of OCD to the bacteria that causes strep throat. This is called pediatric autoimmune neuropsychiatric disorder associated with streptococci, or PANDAS. In this case the antibodies that the body produces to attack the strep bacteria end up attacking brain tissue in the basal ganglia. This results in children developing OCD-like symptoms. When the infection is treated by antibiotics, there is a significant improvement in these symptoms and often they go away. If your child suddenly develops OCD symptoms, or his OCD symptoms worsen, go to the doctor to check for strep.

The progress of OCD is unpredictable. Some children may have minimal symptoms as adults or no symptoms at all. Others have symptoms from time to time. Often the symptoms themselves change over time. The recurrence of symptoms may result from the effects of hormones and stress on our biological makeup.

How Can This Disorder Be Treated?

As a parent there are two things you should do. The first is to join with your child and enter his world so that you know what he is thinking. The second is to lead him out of that scary part of his world toward more normal thoughts and behaviors. However, because OCD is a complicated illness, you will need the help of trained professionals as you make this journey. You and the professionals will need to collect information about the disorder and then decide on the correct treatment plan.

At this time the general thinking is that we approach this illness in two ways. Medication has been shown to be effective in eliminating or muting the obsessive thinking. Second, one should follow a program of cognitive behavior therapy with an experienced clinician, which includes exposure to the frightening obsessive thoughts and acting to inhibit the child from doing his compulsive rituals. As part of this process, one should work with the child to change the nature of these repetitive thoughts, a skill we call positive self-talk (see **Tool Sheet** 7 in Appendix 2).

If the symptoms are severe, it is usually recommended that one start with medication. However, with less intense and controlling thoughts, cognitive behavior therapy may bring significant change.

In order to enter your child's world, you must be alert to what your child is doing. If you feel that there is a behavior that is a little odd, ask your child to help you understand what is going on and what he is thinking. You need to treat these odd thoughts and actions as perfectly normal, and something that you need to know about. *Validate* your child for being aware of what she is thinking and feeling. For instance, you might say, "How clever of you to know what your mind is thinking and feeling. Tell me more." Explain that sometimes we have "sticky thoughts" that we cannot get out of our heads. These thoughts may insist that we do things that we don't fully understand. Reassure your child that there is nothing wrong with having "sticky thoughts," but when they interfere with doing more important things in life, then it is time to help those thoughts go away or become smaller and smaller.

As you learn more about what is going on in your child's head, reassure him that his frightening worries are not him, they are only OCD. OCD is a hiccup of the brain that gets us stuck on worries. Explain to your child that it is not his fault that he has these worries; it is the fault of OCD. Other children have had the same experience he is having. You understand that he may feel self-conscious, or a little different, but he is just fine in your eyes. Together you will figure out what is happening and get help. When you encourage your child to share his thoughts and then show him that you are not scared by these thoughts, you are leading him to health.

Getting Information

In order to help lead your child out of this scary place in his mind, you and your treatment team need more information about the specifics of what your child is experiencing. You need to know what the child is thinking, when he has these thoughts, and what triggers them. In terms of his actions, what exactly is he doing, where and when does this occur, and how long does it last? In some cases, as with Grier, your child will be eager to tell you just what is happening and your job is to appear concerned but relaxed as you hear information that is truly upsetting and scary. While your child is talking about monsters coming through walls, imagine that she is telling you how she makes a peanut butter and jelly sandwich. Remember, this is a hiccup of the brain and can be treated. It is an enormous comfort for a child to finally be able to share with another human being the details of something that has caused so much preoccupation and pain. As you talk about these thoughts and actions, your child will learn that this is not a dark secret but rather a matter-of-fact topic that needs to be understood.

Some children are so upset by their internal thoughts that they don't want to burden their parents with them. They may be afraid that their parents will think that they are crazy. Sometimes children find it easier to talk to a child therapist or psychiatrist who has seen other children with this problem. He can reassure your child that together they will work on getting the thoughts to go away.

Explaining to Your Child What Is Happening to Him

So far you have been trying to be curious and calm as your child tells you his frightening and odd tale. Then you can reassure him that this is actually something that many children experience. You are sure that there are several children in his school who have the same issue, but they may never have told anyone about it.

Then explain that this is not your child's fault but rather his brain sometimes acts in an unusual manner. When this happens the brain gets stuck in thinking about one particular thing, rather like a compact disc that gets caught and repeats the same phrase of music over and over again. This is like a hiccup of the mind. It sometimes insists that you do things that seem a little odd and may even tell you that something bad will happen if you don't do these things. In your effort to distinguish between the child and the OCD, you might encourage your child to try to name his OCD. This will externalize the problem and reassure him that the disorder is not him. Then he can say, "Mr. Worry made me check on the newspapers," or "Soapy made me go and wash my hands." Reassure your child that you and his doctor will help him think this through so that together you can figure out which thoughts and actions make sense and which ones do not make sense.

Getting Ready to Lead Your Child Out of an Unreasonable World toward the Normal World

You are going to help your child as he sorts out what internal demands to respect and which ones to ignore. As you do this, it may be helpful to teach your child how your world works so that he has a better understanding of what is dangerous and what is safe. In an effort to address her compulsion to pray, Grier's parents talked with her about why they prayed. They explained that they prayed in church to understand the message of God to mankind. They prayed before dinner to remind themselves of God's generosity in providing food. They prayed at night to thank God for the joys of the day and plan for the next day. They did not think that God needed people to think about him all day long; God was bigger than that. They felt that God wanted everyone to enjoy His blessings and simply say thank you from time to time. He would not ever punish one for failing to say thank you before eating. Therefore, God would not be angry if Grier did not pray when she had a snack or her friend offered her a piece of gum. They explained to Grier that when worries come into her head telling her that she must pray or something bad will happen, it is an example of that hiccup in her mind. Her brain is playing a trick on her.

Grier's parents also tried to reassure her about germs. They explained that everybody has bad germs and good germs. The good germs fight the bad germs and that is how disease is conquered. However, like all soldiers, they need to practice their fighting skills. Therefore it is very important to have some bad germs in your body at all times so that the good germs can fight them and get really good at destroying everything that is dangerous. Therefore, you would never want to destroy all germs or prevent all germs from entering your body.

Getting Rid of These Thoughts: Exposure to the Feared Object
or Situation and Inhibiting the Urge to Respond

The most successful treatment for obsessive thoughts and actions involves exposing oneself to the feared object or situation until one is no longer afraid. Here the central idea is one of *habituation*. Let me give an example that will be familiar. Imagine that it is a hot day in early summer and you want to go swimming. You dive into the pool and are initially shocked by the cold water. However, as you swim your first lap, your body is getting used to the cold. By the time you get to the second lap, you feel comfortable in the water. By the time you swim your tenth lap, you may actually feel that the water is warm. What has happened is that your nervous system has become habituated or accustomed to the water and no longer finds it cold.

An image of a female warrior fighting bad germs.

Exposure also works in the case of fear. In Grier's case, her family forbade her to read her prayer card unless she was sitting down to dinner with her family. Initially this was very distressful to Grier because she was convinced that God would be angry and bad things would happen. However, her parents practiced this with her several times a day. Grier had to eat breakfast, lunch, and snacks without the prayer. Gradually she became accustomed to the new behavior of not praying and she came to realize that nothing bad had happened when the prayer was not spoken. Remember, preventing a ritual is like having a terrible itch and not being allowed to scratch it. As you think about the itch and not being able to scratch it, the itch becomes stronger and stronger. However, eventually your mind will be distracted and the itch will disappear.

When a therapist does an *exposure,* the eventual goal is that the child will stop having irrational fears. For instance, we want Grier to value prayer, but not fear that she is doing something bad if she does not pray every time that she eats. Yet this is done in baby steps. The therapist will work with the child to develop a *hierarchy of fears.* Here the therapist and the child work together to develop a sequence of 10 to 15 increasingly scary acts or images that the child needs to be comfortable with in order to habituate to her fear. In Grier's case, a hierarchy of fears related to her fear of germs might include doing the following actions without washing her hands afterwards. Note: the therapist starts with items that are mildly worrisome and proceeds to high anxiety items.

Grier's Hierarchy of Fears

1. Talk about germs
2. Look at a textbook picture of a germ
3. Make a collage with glue and glitter
4. Shake hands with the members of her church
5. Put her hand in a stream
6. Touch clothes she has worn

7. Touch clothes worn by family members
8. Sort clothes in the school's lost and found
9. Eat with cutlery in a restaurant
10. Count money from the cash register of a restaurant
11. Walk up and down the stairs at the Metro holding the railing
12. Spend a morning at the Metro touching the fare machines, the turnstiles, the seats, and the support poles in the cars

The next step after constructing the hierarchy is to get the child to figure out how to rate her fear. A helpful device was developed by Edward Wolpe, M.D., a professor of psychiatry at Temple University School of Medicine. His scale is called SUDS. Here is what that means.

S: Subjective
U: Units of
D: Distress
S: Scale

This scale reports subjective units of distress in a range of 0 to 100. The therapist first discusses with your child what a 100 would be. For Grier, this might be going on the Metro and holding onto the pole in the subway car. What is a 50? For Grier this might be putting her dirty clothes in the hamper.

Once you have the hierarchy of fears and the SUDS measure, the therapist gradually exposes the child to the items that he fears. He starts with items that raise the SUDS to at least 50. He then proceed to increasingly difficult items until the SUDS level reaches 85. Note that too much discomfort is better than not enough discomfort. He keeps the child exposed at this level until gradually the SUDS go down. Do not panic; they will go down. Your child may find it helpful to do some self-calming techniques, such as deep breathing as he first manages this increased fear. However, like the cold water, your child will gradually habituate to the fear and the SUDS will decrease. If any of the items goes above 85, the therapist goes down lower on the list to a less stressful item. For instance let's say Grier gets to the point that she can put her own clothes in the hamper but she cannot pick up her family's clothes. Her anxiety soars to 90 when she is asked to do this. The therapist then went back to her handling her own clothes, perhaps taking the incremental step of putting them in the washing machine. She repeatedly did these feared tasks until her SUDS were down at 0 to 20. She was then ready to move up the hierarchy and handle the next difficult item.

Parents can help their children practice what they are learning in treatment. The important thing is to practice the feared behavior daily. We want to change the way in which the neurons are firing, and to do this we need lots of exposure. What you practice will depend on the nature of the problem. Practice working on obsessive thoughts, and the actions that go with them. In Grier's case, she needed to work on both not praying and learning to touch things that she felt would be covered in germs. The boy mentioned earlier needed to learn not to go back and check that he had delivered the papers. Another child would have to work on not touching the mirror before he brushed his teeth.

In addition to practicing exposure to the obsessive thoughts and actions, we also want to stop the child from engaging in the compulsive rituals. Here your therapist will be helpful in developing a plan to gradually inhibit the nonproductive rituals. One does not stop these behaviors all at once. You want to initially act to reduce the behaviors. For instance, her parents encouraged Grier to lead the family in prayer before their nightly meal, but tried to inhibit praying every time she ate. In the case of the paper boy, he was initially encouraged to check that he had delivered each paper one time; however, additional checks were discouraged. He learned to use positive self-talk (**Tool Sheet 17**) to dispute the irrational internal voice, "Hectic Harry," who urged these additional checks. The girl who obsessively organizes her shirts may be allowed five minutes to tidy her room but no more. Again, she will need to use positive self-talk to talk herself out of doing more ordering.

Because it is so hard to practice exposure and response inhibition, it makes sense to give your child a concrete reward for this work. The method of token economy (**Tool Sheet 17**) can be a helpful tool for structuring rewards. You might reward doing the practice session, but also give a bonus if the child can move up the hierarchy of fears. Similarly, reward your child for reducing the number of times that he does his ritualistic behavior. Note that this work is very time consuming. During intensive treatment, one should spend a total of 1 to 2 hours a day on exposure. This is hard work and requires a large commitment from both parent and child; however, this approach works to significantly diminish the OCD behaviors.

Getting Rid of These Thoughts: Positive Self-Talk

We have talked about exposure as an excellent way to deal with obsessive thoughts and response inhibition as a good way of dealing with compulsive rituals. This is all part of cognitive behavior therapy. Once your child does the feared act and finds that there are no bad consequences, he is no longer reinforced for doing his irrational behavior. As he continues to be exposed to the fear and nothing bad happens, he will habituate and no longer feel the fear.

Sometimes when the obsessive thoughts are less intense, we can change them by means of positive self-talk. After identifying what "sticky" thoughts are silly, we need to have a plan for disagreeing with these thoughts. In other words, your child needs to come up with a "reasonable thought" whenever a sticky, irrational thought pops into his mind. Let's see how this might work. Suppose that Grier is obsessing about germs because she just had a bite of her friend's donut without first washing her hands.

She is upset that she may have poisoned herself because her hands were dirty and covered in germs when she touched the donut. She needs to develop positive self-talk (**Tool Sheet 17**) to refute her fears.

An example of this might be: "I have washed my hands already this morning and there are not many germs on them. My body can handle a few germs just fine. I can always wash my hands again before I have lunch."

Let's try a few more examples to see how positive self-talk works.

Irrational Thoughts	Positive Self-Talk
I have not prayed before eating this donut and therefore God will be angry and punish me.	I need to pray to appreciate the beauty of creation. God does not need me to be constantly reminded that creation is beautiful. Furthermore, God would not punish me for enjoying food.
I have forgotten to deliver the newspapers and my boss is going to see that I am incompetent. I will be fired.	I know that I am delivering the newspapers to every house. If I make a mistake, I will make sure to deliver the paper later in the day and apologize. It is not a big deal.
If I do not touch the mirror three times, my mother will get sick and die.	My mother is healthy and goes to the doctor. She will die at some point but not now and not because I am touching the mirror.
I must maintain absolute control over my thoughts and actions so that I can be perfect. If it doesn't look or feel "just right" it is intolerable.	Thinking I must be perfect is unreasonable because no one is perfect. I have a hiccup of the brain that makes me think these thoughts, but they are not true. I need to practice being imperfect for a change.

You can help your child by modeling the behavior that you want your child to learn (see **Tool Sheet 13, Changing Behavior**). Positive self-talk is something you do when the sticky thoughts get in the way. For instance in the case of Grier, her parents might eat a hot dog from a vendor or have popcorn at the zoo. Out loud they would remind her  that the heat from the grill or popcorn machine kills most germs and that your body knows how to handle the germs that remain. They also might remind her that God does not need to hear a prayer just then. Remember to check in with your child to see if she is having sticky thoughts and what she is saying to herself.

Sometimes it is beneficial to have a *positive visual image* in one's imagination to think about. This is an example of positive self-talk, but in this case it is a picture or a mental scenario that the child pulls up to dispute the obsessive thoughts. In Grier's case, she had two images that she learned to summon when she felt anxious. In one she had a secure tree house with a barricaded door high in the tree and a fish pond near by (see drawing).

She could retreat to this house in her imagination when she thought of things that frightened her, such as the monster in the basement. She knew that her mind was playing tricks on her and there was no monster, but going into her tree house helped her feel safe and secure. In another image, Grier imagined making a monster shrink into dust with a shrink gun (see drawing). This allowed her to vanquish the scary thoughts by her own powerful imagination.

In addition to this positive self-talk and the use of powerful imagery, it would be helpful for Grier and her parents to think of a good distraction (**Tool Sheet 6**). Children can learn that at times they may be able to push the distressing thoughts out of their heads by thinking of something else. For instance, she might think about the hero of a story that she is reading and how she wants to be like her. She might think of a pleasurable event that is going to happen, such as making a cake with her mother.

Grier's Safe house and fish pond.

Grier's picture of killing a monster.

Sometimes thinking about a distraction is not enough and it's better to engage in actually doing a distraction. Some distractions are best when they involve actions that one can take to avoid doing a compulsive action. In Grier's case, when she had a desire to pray, she might distract herself by getting a favorite book to read, or singing a song that she liked. Grier herself gave some excellent advice about these overwhelming feelings and how her parents helped her:

> All feelings can be treated. You can tell someone about it and they can help. They can help get your mind on another thing or remind you what is good. Sometimes when I have bad dreams, I tell mom and dad and go in their bed. They help me think of something else. They talk about it. Dad said he used to have OCD and he got over it.

Medications

The medical breakthrough of the last 40 years is learning that OCD has a biological basis and that medication can be effective in reducing the intensity of the thoughts and feelings that drive the compulsive behaviors. At this time the major medications used with children are Anafranil, Prozac, Zoloft, Paxil, and Luvox. Here it will simply be noted that there is increasing research on the use of medication to treat OCD in children. When it is effective, it is remarkable because children suddenly stop doing the behaviors that they themselves perceive to be weird and counter-productive. It is worthwhile discussing medication as an option with a child psychiatrist familiar with OCD. It is important for the child to try to resist the OCD symptoms while the medication is being tried.

Collaborating with Teachers

It is important to keep teachers informed about what is going on when your child has OCD. You may need to educate them about the nature of the disorder and reassure them that your child is working with trained professionals to deal with this problem. Sometimes you can give them appropriate reading material, such as getting a copy of *The Boy Who Couldn't Stop Washing* for the school library. Another helpful resource is the booklet *School Personnel: A Critical Link* by Gail B. Adams, Ed.D. and Marcia Torchia, R.N. Likewise, *Teaching the Tiger* by Marilyn P. Dornbush, Ph.D. and Sheryl K.Pruitt M.Ed. is another valuable book on this topic. Teachers need to know that OCD is a common disorder. They can then begin to pick up on who has the symptoms so that they can be referred for help.

This Is a Family Problem

Having a child with a disorder such as OCD is very difficult because we get frightened when our children are scared. We also are unsure of the outcome. In some cases during treatment the obsessive thinking and compulsions disappear as suddenly as they emerge, in other cases the symptoms disappear only to recur later. Often OCD turns out to be a chronic disease that needs ongoing monitoring and care. It is very stressful to be continually on guard, trying to help your child deal with his unreasonable fears and rituals.

Because of the difficulty of the illness, it is very important that parents look after themselves. They need to get rest, exercise, and entertainment. If you are not relaxed and emotionally fit, you will not be able to give your child the care and support that he needs. Having babysitters is very important so that the parents can have time to nurture themselves and their relationship. Our goal is that your child's OCD becomes just a minor part of your family life. As one father said who had a daughter and wife with OCD, "Around here, OCD is like having a common cold."

Siblings of your child with OCD also are at risk. Whenever there is an identified patient in the home, parents become extremely solicitous of that child and the other child or children can feel unloved or ignored. They may have trouble understanding some of the irrational behaviors of their sibling, or they may feel guilty that they do not share this difficult problem. Sometimes siblings feel that their parents demand that they be perfect, but allow the sibling with OCD to get away with crazy, disruptive behavior. It is important that OCD be explained to these children so that they realize it is a problem external to their sibling. He may not want to run around checking on the lights and the doors. The OCD is making him do it. It is important to remember that siblings are also vulnerable to having hurt feelings and a sense of being second class citizens. Sometimes they are teased or shunned because they have a sibling who does weird things. Other children may feel that the whole family is weird and should be avoided. Thus siblings will need special treatment and attention from their parents.

Children with OCD often benefit from a reward system such as a token economy (**Tool Sheet 17**) that rewards them for not doing compulsive behaviors and using positive self-talk (**Tool Sheet 7**). If you are doing this, make sure that all children in the family have their own token economies. There is always some behavior that needs encouragement, such as getting a budding musician to practice the piano or encouraging a couch potato to exercise.

In some cities there are support groups available for families where one member has OCD. Check with your local hospital to see what resources may be in your community.

Religion

In some cases children develop a belief that God is directing them to act in a certain manner that is clearly obsessive and counter-productive. Different religious traditions have been helpful in figuring out ways of dealing with these destructive thoughts. In the Roman Catholic Church, there is a ceremony for ridding a person of the sin of *scrupulosity*. There is also a service in the Jewish tradition for dealing with compulsions where the child fears that God will punish him if he does not follow certain rituals. These rituals may have meaning for families with strong religious beliefs but they should not be considered as the primary way to treat OCD.

Structure

Children with OCD need a set routine. When there is a change in routine, the OCD symptoms can become much more intense. Post a schedule (**Tool Sheet 22, Providing Structure to the Day**) where everyone can see it. Build your structure around specific times for meals, homework, and going to bed. Holidays and vacations can be disruptive and may need special planning. One might want to make up a special holiday schedule so that your child with OCD knows what the new expectations are around eating and sleeping. He will need help anticipating travel, staying in unfamiliar places, or eating in restaurants. Before you travel, have a discussion about how you can make these experiences more comfortable. Remember not to facilitate your child doing obsessive thinking or compulsive behaviors. For instance, do not bring an extra set of family cutlery to the restaurant. Rather consider this an excellent time for exposure work and reward him for using the restaurant's knife and fork.

Having a set of family rules is important to achieving structure. Rules give clarity and provide limits, which is just what children with

OCD need. Your other children will benefit from these as well. Try to state the rules in a positive tone. For instance, "television after homework is done," rather than "No television unless homework is done." Don't be defensive! Tell your children the rules and observe your limits (**Tool Sheet 15**) as you explain that these rules are necessary for you to create the family atmosphere that you want. Be sure to enforce the rules.

Because stress exacerbates OCD symptoms, think of ways to have a calm family life. Try not to over-schedule the day. Children with obsessions and compulsions need a great deal of time to do things. When they are doing an exposure, they will need extended time to practice this. Therefore, try to streamline your life so that you and your child are not overwhelmed.

Finally, children with OCD often like to use their illness as an excuse to explain behavior that is out of control or annoying. Remember that children with OCD misbehave just like children without OCD. They will need you to use management skills such as **Tool Sheet 14, Teaching Consequences and Repair**, and **Tool Sheet 16, Time Out**, to control their behavior.

Common Pitfalls: Things to Avoid

It is important to think about behaviors that parents should avoid. The commitment to change must come from both parents and children. Parents cannot force their child to change. The child must come to see that it is in his best interest to change because what he is doing does not make sense and is not effective.

1. In general, when working on exposure, a child should not be physically forced to do the feared behavior. Go back to a less anxious step on the hierarchy and keep working on exposure at that level until the SUDS are down. This is a gradual process. Have patience and trust that eventually the child will get where he needs to be.
2. Parents need to stop doing behaviors that reinforce the rituals. For instance, if your child needs many changes of clothes throughout the day, you should limit how often you do the wash so that it is not easy for him to keep changing into new outfits. If your child's bedroom fills up with changed clothes and the closet is emptied, enlist your child in the weekly task of doing laundry and/or refolding clothing for another wear.
3. Parents should avoid being too reassuring while their child is practicing the exposure. It is fine to be present as a way of encouraging the child not to do the behavior. Initially you may want to help your child develop an action plan. However, once the child is acting to avoid the obsessive thinking and maladaptive rituals, you want your child to feel that he can handle this on his own. You do not need to tell him that he will be alright at this point.
4. Avoid criticizing or scolding your child when he slips back into his compulsive behaviors. Instead, be the cheerleading squad, praising him for all of his efforts, no matter how small. Remember that this is a slow process with three steps forward and two steps backward.
5. Finally, parents do not blame yourselves! Remember that this is a chemical and structural problem, nothing that you have caused. Also remind yourself that cognitive therapy with medication has been proven to be successful in treating this disorder. Through your efforts, you are leading your child back to health. You should congratulate yourself that you are reading this book and putting together a plan to help your child.

Summary

Obsessive compulsive disorder affects many children throughout the world. Yet often it is unrecognized because these children are embarrassed by their frightening thoughts and bizarre rituals. They consider it a dark secret. Hopefully you will now be better able to recognize the symptoms of the disorder. Remember, your goal is to join with your child to understand what he is thinking, feeling, and doing, and then once you understand, lead him to health.

In this chapter we have looked at the biochemical causes of this disorder. We have noted the importance of medicine and cognitive therapy for treating this disorder. The cognitive therapy involves exposure, response inhibition, and disputing irrational thoughts. In addition we have discussed other skills that parents can use, such as distracting their child and then helping their child to distract himself. Throughout this book we have talked about the need for structure for children with issues related to self-regulation. This is particularly true of obsessive compulsive disorder. Always remember that OCD is a hiccup of the mind. It is a condition that is no one's fault. There are tools to lead your child to health.

6

He Won't Listen and Can't Finish a Thing!
How to Help Your Child with Attention Deficit Hyperactivity Disorder (ADHD)

Noah: A Creative, Energetic, and Unfocused Child

My kid is really creative and fun to be with. He invents projects from things he finds at the creek. He'll glue pieces of wood with interesting stones, a piece of moss, and hook in a rubber band with paper clips, and voila! He's made an airplane! He's got an amazing sense of humor. He cracks me up with his stories. He can take an ordinary trip to the store and tell a story that captivates the whole family. Everything is alive, magical, mysterious, and surprising in his mind's eye. A plain old leaf can become a fantastic found object.

I can't imagine what it's like to be inside Noah's mind. It must feel like a high speed car riding on a roller coaster like Space Mountain. Ideas popping like popcorn! The body goes with his amazing mind. He is constantly in motion. You should see us at the dinner table. The kid takes a mouthful, gets up and runs around the room, acts out some story he's telling, runs up to his bedroom to show his dad something, back down to the table, another bite of food. That's if he hasn't forgotten what we're there for … It goes on and on. If I happen to say something to respond to his fantasmagoric ideas, it sends him off into another direction, catapulting to new dimensions. You can't imagine!

So what am I complaining about? I'm totally exhausted trying to keep up with this 7-year-old child of mine. I have to get him up early before school, take him down to the track and run a few miles before we have breakfast. If I don't do this, he's so hyperactive at school that he's uncontrollable. You can bet we'll get a call from his teacher saying, "Did you give him his medication?" Do you think I'd forget what he's like off his medicine?

Then there's the part about his sister. He won't leave her stuff alone. He is in and out of her bedroom grabbing things he wants, hiding it somewhere, then acting like Mr. Clean when we ask, "Did you touch Emily's Game Boy?" He's really a good kid so it's hard to get mad at him when he does this stuff. Such a sweet smile on his face. That's not to say we don't punish him. We put a favorite toy of his in the trunk of my husband's car for a whole week as punishment when he took Emily's Game Boy. We wanted him to know what it feels like to have something taken from him without being asked. It doesn't stop him though.

You can't take your eyes off him for a second. When we went to the county fair last week, it was 10 seconds before he had submerged his fingers in every drink at the food stand, pulled the ears on someone's dog, and darted into an exhibit without paying. I've thought of putting him on a leash, but people would scream "child abuse!" at me.

I've gotten Noah to 7 years of age alive! I consider that a feat. I have had to watch his every move as he has grown up, fearing for his life. When he was 2 years old, he was climbing up on the kitchen counter, then on top of the refrigerator while holding a kitchen knife in one hand. My hair stands on end thinking of the life endangering things he has done. One time he bit

into an electrical cord that happened to be plugged into the wall. It was a miracle he wasn't electrocuted. Then there was the time he tried to "fly" out a second story window, a beach towel tied around his neck like Superman. Once he even got under the neighbor's car to "take a look at what's underneath." Luckily I caught him before Mr. Wilson drove over him.

So here I am in every professional's office in town trying to get a handle on his problems and to save my own sanity. I love this kid to pieces. He is a chip off the old block (my husband's, that is). But I'm going to jump off a cliff one of these days if I don't figure out how to get him to stay focused, control his high activity level, and stop touching everything in sight. I would love to have the chance to hug my child for 2 minutes without him in "squirm" mode. The only time he is still is when he's falling asleep, stroking my hair for half an hour. That's my story. I hope you can relate to what I'm talking about.

Noah was a compelling child. After an hour in the therapist's play room, it was a path of destruction. Even with a high amount of structure, almost everything was off the shelves. In this chapter, we will discuss children like Noah, who have problems paying attention. We will explore the different kinds of attention deficits, and the tricks of the trade that can help children with attentional problems.

The Mixed Bag That Makes Up "Attention Deficit Disorders"

What makes a child acquire the label of attention deficit disorder (ADD) with hyperactivity (ADHD) and impulsivity? The typical symptoms that make up this disorder include the following:

- Distractibility by sights, sounds, or objects in the environment, as well as one's own thoughts
- Poor concentration, inattention, and a lack of persistence to stay on-task
- Poor self-monitoring, which causes the child to rush through tasks, miss important details, or make mistakes without realizing it
- Disorganization that impacts how the child uses time and space or sequences activities
- Impulsivity and difficulty stopping oneself from doing things that are off-task

In addition to these problems, many children with ADHD have other learning problems that impact skills such as motor planning, conversational skills, mood regulation, motivation, and self-control (Barkley, 1997). Sometimes it's difficult to sort out what should be treated first. Regardless of this, we know that children with ADHD are at high risk for academic under-achievement and behavioral and emotional difficulties, particularly anxiety and oppositional disorders. As we discuss in our chapter on medication management, when anxiety accompanies ADHD, the child is apt to be more impulsive and respond less well to stimulants that usually help attentional problems. Children diagnosed with ADHD do not fit into well-defined categories; therefore, it is important to sort out what is unique about your child's needs.

Treatment Approaches for ADHD

A variety of treatment approaches have been used in treating children with attention deficits. The ones more widely used that have been proven effective are behavior modification techniques and cognitive training. They are useful in addressing impulse and behavioral control as well as problem solving, organization, and self-monitoring skills (Barkley, 1997). Use of medication to treat symptoms of ADHD often reduces hyperactivity, impulsivity, and inattention. Other approaches that have been found useful include:

- Special education and tutoring to address learning needs
- Language therapy to improve auditory processing
- Sensory integration to address sensory problems that affect attention and activity level
- Auditory training (i.e., Tomatis, Berard) to decrease auditory hypersensitivities and improve auditory discrimination
- EMG biofeedback to inhibit excessive body movement
- Neurofeedback to help the brain focus on relevant information
- Dietary supplements and dietary control of sugar intake

Some of these approaches have limited success, while others have not been fully researched to prove their effectiveness. We support the idea of finding what works best for your child. Every child's nervous system is different and, therefore, what works for one child with ADHD may be very different for another.

> **Tip:** Whatever approaches are used, it is generally accepted that most children with ADHD need a multidisciplinary approach that combines more than one type of treatment. It is a good idea to find a trusted professional who can oversee all the approaches you use with your child and who can provide parent guidance. A developmental pediatrician may be ideal to serve this role.

Not only is it important to find professionals to work directly with your child to address the core deficits that underlie the attentional problem, but it is also important to change how your child interacts with you and family members. You can refer to Chapter 11, which describes child-centered time, to help improve the relationship you have with your child.

> **Tip:** There are things that children learn through practicing activities that improve attention, but it is through play and relationships with parents, siblings, and peers that the child learns to modulate his activity level, to pay attention to tasks and persons, and to feel proud about mastering something new.

In this chapter, we will discuss how children develop the skill of staying on-task, screening out distractions, and containing their activity level. We will focus on how children develop impulse control and motivation to persist in tasks. Lastly, we will share different ideas to help improve your child's attention. Our **Tool Sheet 5, Learning to Pay Attention**, summarizes many things that work for problems of attention.

How Children Learn to Pay Attention

Learning to Focus and Orient to What Is Important

The ability to pay attention begins with the process of registering, filtering, and processing sensory information. Sensory registration is when information enters the senses for processing and learning. Many children with ADD have impaired sensory registration. Usually the problem is one of an over-aroused nervous system. Often children who are over-aroused cannot focus because their nervous system is overstimulated by the many things in the environment. This makes it difficult to determine which information is important to attend to and which information should be ignored. Your child might notice every sound, visual detail, touch, or movement in his immediate environment.

Some children have the opposite problem. They have an under-aroused nervous system and nothing catches their attention. This kind of child needs to have you show him something over and over again and point out important details. He needs sensory stimulation to be intense, otherwise he won't pay attention. Often this under-aroused child will not pay attention the four times that his mother is asking him to turn off the television and get dressed, but when she increases her voice and is screaming, he finally tunes in.

Here are some symptoms of children with impaired sensory registration and some tips about how to help them focus in on what is important.

1. Easily overloaded by busy environments (e.g., classroom, malls, playgrounds)

> **Tip:** Make things simple. Have only a few toys in the bedroom, a desk, or seat near the teacher.

2. Hypersensitivities to certain sounds, especially to:

High-pitched sounds, such as whistles or children laughing
Low-frequency background noises from heaters or appliances
Loud noises, such as vacuum cleaners, toilets flushing, or doorbells

> **Tip:** Sometimes children with ADD need a calm, quiet place to work. Yet other children find the continuous background noise of music or a television calming.

3. Overwhelmed by too much visual stimuli

> **Tip:** Make sure there are clear spatial cues in the environment to help orient your child. For example, draw boundaries around things that are written on the blackboard or on a homework assignment sheet to rivet attention to important details.

4. Hypersensitivities to touch

Bump or push other children when in close quarters and bothered by random touch from others
Complain about tags in clothing; only want to wear certain types of clothing
Dislike face or hair washing and being hugged or patted by unfamiliar persons

> **Tip:** These kids need space. In the classroom they need the structure of a desk and chair and find sitting on the floor difficult. They may not like to be touched by others, and prefer to initiate touch themselves, on their own terms.

5. High need for input to the joints (weight, pressure, traction)

Like to pull and push on heavy objects or crash things together
Like to hang from jungle gym bars or banister
Like to butt head into things
Prefer rough housing activities like pillow fights, wrestling
Loves deep massage on back

> **Tip:** Children often seek things that are organizing for them. If your child likes heavy deep pressure and firm touch, be sure that he gets a lot of this kind of input. It will help him to pay attention.

6. High need for movement activities

May love to swing high for long periods of time
Like to move about, run, or find opportunities to move on playground equipment
Often leaves desk at school to get something

> **Tip:** Watch your child when he seeks movement stimulation. Does he benefit from the movement or does he become overly active after doing it? If he becomes more hyper, limit the amount of time that he can swing and jump. Be sure the movement has a purpose with an activity or goal in mind. That will help to calm his hyperactivity.

7. Motor planning problems

Difficulty initiating and planning new movement activities
Prefer sameness in movement games
Need physical assistance and verbal prompts to learn a new motor activity like shoe tying
   or skipping

> **Tip:** These children may need time to learn new motor skills such as shoe tying or skipping. They may be slow, but with practice they will master these skills.

As you look through this list, see if any of these problems pertain to your child.

Noah's Sensory Profile   Noah's sensory profile was typical of children with an over-aroused nervous system. He became easily overloaded in busy environments and was known to fall apart and explode if his parents planned too many activities in a given day. On the other hand, his high intelligence and need for novelty created a problem for him. He needed cognitive stimulation but the act of seeking out what his brain needed resulted in him becoming overwhelmed. When other children laughed in fun, Noah would cover his ears and exclaim, "It's too loud in here!" This didn't stop him from talking in a loud, boisterous voice. Even the sound of an air conditioning or heater would annoy him. He preferred to swelter in the summer heat than have the air conditioner unit humming in the background. The smallest visual stimulation distracted Noah, particularly if it interested him. "What's that in your pocket?" "Look at the cool emblem on Spider Man's shirt!" Noah is an example of a child with an over-aroused nervous system.

Now let's get back to the nuts and bolts of sensory registration and what you need to know to help your child. The child's ability to focus on sensory information has a lot to do with basic arousal. Arousal operates on a continuum from extreme alertness, to drowsiness, to deep sleep. Sensory information will be processed differently depending upon the person's level of arousal. For example, a person who feels drowsy would be alerted by a loud noise but not a more subtle sound. The importance of this is that you want your child to be at his optimal state of alertness when he is at school, doing an important task, or learning something new.

Often parents puzzle over how their child can be so wired and hyper-alert at nighttime, but be dead to the world in the morning when it's time to get up, get dressed, and have breakfast. These two states of arousal represent opposite ends of the continuum. Many times children with ADHD have two states of alertness—"hyper" mode and "deep sleep" mode, with little in the middle ground. No matter how intense the sound of the alarm clock is, it may not awaken your child. Once awake, your child may enter "alert, hyper" mode. Then he may notice the slightest sound such as the floor creaking and exclaim, "What's that!" Impaired sensory registration is usually the problem when children function at these two ends of the spectrum.

In addition to problems with their arousal switch, children with ADHD have problems with orienting to things that are not important. For example, a mother may tell her child repeatedly, "I said! Turn off the TV!" The child will extinguish her voice from his sensory registration zone. His nervous system responds, "Oh, that old thing. I know what that is and I don't need to respond anymore." This ability to figure out what is important is often distorted in children with atypical sensory processing. At other times everything is novel and worthy of attention. It is extremely tiring for the child. His nervous system is flooded with too much information. It is information overload!

> **Tip:** If your child doesn't respond unless stimulation is intense, pick a few key things that you want him to respond to. Maximize the features of those things. Add high contrast color. Increase the sound of words with soft music playing in background. Add a tactile component to the task. Or have your child sit on an inflatable cushion to give him a little movement while he sits.

Learning to Process Information Effectively

After information enters our senses, it is processed in the brain for the learning of concepts, formation of new ideas, and understanding the world around us. Many children with ADHD have problems with information processing. For example, a child with reading problems may have difficulties processing the sounds of language (also called phonemic awareness) or understanding the spatial configuration of letters and words.

When information processing is the problem, the child often has difficulty understanding the meanings of things. Sometimes the child gets stuck on a particular detail and is unable to redirect his attention to what is most important for the task. This is called perseveration. Along with this, there are often problems with information storage and retrieval for memory.

You can learn a great deal of information about your child by observing the things that interest him or that he notices in the environment. Does he only tune in if the topic is Godzilla and Star Wars, video games, and magic cards? Is this a child who can step over a boat load of toys and dirty laundry on the floor and can't find his back pack amidst an array of things? When children don't tune into something important, usually the person speaking or the task do not offer the right kind of sensory information for processing. We need a match between your child's learning style and how you introduce activities to him.

> **Tip:** Many children with ADHD are hands-on learners and need tasks to be presented on many sensory levels—tactile, visual, and auditory. So the mother calling her inattentive child to dinner may need to go stand beside him, rest her hand on his shoulder, wait until he turns to her, then tell him, "It's time for dinner. You have 5 minutes to turn off the TV. Here's the timer."

Learning to Sustain Mental Effort

Paying attention is the ability to finish activities, to follow through on directions, to give close attention to details, and to listen when spoken to. The child with ADD may avoid tasks that require sustained mental effort. He may lose things or forget to do daily activities. He has trouble with the basics of organizing tasks and activities. When a child has ADD without hyperactivity, he is less apt to have problems with behavior or impulsivity. More often, this kind of child is more likely to be withdrawn and anxious (Quinn, 1997). Girls are more apt to show this profile than boys. Sometimes girls with ADD lack the typical symptoms of hyperactivity and impulsivity. They are often unfocused but not overly active; therefore, they are harder to identify. This is why girls with ADD are often diagnosed at an older age than boys.

> **Tip:** It can be helpful to give your child a reward for actually finishing a task, such as allowing him to watch television if all of his homework is finished.

What helps us to stay attentive longer are two things—the novelty of the task and its complexity. Objects or events that are both novel and complex for a young infant may involve interesting patterns, bright colors, unique spatial orientations, surprised looking faces, and meaningful events such as feeding time. If an object, activity, or event is not complex, the child will perceive it as boring and he'll turn his attention off.

The formula to success in building attention is to come up with tasks that are moderately complex. This way the child will expend effort for learning but will not be overwhelmed. Motivation also plays an important role in this process. There are children with low levels of motivation who present a great challenge to parents and teachers because nothing seems to hold their interest. Some parents exclaim, "I have wracked my brains to come up with things that will interest my child, but to no avail. All he wants to do is watch TV or play Game Boy."

Here are some ideas to help capture your child's attention.

How to Help Your Child Pay Attention Longer

Offer novelty or something new to do.

Add variety or make the task more complex in some way, requiring your child to think more.

Present a conflict so that something isn't quite right with the task; a problem needs to get solved.

Create a surprise by introducing something that isn't what your child anticipates.

Vary the activity so that it is less predictable and more uncertain.

Think about which sensory channels your child uses for learning.

Don't just talk to your child. Make the task visually compelling. Is there a way that the task can be made more "hands-on" for him?

These are the things that cause us to remain interested in an activity. The more novel, complex, and interesting the stimuli are, the more learning will occur. When your child gets bored quickly, it could be that the task is presented too quickly for him to process the information and he gives up. Make sure that the sensory features of the task are right for your child and give him enough input to be engaged.

Learning to Curb Impulses

Impulse control is the skill that children use to stop themselves from touching things when they need to be still and concentrate. When a child has problems with impulse control, he or she may show any of the following symptoms.

1. Increased activity level:
   Fidgetiness, difficulties remaining seated, and restlessness
   High need for movement such as running and climbing
2. Poor impulse control:
   Excessive talking
   Interrupting others
   Demanding
   Inability to wait his or her turn or for events to occur

Need for immediate gratification

Responding too often and too quickly during tasks that require vigilance, waiting, or careful work

High need to touch things before thinking

3. Difficulties making transitions in activities:

Resistance in changing from one activity to another

Tendency to rush into the next activity without thinking about the sequence

4. High need for novelty coupled with a short attention span:

Getting bored easily with toys

Play only briefly before moving onto something new

5. Problems organizing and sustaining play:

Once focused and on-task, unable to think of more than one thing to do with the toy or game

Need help to elaborate on what they are doing

Difficulty taking in other people's ideas

Difficulty figuring out what to do with toys without a lot of help; video games and television are often favorite activities because the child doesn't need to be inventive

Noah's Impulsive Side   Noah was a highly impulsive child. At mealtimes he was in and out of his chair numerous times. He hated sitting and would get up to show his parents things or to go do something that he suddenly remembered. If he had his way, he would have preferred to stand for meals or to snack at random times. Holding a conversation at the dinner table was next to impossible for Noah's family. Noah needed to monopolize the discussion and he constantly interrupted his parents' and sister's conversation. If the topic was something he was not interested in, the problem was worse. Then there was the issue of getting Noah to come to the table for dinner. If he was involved in playing on his Game Boy or creating a project, it was the familiar lament, "Just 5 more minutes! I'm not finished!" He hated to be rushed and would become controlling and bossy to prevent having to accommodate to another person's schedule. Even though he loved projects, the process was long and convoluted, taking forever to finish whatever he perceived the end product to be. When you looked at his projects, it was hard to distinguish between works in progress and ones that were complete.

Learning to Get Organized

Executive functioning is the ability to organize and monitor actions as the task demands change. The child with this problem relies on old behaviors that he already knows. Sometimes the child becomes repetitive in his actions because it is more comfortable. It does not require him to adapt and do something new. There is little self-control and self-monitoring. This causes the child to rely on mom or dad to set the controls. The challenges of organizing a child with executive functioning problems are discussed in detail in Chapter 19 on The Curious and Clueless Child.

For example, Noah had problems with sequencing. He had significant problems with executive functioning. On the surface he looked like a child with lots of creativity, and indeed, he was. But he fell short in finishing things. He could not follow a planned sequence. And he was unable to accommodate to variations in a plan. Working in groups of children was extremely hard for him. It was his agenda or no one's plan. He quickly alienated peers and would often be the last one picked for team sports because of his rigidity, bossiness, and high need to control things. Sequenced activities like following a recipe for cookies was a real struggle for Noah. As he grew older, activities such as writing a book report were his worst evil, resulting in prolonged tantrums. He was known to hide his assignments from his parents. His motto was "Out of sight, out of mind!"

Tip: It is very organizing to reach closure on an activity or to end a task in progress in a way that you are able to pick it up where you left off. You might help your child to do this by writing down what's next, organizing the materials in a stack, or making a list of "to-do next."

Learning to Put More Effort into Tasks

We have a limited supply of mental energy and can only do so much at any given moment. Because we have a limited capacity to process information, there are times that we will feel mental overload and fatigue. The things that consume our mental reserves are how much of a processing load is imposed by the task (e.g., number of choices or decisions), the demands on performance, and your level of physical energy and mental stamina. Usually the greatest challenge to our mental reserves is when we have to do two tasks at the same time, what we call multitasking. That's when we tend to make absent-minded mistakes because we are dividing our attention into several areas. For instance, many parents experience this when they are trying to talk on the telephone and their child is telling them something at the same time.

One thing that helps us to keep at it on tasks is becoming automatic. Once a skill is learned and becomes automatic, our attention may be directed towards more complex activity. For instance, once a musician has learned the notes of a musical composition, he can concentrate on musical expression rather than focusing effort on reading the notes. Or, once a child has learned a skill such as running, he can engage in complex games of football, soccer, or tennis.

Here are some ideas to help your child put more effort into tasks.

Helping Your Child to Put More Effort into Tasks

Does your child do better if you streamline the task to one sensory channel (i.e., just listening in a dimly lit room) or does he engage better if there is a lot of stimulation from many sensory channels?

Present difficult or challenging activities when your child is at his most alert. For example, do homework after a physically active game or task breaks every 15 minutes to go sharpen a pencil or get a drink of water.

Provide repetition of information in a variety of ways so that your child learns and processing the information becomes automatic.

Avoid cognitive activities when your child is tired and on mental overload. Make sure he gets enough rest.

Learning to Screen Out Distractions

As we have mentioned, the child with ADD is easily pulled in different directions. Here are some ideas on helping him screen out distractions and remaining focused on one thing at one time.

- Set up tasks and offer directions so that all distractions are kept to a minimum.
- Be clear and concise when you speak to your child.
- Keep all peripheral distractions out of sight, ear shot, or touching zone.
- Use a well-organized work space.
- Make sure the task is at the right cognitive level for your child. If you simplify the tasks, make sure that they still are interesting for your child.
- Provide structure, sequencing the task into clear steps.
- REMEMBER: Less is better!

Helping Your Child Be Better Motivated and Have Better Self-Control

A key feature of developing the capacity for self-control and good impulse control relates to the ability to delay one's own actions and to comply with caregiver requests or social expectations. This capacity has a lot to do with the child's ability to reflect on his own actions and to think through strategies when the situation changes. This first develops when a child uses a strategy that his parents have taught him. For example, mom might tell Sam not to touch the fragile objects on Aunt Nelly's coffee table. If he has learned some tricks like putting his hands in his pockets or holding something else in his hands, he will be better able to stop the urge to touch the crystal figurine. But if the object is too compelling to Sam, like a chocolate treat, he might grab it quickly and pop it in his mouth.

> **Tip:** Practice taking breaks in activities with your child. Make the breaks have a purpose to keep your child organized. For example, take a break to get a drink of water, to get supplies for the project to the storage room, or to do a "mad minute" of clean-up. Taking breaks helps your child to learn how to pace himself, not to become overloaded, and to take stock of what he has done so far and what comes next.

In addition to internalizing strategies to control and stop behavior, the child also needs to learn to use language for self-control. When the child uses the "little voice in his head" or talks through what he is doing, it helps not only to organize the behaviors but to regulate actions. **Tool Sheet 7, Positive Self-Talk**, is a good skill to teach your child. When he is in a new situation such as his aunt's house, he needs to remind himself what to do in a positive way. "I must keep my hands in my pocket." "I must ask permission before I take anything in another person's house."

Here is a summary of the ways that you can help your child be better motivated, more persistent, and less impulsive

- Repeat experiences you want your child to engage in with variations on a theme so that it holds his interest.
- Integrate these experiences into everyday sequences to develop a habit strength. For example, do "quiet time" after dinner and your child will learn that is expected of him.
- Help your child anticipate upcoming events and get ready for them. Make a schedule of activities, a pictorial list of event, or other kinds of charts to cue your child.
- Offer verbal praise when he uses good strategies to get ready, stay on-task, and finish things. This will help build a sense of time management.
- Link verbal labels or language to sequences by describing or narrating what your child is doing.
- Reflect back on past activities and problems that came up. Ask questions to prompt your child's thinking and problem solving for what he will do if that happens again.
- Provide structure and rules so that your child knows what he can and cannot do.
- Help your child understand how certain behaviors lead to certain outcomes or consequences.
- Provide positive feedback while your child is engaged in an activity about how well he is staying on-task, how motivated he seems, and his good capacity for self-control.

- After an activity is over, talk about what happened to build the skill of analysis of one's own behavior. Break the behavior into its parts and act it out, draw a comic strip of what happened. Think through a range of possible responses that could have happened or what might happen the next time. Ask "What if this happened?" kinds of questions to promote thinking about consequences.

In addition to the tips that we have offered in this chapter, our **Tool Sheet 5, Learning to Pay Attention**, provides many more ideas that will help your child at home and school to be better at focusing attention.

Summary

Because there are many different factors that contribute to a child being well-focused, it is important to tease out what makes your child unique in his capacity for attention. Is he over- or under-aroused in his sensory registration? When is his best quiet alert state? Does he crave novelty or does he get overly fixated on the same things? How does he keep his effort going on tasks? Can he screen out distractions? Lastly, how does he organize himself and get motivated for a variety of learning and play activities? All of these are important and require different strategies to help your child.

This chapter offers ideas to help you identify your child's attentional needs and how to intervene at home. A psychologist can further assist you in coming up with a good treatment plan. Your child may also need interventions such as occupational therapy to help him be better able to modulate his arousal and processing of sensory information. Special education tutoring is often helpful in furthering your child's organizational skills for learning school work. Finally, a child psychiatrist or pediatrician may be needed to guide you on whether your child would benefit from medication. Putting together a comprehensive plan that integrates your child's overall attentional needs should make a difference for your child.

7

The Oppositional Child
You Are Not *the Boss of Me!*

One of the most frustrating challenges facing a parent is a child who refuses to get with the program. A child who is oppositional is basically trying to be in control of his world even if it means disregarding the needs or desires of others. He may refuse to do what others ask him, or he may be more selective, refusing to do what particular people ask him to do. The oppositional child often insists that others do what he wants and he is prepared to be intensely argumentative to get his way. These children frequently refuse to accept responsibility for their actions and instead blame others when things go wrong. They tend to be intensely reactive, often becoming angry and annoyed when they do not get what they want.

Developmentally, it is natural for infants to want to be fed when they are hungry or cry when they are wet, crying to get what they want in both cases. We expect them to be demanding. However, as children grow up, we anticipate that they will learn that their proper needs will be ultimately met, and that they will be able to tolerate the modest frustration of not having those needs met immediately. We also expect our children to develop empathy and concern for the other members of their family and understand that sometimes another person's needs must take precedence over their own. The toddler may still assert himself by crying and physically lashing out when he is frustrated. However, as a child begins to speak, he learns to control a situation through language rather than aggressive acts that hurt others. He may want what he wants, as in the classic statement of a 4-year-old, "You are not the boss of me!" However, by the time the child is in kindergarten, he should be able to do what those in authority tell him to do. Physical acts of aggression should be reduced and occur rarely, certainly not in the school environment. Children who continue to be oppositional as they move through school are at risk for developing a variety of social and academic problems.

In this chapter we will talk about why children become oppositional, and how you as a parent can effectively help them become more cooperative and responsible. Henry provides a good example of an oppositional child. We will consider strategies that his parents used to help him and then consider what other strategies may work or not work with these intense, strong-willed children.

Henry: An Out-of-Control Four Year Old

Henry was an appealing 4-year-old, with fair hair and a penetrating gaze. He was big for his age and rather stocky. He was referred to a psychologist by his teachers because of his difficulty getting along with other children and his aggressive behavior. In class, he moved from activity to activity, avoiding art projects but enjoying blocks and cars. Henry had one favorite friend, William, but often he played by himself. With William he was verbal, describing in detail his plans for the space ship that they were building. However, when a child other than William came into his space, Henry became agitated, taking the child's toys and throwing them to the other side of the room. Sometimes he would literally push the other child away from the activity he was doing. At recess, Henry loved to dig in the sand area. On one

occasion he went behind the playhouse where another boy was digging. For no apparent reason, Henry started to hit the child with his shovel, aiming at the face. When the teacher heard the child scream, she rushed over and asked what had happened. Henry had nothing to say and showed no remorse. The other children did not know what to make of Henry. He scared them and they rarely invited him to play.

At home, Henry was unpredictable. His parents were divorced and Henry's behavior varied, depending on where he was staying. At his father's house, he loved playing Batman and would gleefully put on his cape and cast his father as Joker. He and his father were interested in battles and as he got older, they enjoyed visiting Civil War battle fields together. His father did not report any behavior problems. However, at his mother's house, Henry often had trouble when he was asked to do things. He refused to follow his mother's rules or requests. On one occasion as she talked to her neighbor, Henry ran into the street. He stood there looking at her and refusing to return to the sidewalk until she left the neighbor and came over to physically move him. When she told him to take a bath, he would hit her and tell her that she was a bad mother. She also found it hard to soothe Henry. He did not like back rubs or hugs. He would often butt into her with his head when he wanted her attention.

Henry was intense and emotional. If he had an idea of what he wanted to do, he became very frustrated when that plan was thwarted. He would act before thinking and did not seem to care that others were mad at him or did not want to play with him. He simply wanted what he wanted, when he wanted it. While he was cavalier in regard to most people, he seemed to have a very different agenda in regard to his mother. He desperately wanted her attention and he wanted her intensity. He almost seemed to enjoy getting her angry, because then her attention was at its most intense, even if that attention was negative.

Why Do Children Become Oppositional?

Biology

Henry is a good example of an emotionally dysregulated child who is biologically predisposed to be intense and reactive. As described in the Chess and Thomas temperament criteria (see Chapter 2 on Anxiety), Henry is an example of a child who has been intense since he was an infant. His moods have gone

up and down, sunny one moment and thunderous the next. He also has lacked the ability to be adaptive. He has always been quite rigid in his thinking and once his mind is made up, it has been hard to get him to change direction. He also has shown a constitution that is reactive in a quick, impulsive manner. A small irritation could trigger a rapid emotional response that might accelerate until he was completely out of control.

In addition to having an intense, reactive, and moody temperament, Henry also shows the pattern of sensory integration difficulties outlined in Chapter 8. He simply could not tolerate more than one child in the block corner. He had trouble receiving touch on any terms other than his own. Much of his anger towards other children was seen when they crowded him or inadvertently touched him if he was standing in line. At other times, it was hard to know what had set him off. When he hit the child in the sand area, it seemed to come out of the blue.

Another aspect of his emotional difficulty was that Henry had trouble reading what other people were thinking and feeling. He was aware of how *he* was feeling and what he wanted, but he had much more trouble reading the feelings and wants of other people. He could not perceive what his parents were experiencing and even if they were feeling sick, he still wanted them to play what he wanted to play, when he wanted to play it.

Because of this insensitivity, it is hard to communicate with children like Henry. A positive approach often seems too mild for them. "You did a great job clearing the table," does not get the child's attention, but an irate parent shouting, "I told you five times to put on your pajamas!!" comes in loud and clear. In their sensitivity, these children may overreact to an authoritative voice and escalate from upset to crying, to going rigid, to shouting bad words, etc. Unfortunately, this is often effective in getting parents to back down. Parents find continued contact aversive. It is easier to get mad at the child or leave him to his own devices than to teach him to have a sustained, back-and-forth discussion where everyone gets heard.

Part of the problem with a child having intense feelings and not reading social cues is that your child's thinking suffers. When these children are feeling upset, they are very unreasonable because they are overwhelmed by emotion. Often they cannot understand turn-taking and compromise. Basically the child wants to get his own way at whatever cost and he is willing to take more and more outrageous actions to prevail. He wants others to make his world right and calm him down because he has no internal capacity to self-regulate.

There are, in fact, a variety of biological factors that are making Henry vulnerable. His intense temperament, sensory integration issues, failure to read social cues, lack of empathy, and poor thinking all make it hard for him to get along with others. Such a child can easily dig in and become oppositional as he tries to control his environment. We need to understand and respect this vulnerability as we try to help him learn to cooperate and become a little more flexible.

Henry's parents reacted to his temperament in different ways. His dad saw him as an energetic child who would be successful. His mother saw him as an out-of-control child who would get into a world of trouble.

Characteristics of an Oppositional Child

1. Intense reactive temperament which is inflexible and has trouble adapting to new situations
2. Angry and negative mood and actions
3. Sensory integration issues leading to physical discomfort and irritation
4. Difficulty reading social cues and limited empathy
5. Poor thinking
6. Uncooperative

How Does the Environment Contribute to a Child Becoming Oppositional?

Some children become oppositional because of an environmental stress. Early life experiences can make it hard for children to learn to deal with their world in an easy-going, interactive manner.

Attachment   At times oppositional behavior develops because children are not attached to their primary caregiver. The oppositional child never learns that he can count on the central people in his life to understand what he is feeling and needing and provide consistent care. Because of this, they learn maladaptive ways to get what they want. When this happens there is an attachment disorder.

Attachment problems can develop when a parent has difficulty understanding his or her child. Many children with the unique sensitivities that Henry had are hard to figure out. In some cases the child may simply have a temperament that is unfamiliar or uncomfortable to the parent. When a child cries for a sustained time, one parent might think, "Boy, my baby is strong and is telling us what he wants. This child is not going to be any push-over. He's my man!" Yet in response to the same child, another parent might think, "This baby is just trying to drive me crazy. Nothing I do is ever enough. He can never be satisfied and just wants more and more."

Family Dynamics   Sometimes oppositional behavior can develop as a response to the dynamics in a particular family. In Henry's case, there was ongoing conflict between the parents that resulted in the mother leaving the home when Henry was three and a half. She continued to see Henry and wanted him to live with her, but initially he lived primarily with his father. Once they had a separation agreement, they accepted 50/50 visitation. This was confusing and difficult for everyone involved. When Henry asked why his mother had left, his father told him that she did not want to live with them. Henry, with his inflexible thinking, believed that there was something wrong with him that had caused his mother to leave him.

It took years of consistent parenting and reassurance for him to understand that she was leaving his father, not him. However, deep within him, there had been planted a seed of doubt and a feeling that she did not really like him or want to live with him. This doubt fueled his anger towards her. "You can't tell me what to do! You are a horrible mother. I hate you."

Parents' Own Issues   In some cases maladaptive parenting styles develop because the parents have their own issues that affect the way that they parent. This was seen in the family of Kim.

Kim was referred to a psychologist in the fifth grade because he was refusing to do anything at school and he was cheating on tests. It turned out that Kim's mother had a brother who had committed suicide. She had always worried that on some profound level she could have prevented the suicide. She blamed herself for not having been sufficiently available and loving to her brother. Therefore when her intense, reactive baby got upset at night, she would never leave him to cry it out. She had to sit with the baby and hold him so that he would know that she would always be there for him. As the boy grew older, her failure to observe limits led the child to become demanding and develop a sense of entitlement that he deserved to have what he wanted. This intense boy would yell at his mother and insist that he have his way and then reward her with hugs and kisses. By the time that the mother realized that she needed to take a stand, it was too late.

School Difficulties   If a child has trouble learning, he may refuse to do what he is asked to do. This is often seen in bright children who realize that they are not catching on in their school classes as rapidly as other children are. In some cases, they may try to hide the fact that they don't know how to do something by refusing to do it. Because they are worried that they are having trouble learning, they may become cranky and irritable and take their frustration out on others.

Environmental Stress   Children may also be affected adversely by other events in their world. With a young child, there might be distress caused by the birth of a sibling or being put in preschool and missing one's mother. An older child might become angry because of something beyond his control, such as a divorce, a move, the death of someone dear, or an illness. Social problems are a frequent cause for emotional distress. If a best friend starts hanging out with another child and then refuses play dates, or if there is no room on an after-school team, a child may become distressed.

Perceptions of loneliness and rejection often trigger feelings of anger or shame, which in turn can lead to oppositional behavior.

Whether the cause is biological or environmental, oppositional behavior needs to be dealt with in a calm, consistent manner. When parents try to do everything the child wants, the child will feel increasingly entitled to having things go his own way. This entitlement can lead to demanding, oppositional behavior. When parents set rigid limits and come down hard on their child with every infraction, children may feel rejected and unlovable and as a result become angry and oppositional. Once oppositional behavior patterns develop, they are hard to change, but they can be changed. You simply need to be patient and try a variety of approaches until you find what might help your child. Bear in mind that oppositional children are at risk. Because they often act in an obnoxious manner, they are aware that many people do not like them or are irritated with them. These children are therefore in danger of internalizing negative views about themselves and having negative self-esteem and depression.

Techniques that Parents Can Use to Deal with an Oppositional Child

Accept that your child has good reasons for feeling the way he feels. It is very important to validate your child for the way that he is feeling. This does not mean that you agree that his feelings are justified. It simply means that you understand why he feels the way he does. Much oppositional behavior is rooted in a child's sense that his parents don't understand him and furthermore don't want to understand him.

At times, it is hard to be positive because the child is behaving badly and is in a foul, unreasonable humor. However, even at these moments you can always validate how the child is feeling. With Henry, his teacher might say, "I can see that you wanted to play with the blocks and you did not want to have Ivan around you. You must have felt very frustrated." She is not condoning the fact that Henry yelled at Ivan and pushed him out of the block area, but she is saying that she understands the strong feeling that Henry was having. Henry needs to know that she understands how hard it is for him to play with other children, even though she may insist that he not push them. (see **Tool Sheet 10, Validation** in Appendix 2).

Point Out What Your Child Is Doing Right

All children respond to positive words and actions and with these biologically extreme children, this is especially the case. Keep in mind that what works best is acknowledgment of what is going right rather than simply telling the child that he is a good kid. The parent should aim to say five times as many positive comments as negative comments. This is a lot harder than it appears. When a child picks up his back pack and heads to the car, we normally don't say anything because the child is doing what is expected. In the case of the cranky child, however, we need to help the child understand what he is doing right and tell him that: "Henry, I'm impressed that you remembered your backpack when I had forgotten it!" A positive parenting style includes actions as well as words. Often a hug or a smile goes a long way toward helping a child feel appreciated.

Being positive is hard because these children often have trouble with the smallest task. Try to ignore ill-advised behavior. Because this child is apt to make many bad choices, we need to be selective about the behaviors to focus on; otherwise, family life becomes an unrelenting war zone. When you reward your child for what he is doing right, or give a positive comment to the sibling who is doing what you want, you are actually shaping your child's behavior toward the behavior that you want. Refer to **Tool Sheet 13, Changing Behavior**.

Occasionally cranky kids, particularly very smart cranky kids, react negatively to positive comments. It is likely that they are feeling patronized. If this is happening, cut back on the verbal praise and increase the nonverbal signs of approval.

Show Your Child That You See Him

Oppositional children are emotionally inflexible. However, their refusal to cooperate is often related to wanting their parents' undivided attention. Henry stood in the street and stared at his mother with the express purpose of getting her to stop talking to the neighbor. The strategic parent will make sure that her child has intense undivided attention *without* having to dig in to get it. If the parent can provide undivided attention to the child on a regular basis, he may find that his child is less oppositional. Related to this is the need to move at the child's pace. In child-centered time, the parent moves at the child's time. Take 5 minutes to watch as your child makes a sandwich or pause on a walk to watch a caterpillar. The techniques reviewed here are covered in more depth in Chapter 11 on parenting.

Child-Centered Time (**Tool Sheet 11**) is a valuable tool to get a parent positively connected with his child. It requires that the parent enter the child's world, where the child is the center of attention and the parent is a supporting player. In the case of a young child like Henry, the parent needs to get down on the floor with the child while he is playing and let the child direct the play. The parent is the proverbial putty in the child's hand. He follows the directions of the child and (listen up, fathers!) he makes no suggestions about what should happen. The odd thing about this activity is that the parent narrates  what is happening, rather like Howard Cosell reporting on a football game. This will irritate some children and if this happens the narration may have to be simplified, but most children love it. The principle behind this running commentary is that you are providing a verbal mirror for the child. You are telling him what you see and in the process helping him see himself. This is affirming and centering for a child. Believe it or not, most children have no idea that we spend so much time observing them and thinking about them.

Tip: Child-Centered Time

1. Happens daily.
2. Both parents do it.
3. Lasts 10 to 30 minutes. Do as much as you can every day.
4. There are no interruptions—no phone calls or talking to other people.
5. Activities change as the child gets older, but maintain one-on-one focus.
6. It is OK to be silent. Just be present and attentive.

Here are some examples of how child-centered time can work for an older child.

Alvin: A Silent, Withdrawn Eleven-Year-Old   Alvin's father was feeling increasingly isolated from his son, who used to be his buddy. Alvin was getting increasingly moody and he had started to refuse to do minor chores around the house. Alvin's father was worried that he was losing connection with his child. He therefore devised a novel child-centered time for this pre-adolescent. He found that a way he could connect to his son was to give him a back rub while they watched football together. This child loved back rubs and he also loved sports. These afternoons of sitting together in front of the television forged a strong connection between father and child. Even when the son became upset and was refusing to comply with the family plan, he always knew that his father was there for him. The key thing to remember is that this is the child's time. If the child wants to talk, fine; if he wants to remain silent, fine. The parent is simply there to listen, be with the child, and make no demands.

Howard: A Twenty-Three-Year-Old Reflects on Child-Centered Time   Dr. Anne Wake, a respected child psychologist, recounts her work with the parent of an elementary school-aged child who was at loggerheads with the family. This child was very active. Dr. Wake instructed the mother to try moving while she did child-centered time. The mother invited her son for a walk and then asked him where he wanted to go. This was unexpected and at first the boy did not know what to say. He wanted his mother to make the decision. However, the mother was quietly insistent that it was his walk and he should decide where to go. Years later this same fellow returned to Dr. Wake's office for an evaluation to see if he qualified for accommodations on graduate school testing. To her surprise, he reminded her of their work together years before. In particular he mentioned the fateful day of the walk. He said that that walk had been a pivotal moment in his childhood when he realized that he could be an independent person who had the power to decide what he wanted to do for himself.

In interacting with children, remember that they are different from adults. A walk for them is not the same thing as a walk for us. The little child may become fascinated with a caterpillar and spend 5 minutes looking at it. An older child may want to know why the leaves turn yellow. It is critical that parents recalibrate to child time and move at a slower pace that allows time for these observations and reflections. Often we are hassling children to fit our schedules and it is a little like fitting Cinderella's step-sister's foot into the crystal slipper. No wonder they become frustrated and angry.

Teach Your Child to Calm Himself

Oppositional children are frequently irritable. They can be taught to soothe themselves, even when they are infants. In Chapter 4 on sleep, we described several strategies for helping infants to calm down and go to sleep without parental interference. One strategy was wrapping the infant very securely in a receiving blanket so that he felt snug and could let himself relax. One family had luck putting their child in his car seat on the dryer. They ran the cycle without any heat and the noise and vibration soothed the child.

Toddlers are notorious for wanting what they want right away. Often we start out calming them down by holding them or distracting them. However, as a parent your job is to try to figure out what could calm your child on his own. Some toddlers calm themselves by holding a blanket or sucking their thumb. A beloved stuffed animal can be very soothing. Other young children can be calmed down by an attractive activity such as looking at a favorite book or listening to a tape or drawing. As a parent, you need to think about what is appealing to your child. **Tool Sheet 1, Self-Soothing**, will help generate more ideas for you.

For example, Henry, the 4-year-old mentioned at the start of this chapter, was in desperate need of learning some self-calming tools. He got angry quickly when he was frustrated and then continued to spin out of control, hurting others and yelling ill-advised comments. His teacher was perplexed about how to get him back in control. She had noted that Henry loved to look at picture books, so when he was beginning his emotional wind-up, she would take him aside to a quiet corner of the room and give him a book to look at. It was odd. Miraculously, Henry would comply with this request and would sit for long periods leafing through the pages. This teacher had found something that helped Henry distract himself from the irritants that were making him wild, and calm him down without his even being aware that this was happening.

> **Tip:** Calming activities often involve some form of counting or other rhythmic activity. Sudoku, knitting, or singing a repetitive song are calming for this reason.

For elementary school children, calming is usually tied in with distraction. If you can become focused on another task, you cease to focus on the things that are irritating. Often doing something different takes your mind off bothersome internal thoughts. What the child chooses to do will depend on the child and what he finds absorbing. You can help your child identify these things. For one child it might be thinking about or stroking his pet, for another child it might be reading a Star Wars book. In the process, your child is learning to control his emotional state. **Tool Sheet 6, Distraction**, is a good resource for generating ideas that might work with your child.

School-aged children need to learn not to dwell on what is upsetting. They can learn meditation skills that will put these negative thoughts out of their minds. The **Tool Sheet 8, Mindfulness**, is helpful in showing you how to help center your child. One young boy tried to defend against his angry thoughts by imagining that he was a goalie. Every time a negative, irritating thought entered his mind, he would rush to it and try to kick it as far away as possible.

As you work with the child to develop his own ways of calming himself, you must be calm. You need to speak slowly and gently. If you are feeling agitated yourself (and with these children feeling agitated is a daily if not an hourly occurrence), try deep breathing. Nothing works faster for getting oneself back to a calm, centered state. Just take three deep breaths, counting to three on the intake of air and three on the exhale of air. Think of a place in your experience where you were very calm, relaxed, and happy. Pull this image into your mind to remind yourself that you are going through a trying time and that this, too, will pass. Your child is a child and he will be more cooperative as he grows up. If you are still riled, take a few more deep breaths. This process of deep breathing does not take long, but it may help you get the self control to deal with your demanding child. You are modeling for your child that one can calm oneself down and then act in a reasonable manner. Practice Mindfulness exercises with your child as you both learn new ways of calming the spirit and the body and feeling peace.

Teaching Your Child to Solve Problems

Problem solving is difficult for the oppositional child because of the intensity of his emotions. It will take a while to learn to be an effective problem solver, but if you model this skill when you are trying to resolve family conflicts, your child will gradually learn it.

Steps to Problem Solving

1. What is the problem?
2. Brainstorm alternatives, the more the better.
3. What are the pros and cons of each alternative?
4. Which one has the best chance of working?

Here is an example of how problem solving works. Henry is furious that his older brother Rex has turned on the car radio and is not letting him play his favorite tape. He starts screaming at Rex and telling him in colorful terms that he is loathsome. What is the problem-solving parent to do? As a parent you may need to help the boys articulate just what the problem is. Henry might say the problem is that Rex is an idiot and always does what he wants. Rex may feel Henry is a baby and cries when he cannot have his way. You as the parent might suggest that the problem is that they both want to listen to different things at the same time. How can they solve their problem? Do not be tempted to rush in and provide a solution. Explain that you want them to be reasonable and creative in thinking what might be a fair solution. You might even model explaining the pros and cons of the solutions they generate. Once they have a plan, try it out for a trial period to see how it works. Your job is simply to chair the meeting. If they cannot solve the problem, there will be silence in the car as you drive them to school.

Your oppositional child probably already knows that there are tried and true ways of solving problems such as the example above of listening to music in the car:

- Equal time
- Coin toss
- Alternate days

- First one in the car gets first pick
- The person dropped off first gets first pick

The trick is to think about what would be effective rather than who is right or who wins.

Encouraging Your Child to Be Cooperative and Responsible

It is tempting to focus on what behaviors you want stopped—shouting, arguing, snide comments, hitting, etc. However, in dealing with these intense children, you also want them to focus on what behaviors might work for them. Children learn responsibility and cooperation by being responsible and cooperative. However, the expectations for what is an appropriate task vary by age. Ideally, being responsible should be rewarding rather than drudgery. Try to think up tasks that are attractive but that nevertheless help the family. Give your children choices about what they want to do and change the tasks when they are no longer appealing. Be careful not to overwhelm your child. As he gets more competent and more calmed down, he will be able to handle more responsibility.

When you start instituting these tasks, you will need to do them with your child so that you are showing him what to do and giving him support. As the child gets older, he will be able to do these things independently. If your oppositional child refuses to do these tasks, simply work alongside him and if it makes sense, give him a concrete reward for task completion. You might want to have a chore list with a value for each task. For instance, you can earn fifty cents for emptying the dishwasher or five dollars for washing the car. Then the child can choose what to do when he needs money. Or you can insist that he do the task at a proscribed time and if he doesn't there is a consequence. In general, try to stick with positive reinforcement and avoid being punitive. If you give a consequence, try to make it a natural consequence. For example, if you help clean up the kitchen, we might have time for an extra story. The following lists may spur your thinking about appropriate tasks for your child.

Teaching Responsibility: Tasks for Children Eighteen Months to Three Years Old

- Feed the fish
- Water the flowers
- Pick up toys with parent
- Send valentine or birthday card to grandparents
- Make decorations for holiday
- Put newspapers in recycle bin
- Empty the wastepaper baskets
- Wipe the table
- Set the table
- Wash vegetables and fruit
- Put away cans
- Turn off lights while being carried
- Help pull up covers on the bed
- Get own snack or cereal
- Run simple errands around the house

Tasks for Four to Six Year Olds

- Pull up covers on bed
- Put dirty clothes in the hamper
- Straighten up room, perhaps with parent's help
- Put away toys
- Write name or other information on birthday invitations
- Pick out appropriate presents for friends and family members
- Help do the grocery shopping by finding certain items
- Help to bring in and put away groceries
- Help in cooking, for example making brownies, supervised cooking, learning to use kitchen tools
- Give back or foot rubs to tired family members
- Sort clothes for laundry
- Fold clothes
- Put away clothes
- Plant and water own garden
- Help younger children
- Put dishes in the dishwasher

- Measure soap and start the dishwasher
- Rake leaves
- Walk pets
- Pay for an item at the drug store and try to count change
- Have an allowance and save some of that money

Tasks for Seven to Twelve Year Olds
- Record homework
- Figure out where to study
- Figure out how one concentrates best
- Figure out a method for keeping track of homework
- Care for pets
- Take responsibility for a household task, such as unloading the dishwasher, taking out the trash, or sweeping the kitchen floor
- Make a dish or a meal on one's own
- Run the washing machine and dryer
- Cooperate with parents when they need help
- Help with household tasks, such as painting a fence
- Wash the car
- Change sheets on bed
- Read to younger siblings or play games with them when they are sick
- Look after parent who is sick in bed
- Babysit younger sibling while parent is present

Changing Your Child's Behavior by Behavior Modification Techniques

We have talked a lot in this book about the value of positive reinforcement and ignoring behavior (see **Tool Sheet 13, Changing Behavior**). One characteristic of many oppositional children is that their own emotions are so intense that they frequently have trouble taking another person's point of view. When this is the case, try to reinforce more socially acceptable behavior. One strategy to try is to identify when your child is sharing and then compliment him for the fact that he is being generous. Similarly, you could reinforce him coming up with a plan that takes into account the needs or desires of  other members of the family. When he reverts to shouting and arguing that he should have what he wants, try ignoring him. If he does not get what he wants by yelling, he will hopefully learn that this is a strategy that does not work. This principle is called extinction or ignoring. You often can be very successful by not paying attention to behaviors that are not productive.

> **Tip:** It is always reinforcing to your child to know that you see areas of competence. He doesn't have to be a star little league pitcher. He might simply make fabulous chocolate pudding!

We have also talked about shaping behavior. Shaping refers to reinforcing the small steps leading to a big behavior. In the case of Henry, his teachers might want to reinforce him for letting another child come into the area where he is playing. Then when he actually interacts with the child, they would tell him that he is a good friend. When he initiates an interaction with another child, they would also praise him. Finally if he uses his words to express displeasure rather than pushing a child out of the way, they would reward him. The theory is that as Henry gets accustomed to interacting socially, he will not be so reactive and negative. The play itself should become reinforcing and require much less teacher involvement. Shaping takes time but is worth it.

Making a Repair

When a child does something to hurt another child, he needs to make the situation better and try to repair the harm that he has caused. Many of our oppositional children appear to be oblivious about what another child is feeling. Making a repair (see **Tool Sheet 13, Changing Behavior**) is a good place to start thinking about how the other person feels.

The tricky thing is to figure out what that other person might like. Empathy varies enormously in children. Recent research shows that before age seven a child may not be capable of taking another person's perspective. However, the parent's job is to show that taking another person's point of view is important, even if one cannot always do it. When you ask the child to make a repair, you are actually asking him to think about what the other person would like and in the process you are teaching him empathy. In Henry's case, having hurt his mother by hitting her, what could he do that would please her? If he does not immediately know, ask him what his mother likes to do, what makes her smile, what does he do that she likes? What we are trying to achieve is to get the child to think about the other person in that person's own terms. He then needs to take an action that reflects his knowledge of the other person and what would please him. Repairs will vary as much as the individuals involved. Drawing a picture, giving mom a back rub, making her a piece of cinnamon toast, would all be fine repairs.

It should be noted that there are a small group of children with biologically based relationship issues, such as autistic children or children with Asperger's syndrome, who will continue to find it hard to take another person's perspective. However, even these children can learn to repair hurts that they have caused. Even if the child does not himself perceive why the person would feel hurt, he can learn that if someone says they are hurt he needs to make the situation better. You may want to refer to **Tool Sheet 13, Changing Behavior**, for a more complete review of these principles.

Stopping Oppositional Behavior with a Time Out

When children are behaving in an obnoxious way, parents need to draw a line in the sand. When faced with oppositional behavior, they need to decide what they will or will not tolerate. In Henry's case, the parents decided to draw the line at hitting and physically hurting. With an older child, it might be valuable to draw the line at any hurting behavior such as nasty put-downs or insults. With another child, the line might be drawn with school refusal.

Once you have drawn the line, there you need to communicate this to the child and then plan to reduce the oppositional behavior. **Tool Sheet 16, Time Out**, is a good way of doing this. We will outline the steps in this procedure:

- Identify exactly what the inappropriate behaviors are that you want to stop. Define them in a way that is concrete and can be counted. For example, a parent can outlaw hitting, spitting, swearing, and making nasty "put-down" comments. In general, words such as "inappropriate, aggressive, unkind" are too vague to be helpful.
- Set a reasonable goal of behaviors to work on. Starting with one behavior is a good idea, so that there is a higher chance of the child learning self-control. One should avoid ever having more than two or at most three things that you are working on at one time. Remember, pick a target where you have some chance of success. Making your messy child neat is probably an unrealistic goal, but putting dirty clothes in the hamper might be achieved.

- Have a family meeting with the parents and the child. When there is more than one child in the family, the parents should have a similar meeting with each child, with the idea that everyone in the family has something that he needs to be working on.
- The first agenda item is to tell the child all of the things that he is doing right. In Henry's case, one might mention that he is a great builder, he shows his wonderful imagination in his Batman plays, and he is a good friend to William.
- The parents then explain that there is one thing that is not working well for the family. Note that here you are not saying that the child is "out of control, nasty and brutish, an evil creature." Rather you are saying that his behavior is not working for the parents or the family: "I am uncomfortable when you hit me

and it makes me want to be in a room by myself." This is called observing your limits. Because you cannot allow yourself (or others) to be hurt, you have a plan that you think will help the whole family.

- You clarify what the outlaw behaviors are by giving examples. For instance, you might say, "There are two things that are not working well. You are hitting and shouting."
- Try to get your child's commitment to change: "Do you think that we can work on both of these behaviors or is that too much? Should we start out just trying to make headway on one? Which one?"
- Next you explain how the plan will work.

One, after the first occurrence of an outlaw behavior, the parent says "One," which is giving the child a head's-up that he is moving in a direction that is a problem for his parent. Ideally, the child is at the very beginning of a bad path and there is still a chance of averting a crisis.

Two, when the child commits the offending behavior a second time, the parent says, "Two" and requests that the child leave the room and do something that will calm him down.

Three, if the child comes back and for a third time acts in an outlawed manner, the parent says "Three" and at this point takes control of the calming down. With a young child this may mean holding the child until he is calm; with an older child this may mean asking the child to sit on a stool, sit on the stairs, or go to his room. In the family meeting, depending on the age of the child, the parent can ask the child what might work best for him. The traditional rule is that children are asked to stay in the prescribed place for one minute for each year of the child's age. For example, a three-year-old would sit on a stool for three minutes. With these oppositional children, a further consideration is that sometimes the parent also needs to calm down, so the time out might be a little longer simply to let the parent relax and regain control.

> **Tip:** "Two" is the most important step. It teaches your child that you expect him to be able to calm himself down. He is in control and can return when he is ready to be cooperative and avoid the outlaw behavior. Together you will figure out what might help him calm down. You will keep trying things until you find what works.

In step "Two" the parent is teaching the child emotional self-regulation. Here is where the parent's knowledge of the child will guide finding the activity that will distract and soothe the child so that he is able to participate constructively with the family. The range of alternatives is endless. In the case of Henry, looking at a book was a great tool because it distracted him from the irritation that was bothering him and immediately made him calm.

Here are some examples of what other children have done at step two in order to become emotionally regulated.

Pam: A Run-Away Who Needed to Calm Herself One 7-year-old girl ran out of her house whenever she became upset. The family lived in an urban area, and if the child got away fast enough and turned down a block, it was hard for her parents to find her. What helped this girl get emotional control was building a fort in the basement. She put a blanket over a table and her mother got her a very soft rug. She brought two of her most trusted stuffed animals to live in this fort. When she was upset, she was given permission to go to her fort until she felt better.

Chris: Doing Tantrums When Asked to Do Homework   Chris was a 10-year old boy who had terrible tantrums any time his mother asked him to do something, usually homework. He discovered that he felt better when he went into the family room and snuggled into a large chair and completely covered himself with a quilt. When he had calmed down, he was able to start thinking and do the assignments. Having permission to go to the chair was helpful so that soon he needed much less calm down time.

Lance: Furious with His Brother   Lance was a 9-year-old boy who lived in the suburbs. He had frequent angry outbursts with his younger brother for no apparent reason. When asked, he said that he felt that his brother got special treatment from their mother and that he was always acting like a baby. Lance found that when he got frustrated it did not work to take it out on his brother because he ended up in his room. On the warning of "Two," he ran around his large yard two times and always felt better. Sometimes a parent would join him, explaining that he appreciated a chance to get some exercise.

The point of these anecdotes is to show that what calms a child is idiosyncratic to that child. However, once the child learns a soothing device, he is on his way to learning to regulate his moods and then the intense negative feelings that lead to his oppositional behavior should become more manageable.

The important thing about time out is to tell the child that *you are working with him* to control his behavior and you are confident that he is going to find a way to calm down and become more cooperative. You know that when he gets overwhelmed he can be controlling, but when he feels relaxed he can be generous in what he does for others. If you believe in your child and see him as capable of kind, considerate action, he may come to value these characteristics in himself and be less prone to more selfish, self-centered behaviors.

Stopping Oppositional Behavior with Consequences

When there is a bad behavior to stop, it is preferable to be positive rather than negative. However, occasionally there needs to be a negative consequence in order to pull the child up short. Ideally this negative consequence should be a natural consequence. For instance, if the child refuses to get out of bed to go to school, the parent might pick him up, put him in the car with his clothes, and drive him to school. It is up to him to decide whether he wants to get dressed along the way or go to class in his pajamas. Another child refused to put on a dress to go to her brother's graduation. In this family, appropriate dress was a priority. The consequence was that she did not get to go to the graduation. If a child throws a temper tantrum because there are no cocoa puffs, the parents warn the child that there will be a consequence, for example that if it happens again there will be no cocoa puffs for a month.

In some cases there does not seem to be a natural consequence. In the case of Henry, his mother did not know what to do when he hit her. Initially she talked to him and told him that he was hurting her. This did not work and he continued to hit her whenever she asked him to take a bath and started to undress him. Because she was concerned about his safety in the bathtub, she did not want to leave the room when he hit her. She also did not want to reinforce the behavior by saying that he did not have to take a bath. However, she explained to him that if he hit her, he lost his story that night. In this case, she knew how much he liked his story, but she was in no mood to read when he had been hurting her. She used the reading time because it was immediate, even though this was her favorite time of day and a personal loss for her. Henry stopped hitting her at bath time.

Other consequences that she could have used include:

- Going to bed 30 minutes earlier
- Not having his favorite cereal for breakfast
- Loss of screen time—television, computer, DVD
- Restricted use of bicycle or skate board
- Mother not taking him to a preferred activity

The goal here is to have a consequence that gets the child's attention but is not so punitive that it increases the child's anger so that he is further agitated. See **Tool Sheet 14**.

Provide a Predictable Structure

Oppositional children are so sensitive and reactive that one wants to minimize the confrontations of daily life. Because these children have huge difficulty controlling themselves and getting organized to do what they need to do, their parents need to help regulate them. This is not easy! These children do best when they are in a structured routine yet often they seem to resist structuring. They should go to bed and get up at the same time every day. As far as possible, they need to eat at regular intervals, and at predictable times. Many a meltdown is in fact brought on by low blood sugar. At meal times, there need to be clear expectations about where they eat, how long they eat, and what they eat. An evening schedule helps the child relax and let go of the day. There need to be clear expectations for staying in bed at night. But while it is easy to say, "Just structure the day," figuring out a structure that will work is very difficult.

Every plan needs to be individually tailored to your child and often evolves after a prolonged period of trial and error. Both parents need to agree to the plan, even if they are divorced. Furthermore, one needs to try to get the child to buy into the plan as well. Use **Tool Sheet 22, Providing Structure to the Day**.

Teach How to Ask Rather Than Demand

One of the reasons that Henry was trying his teachers was that whenever someone did something he did not like, like sitting next to him when he was building his space ship or not passing him a cookie, he screamed at them to tell them what he wanted. It is clear that Henry was not aware of his voice tone, he simply had an intense feeling and reacted in an intense way. He also did not know how to ask for what he wanted in a way that the other person could hear.

> **Tip:** If your child's voice tone is too loud, try whispering. When he is trying to get someone's help, teach him to make his voice tone go up at the end of the request. Otherwise the voice tone suggests a demand. Make a game of this until he understands.

One goal of the parent is to help the child to understand that his voice may be too loud or strident. The parent can try whispering to the demanding child because sometimes a young child will lower his voice to the same tone as the parent. The converse is also true. If the parent yells, so will the child.

With a toddler, the parent needs to encourage the child to try to articulate what he wants verbally because these children are just developing language skills and they may be having trouble with the language of asking. Often you need to suggest what might be bothering them as their ability to understand develops faster than their ability to speak. As mentioned before, when one is upset, thinking goes out the window. So do recently acquired language skills.

For instance, in preschool a child may need to be taught to say, "May I play? May I have a cookie? May I have a turn?" There is a reason that parents work hard on the words "Please" and "Thank you." These words are powerful and always ease social interactions. The intense child needs these words more than most and so even though it may take longer to teach them, keep at it. These phrases are best taught when the child is calm, not when he is screaming. Remember, language acquisition may take a long time and need many repetitions and much modeling. Being calm and understanding will aid in learning how to ask and not demand.

For the elementary school-aged child, one can work on higher levels of communication. One technique that children may find helpful is **Tool Sheet 23, the Ice-Cream Sandwich**. The goal here is to ask for something in a way that another child can hear and accept. By the way, this is also a good technique for parents when they are communicating with their child, their spouse or their own parents! The top layer of the ice-cream sandwich is chocolate. Chocolate is always positive. On the top layer one tells the other person what they are doing that you like.

Chocolate wafer = positive comment   ice cream = ask for what you want

For example, a child might say, "Henry, I really like playing with you." Then you go for the vanilla ice cream, which involves expressing what you feel and want to happen. "Henry, I hate being pushed and I really want you to stop pushing me." Finally, you go back to the positive chocolate by saying how this will make everything better, "Henry, I really want to be your friend."

This is a major undertaking for an emotionally dysregulated child, but these children should be encouraged to practice when they are not upset. They can learn to ask for a snack this way. "Mom you are such a good mom. Can I have a cookie? I like eating a snack with you."

With practice and maturity, they may even get more skillful, but for starters we simply want chocolate, ice cream, and chocolate. Of course, asking in the right way may not lead to a snack, but it will lead to mom telling you how clever you are, how persuasive you are and how deserving of an apple you are. The child might even get a hug!

For the reader who might deplore such tactics as manipulative, it is necessary to remember that these children often have a deficit in their ability to empathize. They are also intense and reactive, which leads to demands and argument. They become so easily undone that they cannot get what they want without using the extreme means of being demanding and oppositional. We are trying to teach them to become effective, by practice, so that they have more positive interactions with others.

Summary

These oppositional children are really in a tough spot. They often do not feel good. They have strong negative feelings, they act in an intense and often negative manner, and they are constantly experiencing that people are mad at them. They strike out because they are frustrated and they are not thinking very well. As parents our job is to get them to calm down and change their behavior so that they are more cooperative. The various techniques in this chapter are trying to do that. Validating these children is essential because they take in the negative feelings transmitted from their frustrated parents and often begin to believe that their parents don't want them. Child-centered time is a helpful, preventative technique. If you can give children undivided attention when they are doing their own thing, they may come to believe that what they are doing has merit. You need to teach these children self-calming techniques and how to exercise mindfulness. You also need to shape their behavior so that they start becoming more cooperative and responsible. When all else fails, you need to modify destructive behavior by means of positive reinforcement, ignoring bad behavior, repair, time out, and consequences. We also want to help our children to ask for things in a way that other people can hear. All of these strategies take time to learn. Your child will eventoally learn them over time and become more self-controlled and effective.

8
Children with Sensory Overload

Children learn about the world by exploring with their senses. They touch and move objects in their hands to process texture, weight, shape, and contour. They move their bodies in new positions to map their body in space in relation to the world around them. Children listen to words and experiment in making sounds of their own. They smell and taste flavors and scents, sometimes using these to self-calm. The sense of vision provides the child with a world of color, shape, dimension, texture, depth, and movement. Our brain maps these senses in such a way that they are linked with one another. For instance, simply looking at an apple calls to mind visual, olfactory, taste, and tactile maps in the brain about the apple's attributes—the color, form, texture, weight, taste, and smell. Almost every experience is processed through multiple senses.

As children mature, we discover what kind of learner they will be. Some children are strong visual learners and like to study the visual aspects of things; others are auditory learners, preferring to hear a story rather than reading about it. There are some children who are "haptic" learners—learning by touching and feeling. Other children need reinforcement in multiple senses to learn—touching, moving, smelling, looking, and listening. It is important to understand which sensory channels your child uses for learning and provide those experiences for him. As children grow older they depend less on needing to process the world through the body senses of touch and movement and learn to use the distal or far senses of vision and hearing as their cognitive abilities develop.

Some children with learning disabilities have processing deficits in certain sensory channels. When a learning disability is present, the child may rely on learning through the body senses of touch and movement and less on the far senses of vision and hearing. If visual processing is compromised, the child may have to compensate and learn through auditory, touch, and movement channels. The child may have a combination of strengths and weaknesses in one sense. For example, the child might be very good with visual-spatial skills but weak in visual memory. There are many ways that this can play out.

> **Tip:** To explore what kind of learner your child might be, try a variety of different tasks with him. Pay attention to his style of approaching the task and what helps him pay attention. Does he need to study the materials carefully using vision? Does he need to touch the materials in his hands? Does he need the toy to make a sound or want you to talk to him? Is his body in motion while he plays?

There are children who have sensory integration disorder. They struggle with processing sensory information and either cannot process certain sensory inputs and/or they may react in adverse ways to sensory information. This chapter will describe the common types of sensory integration problems and help you to better understand and help your child with these problems. We will also discuss how sensory problems impact mood and emotional stability.

Sammy: A Child Who Reacted Strongly and Negatively to Sensory Stimulation

Let's begin with the story of Sammy. She is a child who had one type of sensory integration dysfunction. She had what we call sensory defensiveness. This is a condition in which a child reacts in a strong, negative way to most or all of the senses. Her mother described some of the things that set Sammy off.

"When Sammy was a little girl, I didn't think anything was wrong with her. She was content to lie on the floor, looking about the room and listening to sounds. It wasn't until she was about 9 months of age that it occurred to me that her stillness might be a problem. She didn't crawl to explore the room and she barely reached for objects. Everyone said, 'What an easy baby you have!' By the time she reached 20 months, things began to change. If I touched her wrong, she recoiled. If there was a loud sound like a doorbell or vacuum cleaner, she shrieked as if in pain. We had to hold her gingerly because the slightest movement would set her off. And when we took her out in public, she continually asked to go home where it was calm. Now, in hindsight, I realize that the reason that she was so quiet and still was because she had no idea what to do with toys and that she was completely overwhelmed by sights, sounds, touch, and movement. It has been a very long journey for Sammy. We still battle with the effects of her devastating sensory defensiveness, but at least now we know what is wrong with her and she is learning what to do to make her life livable."

Many children who experience irritability and problems regulating their mood also experience sensory integration dysfunction. Usually the problem is one related to the ability to modulate sensory input. Sensory modulation is the nervous system's ability to balance the person's level of arousal with the intensity of stimulation being experienced. For instance, if a person feels sluggish, he may exercise, chew gum, or listen to energizing music to increase his arousal level. After a stimulating day with many activities, Sammy was so overwhelmed that she would shut down, going to her bedroom and secluding herself under her comforter. If her brother or other family members tried to interact with her, she would scream at them to go away. She was so wound up from a day at school that she couldn't settle herself to fall asleep at night.

This chapter will provide an overview of the common types of sensory integrative problems. We will talk about how sensory problems impact irritability, anxiety, and other mood disorders. Strategies to help children with these problems are described, with an emphasis on how to help your child.

Common Sensory Integration Problems

Sensory integrative disorders are fairly common to children and adults with learning disabilities, autism, mood disorders, and schizophrenia. In fact, it has been estimated that approximately 70% of children with learning disabilities have sensory integrative disorders, and that many children who have sensory problems also have high irritability, anxiety, or other mood disorders.

The early symptoms of sensory integration disorders are often related to regulatory problems such as sleep difficulties, poor self-calming, very low or high activity level, and an under- or over-responsiveness to sensory stimulation. These problems can persist as the child grows older. The perplexing part of this is that children with sensory integration problems are highly variable. They may hardly notice certain sensory stimulation in some situations, then in others, they over-react.

Sammy's Response to Sensory Stimulation

Sammy seemed to hold it together at school but if her teachers had looked closely, they would have noticed that she was very stiff, almost robot-like in her movements. She hardly interacted with peers and kept to herself as much as possible to avoid any extra stimulation. At home, she showed her true self, which was a child who was over-sensitive to almost every kind of sensory stimulation. At one point, her parents opted to home school her because the toll of going to school and holding it together was just too much for her.

Usually children with the combination of mood and sensory integrative dysfunction show a range of problems during the preschool years. The toddler with hypersensitivities usually displays discomfort by actively fleeing from the stimulus, retreating to a safe space, or by lashing out at the person or object that they perceive as bothering them. Hitting, biting, and throwing are behaviors that may be related to hypersensitivities. A hypersensitive child might be sitting at the lunch table and feel annoyed by the movement and random touch of other children sitting nearby. His touch system becomes agitated and before he knows it, he shoves the child sitting beside him to push away the annoying stimulus.

There are children with sensory integration problems who quickly escalate from a content, happy mood to a full-blown temper tantrum, sometimes without warning or a particular stimulus or event. These children have low frustration tolerance and quickly become upset when they are unable to problem solve how to manipulate or handle a particular toy.

Sammy's Response to Frustrating Experiences

When Sammy was two and a half years old, she completely fell apart when a puzzle piece wouldn't fit properly, if a cookie broke in half, or if she couldn't get her shoe on or off. Her parents often

anticipated her frustration and made the common mistake of rushing in and solving her problems to avoid a tantrum. As a result, Sammy ended up not knowing how to tolerate frustration or distress because she couldn't figure out how to solve simple problems.

The ability to self-calm is often a major problem for children with difficulties with sensory integration. Parents find that they must constantly give the child warning about changes in activity (e.g., going to another place, changing clothes, doing a new task). Often the child with these difficulties relies upon his parents to help him find ways to self-calm. The parent may give her child a special toy to hold in situations where impulse control is needed and offer constant verbal help. At the crux of the problem is the child's inability to tolerate the sensory stimulation and to problem solve and organize what to do for that particular task or situation.

> **Tip:** Find props or activities that will organize your child, soothe his sensory systems, and prevent melt-downs before you enter the potentially frustrating or over-stimulating experience.

Sensory difficulties can cause children to have trouble with separation, particularly when the parent is the only person that provides a predictable sensory world.

Sammy's High Need for Her Mother's Reassuring Presence

This was certainly the case for Sammy. She was unable to tolerate being in a play group with other children and had no idea how to engage in interactive play with other children. The result was her screaming, clutching at her mother's body, and asking to go home. Her mother was enormously frustrated by this experience, which often occurred at family gatherings. Other parents seemed to think that her mother had no idea how to keep Sammy calm and sometimes made remarks that cut deep into her heart. Family members often asked "What in the world is wrong with her? You must be coddling her too much." Little did they know how extremely difficult being out in the world was for Sammy. As the years passed, Sammy's parents often isolated themselves from group gatherings, community activities, and family events to avoid Sammy's unraveling. They wanted to avoid the unwelcome comments of others who clearly didn't understand. Because Sammy did not have many opportunities to be independent and go off with other children, she developed considerable problems with separation from her parents.

Identifying Sensory Processing Problems

Many children with sensory integration problems fluctuate between an under-reactive and over-reactive response to sensory input. A child who is over-reactive to sensory input may withdraw from stimulation (retreating under the table, covering his ears, pulling away from touch), avoid tasks or situations that evoke a reaction, or react with intensity (hitting or throwing things, yelling at others). In contrast, the child with an under-reactive sensory response may not perceive the sensory input unless it is very intense. Jamie was a child who was under-reactive to sensory experiences. He often hurled his body into other children or his parents like a football player, craving intense body contact because he did not seem to register touch in normal ways.

Often there is a combination of under- and over-reactivity in the same child and sometimes there is considerable variability that makes it hard to establish a pattern. When this happens, we refer to it as a sensory modulation problem. For example, 4-year-old Conner would sometimes wedge himself between furniture and the wall in new situations, then, once comfortable, he would run wildly about the room pulling toys off counter tops, bumping into other kids, and being out of control. He might then suddenly withdraw again, retreating under a table, screaming for others to keep away. This is a more difficult type of problem to treat because of the high variability and unpredictability of the child's responses.

To help you identify whether your child has problems with sensory modulation, a questionnaire is provided in Appendix 1. If your child scores in the at-risk range, then you should enlist the help of an occupational therapist trained in sensory integration who can evaluate your child and help develop a program to normalize his or her sensory responses.

Common Problems of the Touch System

The tactile or touch system is a dominant sensory system at birth. It remains critical throughout life as a major source of information about the environment to the central nervous system. It is a survival system that helps the young baby orient towards his mother's breast to feed, to avoid noxious touch, and to seek soothing contact with his caregivers. This system, along with vision, is essential to building attachment. As the child develops, the tactile system provides perceptual information about objects—their texture, weight, shape, and other detailed information obtained through the hands.

The tactile receptors in the body involve the sense of touch, pressure, pain, and temperature. The most sensitive parts of the body are the face, palms, soles of the feet, and the genitals. The least sensitive area of the body is the back. For example, if a person has an itch on her back, it may be hard to tell someone exactly where to scratch but if the itch were on her hand, she could be very specific about it.

The tactile system has two main functions, protection and discrimination. The tactile protective system is activated by temperature changes of the skin, light touch, and general contact with the skin. Light touch, such as a tickle on the face or a light stroke on the shoulder, might cause someone to react with alarm if the touch occurred without him seeing it. Light touch acts as a protective mechanism to the central nervous system by giving warning if an outside stimulus is too close for safety. This is why so many children with sensory integration problems become very upset when tickled, touched lightly, tapped unexpectedly, or exposed to other types of light touch (i.e., wiping the hands and face).

In the newborn child, this protective reaction is in place until the baby becomes accustomed to being touched and can discriminate between good and bad types of touch. Through holding and cuddling, infants learn to become less sensitive to touching experiences. Swaddling an infant or wrapping the baby tightly in a blanket is often necessary to help the infant remain calm and organized. Learning to tolerate these early touch experiences is one aspect of developing early self-regulation. It is the skill of being able to take in sensory stimulation from the world and take pleasure from it.

The tactile protective system matures quickly. By the time the child has reached the preschool years, it no longer dominates. However, if the person is in a dangerous situation, the tactile protective system switches on again. For example, suppose you think that someone sneaks up behind you and covers your eyes. You are likely to be more alert to this unexpected touch. Children who are unable to tolerate light touch and are highly sensitive to touch experiences are termed tactually defensive. Things like standing next to another child, wearing a long sleeved shirt, or having their hair washed bother them. We will talk more about this problem and how to help it.

> **Tip:** If your child is overly sensitive to touch, be sure he sees you approaching him. Tell him that you are about to touch him to prepare him for the touch, then touch him with a firm reassuring pressure. Avoid a light, tickly touch.

A second important function of the tactile system is discrimination. This is the ability to tell the difference in various textures, contours, and forms by feel. You use this sense when you reach into a bag and identify your car keys by feel. This sense of tactile discrimination plays an important role in starting a sequence of actions and planning movement as you do a skill. It also stimulates the desire to explore the environment. Tactile discrimination is important for being able to localize where you have been touched on your body and to recognize shapes by feel. It helps the brain map out where the body parts are in space and to form an internal sense of the body for what we call body scheme. The hands have many tactile receptors that help our fingers move in discreet ways to manipulate objects. If a child has poor tactile discrimination in his hands, he is likely to have fine motor problems. For example, tying shoes, buttoning, and handwriting are often difficult for children with this problem.

When there are problems with tactile sensitivity, the child often links a negative emotional meaning to touch. For example, when children are playing with peers, they attach a meaning to bumps, hugs, or tickles. Pleasant or aversive types of touch have an emotional tag put upon them. The mother who burrows her face on her baby's tummy in a game of touch should elicit smiling and laughter from her baby. The infant or child with poor tactile discrimination may avert gaze, pull away from the contact, or even cry. The toddler or preschooler who is sensitive to touch may not tolerate playing in close proximity with others and may respond by fleeing or engaging in aggressive actions.

Sammy's Response to Being Touched　　Sammy would respond by stiffening her body when others approached her, fearful that she might be touched. When she was 7 years old, she would run into my play room and hide. As I entered the room, she would scream at me, "Stop touching me!

You're hurting me!" even though I stood at least 10 feet away from her. If I responded, "Sammy, look how far away I am from you! My arms aren't long enough to touch you from here!" she would only scream louder, "You're touching me!" The best way to deal with it was to not talk to her and sit calmly at my table, doodling on a paper until she settled down. She inevitably would come over to my side and ask, "What are you drawing?"

In normal development, the touch system develops in a balanced way. The child rarely is overwhelmed by negative touch. As the child naturally explores his world, he learns to discriminate texture, weight, contour, and shape. This balance does not occur in children with sensory modulation and mood disorders. Instead, the nervous system regresses to a developmentally earlier response, one that has greater survival value. The touch system switches on the tactile protective system, making the child over-aroused. Then the child experiences normally pleasant tactile stimulation as irritating or threatening. These behaviors have important implications for emotional development.

> **Tip:** When children are highly sensitive to touch, they anticipate what a touch might feel like to such a degree that they can think that the touch has happened even when it hasn't. Give your child enough space between you and him. Let him approach you on his own terms so that he can "get ready" for the impending touch experience.

The Meaning of Touch for Sammy and Impact on the Parent–Child Relationship When Sammy's mother or father tried to hug her or cuddle during story time, she would react by screaming at them, "Stop hurting me!" Imagine how her parents might have felt. They frequently talked about their feelings of rejection that they couldn't even touch their own child in loving ways. Soon they found that they avoided being close to her, talking to her instead to keep a connection going. When a person isn't touched, then the touch system becomes even more insulated and accustomed to a "No touching zone." The problem only gets worse.

When children develop sensitivity to touch, it is not only caused by being touched by people, but can also come from the environment. For example, a child who is sensitive to touch may flee from contact with a chair or feel discomfort from the clothing he is wearing.

How Sammy's Touch Sensitivities Impacted Dressing and Eating Sammy couldn't stand wearing clothes with buttons, zippers, or snaps. She hated to wear tight underwear and insisted that the tags be cut out of her clothing. Her favorite clothes were the same blue sweat suit that she wore day in, day out. Of course it had been washed over and over again, and she particularly liked it after it had been worn several days in a row. Getting the sweat suit into the wash was a big battle as was getting her to try wearing anything else. Her aversion to elastic on her body caused her to stop wearing underwear when she was 9 years old. The sensitivities to touch often extend to problems touching textured objects and allowing textured foods to enter the mouth. Sammy avoided all art activities because anything wet and slimy set her off. She preferred hard objects and selected toys that had a firmness and weight to them. Her diet was highly restricted because of her aversion to textured foods. Favorite foods included ones that were firm or hard, like crunchy pretzels, popcorn, crackers, chicken, and cheese.

> **Tip:** Some young children with tactile defensiveness do best when they are put to bed in a clean sweat suit and then don't have to change when they get up in the morning. They can change later in the day, after breakfast or at another point when they have fully awakened.

This acute sensitivity can result in strong emotions. When children with sensory sensitivities are uncomfortable, they may react intensely by hitting or kicking, or physically retreating (e.g., hiding under furniture).

Sammy's Emotional Response to Touch   Sammy was known to clobber a playmate on the playground if she was bumped accidentally. She sometimes would pinch her mother when she was helping her bathe or dress. At other times, Sammy's instinct was to hide. She especially loved to go into a pup tent and bury herself in the pit of plastic ball. Tactually sensitive children react much more intensely when someone else is initiating the touch. These children like to be in control of what they touch. Sammy would often respond by running away or removing herself from the situation, then saying, "I hate this game, it hurts." Even if she was touched slightly, she might exclaim "Don't push me!" or "Watch where you're going!" The problem can build to the point that the child develops a strong sense of anxiety about being touched by others. This can cause the child to look hyperactive or distractible, running about to avoid touch or constantly looking around to see what might be coming her way.

Below we present some of the symptoms of tactile defensiveness. If your child has three or more symptoms for his or her age, then it is possible that he or she has problems in this area.

Symptoms of Tactile Defensiveness
Infancy and Early Childhood
  • Arching away when held (not high muscle tone)
  • Fisting of the hands to avoid contact with objects
  • Curling of the toes
  • A dislike of cuddling
  • Rejecting nipple and food textures (not oral-motor problem)
  • Strong preference for no clothing or tight swaddling
  • Preference for upright or sitting position rather than lying on back or stomach
  • A dislike of face or hair being washed
  • Hating the car seat and other confining situations
Preschool and School-Aged Children
  • Dislike being touched or cuddled by others: pull away from being held, cry or whine when touched, or hits back
  • Distressed when people are near, even when they are not touching (i.e., standing nearby, sitting in a circle)
  • Avoid touching certain textures. Hates getting hands messy (i.e., fingerpaints, paste, sand)
  • Like firm touch best and may enjoy games where there is very intense, high contact (e.g., jumping into stack of pillows from a height)
  • Prefer touch from familiar people
  • Dislike having face or hair washed; especially dislike having a haircut
  • Prefer long sleeves and pants even in warm weather, or prefer as little clothing as possible, even when it's cool
  • Touch everything in sight
  • Bump hard into other people or object
  • Withdraw from being near others, particularly groups
  • May hit, kick, or bite others and are aggressive in play
  • Have a strong preference for certain food textures (i.e., only firm and crunchy, or only soft)

- Dislike being dressed or undressed
- Bite or hit self
- Like to hang by arms or feet off furniture or people
- Use mouth to explore objects

A less common tactile problem, but one that is quite serious, is the child who doesn't respond to touch unless it is very intense. This problem is one of under-reactivity. Despite the fact that Sammy was so tactually defensive, there were times when she showed this tendency. As a toddler, she enjoyed throwing gravel in the driveway and as she grew up, she often sought play activities that had heavy weight and rough texture. She especially liked playing with heavy soccer balls. Children with an under-reactivity to touch are less sensitive and do not experience touch unless the experience is very intense. Such a child may laugh and actually enjoy a firm pat on the buttocks when being disciplined. It is as if their thresholds for noticing or reacting to tactile stimuli are very high. Often these children do not seem to experience pain.

These under-reactive children may be more passive and not explore the environment. Because the child doesn't seek out typical sensory experiences, the nervous system and body are deprived of sensory stimulation that is crucial for learning and development. It is common for these children to seek heavy touch-pressure on their bodies. For example, 7-year-old Kevin enjoyed throwing himself against anyone or anything. He loved heavy contact sports, but often sought out contact when it wasn't appropriate. Sometimes children with this problem develop self-abusive behaviors in an effort to "feel" their body (e.g., biting, head banging). Some children may bite themselves very hard, actually breaking skin without reacting. There are children with this problem who engage in self-injurious behavior such as biting their nails down to the quick, cutting themselves with scissors on purpose, or pulling out their own hair.

The tactile system is easily affected by traumas that a person might experience. For example, a premature infant who is hospitalized and has invasive medical procedures (e.g., oral intubation, heel sticks) might become sensitive to the part of the body that was intruded upon. Some children outgrow these sensitivities as they get older while others continue to remain sensitive throughout their life. Children who are in environments where there is a minimum of holding and carrying from a loving caregiver may also experience a state of sensory deprivation. The effects are often seen in children who have been in orphanages in their early years. These children may not have been encouraged to explore through their senses and may have been put in situations where they had to sit and wait for long periods or were prevented from touching things.

> **Tip:** If your child has experienced a physical trauma because of a medical procedure, injury, or illness, find pleasurable sensory experiences that he can enjoy to stimulate the part of the body that was affected. For example, if your child has reflux, provide him with fun blow toys like plastic horns that will vibrate the entire oral tract.

Sometimes a caregiver experiences mental illness such as severe postpartum depression that impacts her capacity to interact with her young baby. When the infant is not held and touched early in life, the child can develop tactile sensitivities even if he was born with an intact nervous system. If treated early enough, the negative impact of not being held in loving ways can be reversed. It is very important for parents who recognize that they are depressed and unable to provide basic care to get help to prevent problems that will develop for their child and to get support for themselves. It can be devastating for both parent and child when the relationship is void of touch and intimacy.

> **Tip:** If you are depressed and find that you have no physical and emotional energy to touch and play with your child, get emotional support through counseling and get evaluated for medication for yourself. While you are getting your feet on the ground and beginning to feel better, find people who can play with your child in fun and engaging ways. Make sure the play provides good sensory experiences that are appropriate for his age. This chapter has many ideas that could be used.

When children are uncomfortable with tactile experiences, the problem becomes heightened as they grow older. Not only does the child have difficulties processing and tolerating touch, but with maturity, he encounters more challenging and varied tactile experiences. For example, the child must accommodate to the touch of playmates and adults other than mom's or dad's familiar touch. Although the child's own parents may have found ways to approach and touch their child in ways that feel acceptable to the child, other children and adults have not made this accommodation. As a result, the child's tactile problems may appear worse. This is why some children are not identified as having tactile sensitivities until they enter school.

Problems with play skills are common among children with tactile hypersensitivities. Destructive or aggressive play occurs frequently when the child is required to play with other children in close quarters The child may touch other children with force even when trying to be gentle. If given a choice, some children withdraw from other children or find spaces to play that provide them with tactile security, such as a corner of the room. Frequently one sees children who are avoiding touch playing alone on the playground, which results in social problems in addition to the tactile problems.

> **Tip:** If your child likes to bang and throw things or engage in aggressive play like bumping into things, find an appropriate way for him to get the body feedback he needs. For example, you can set up a heap of pillows that he can run and dive into instead of him crashing his body into people.

Helping Your Child to Process Touch and Overcome His Tactile Problems   Children with problems of the touch system, whether it is a hypersensitivity, undersensitivity, or a combination of the two respond well to touch activities designed to help the child. We encourage you to have the guidance of an occupational therapist as you embark on these activities. We summarize a number of principles along with accompanying activities that might help your child in **Tool Sheet 2, Activities for Problems of Touch,** which includes ways to help the tactually sensitive child and children who are undersensitive to touch. These activities can be incorporated into daily routines and fun games to make them more meaningful and acceptable for your child.

The Movement Sense

Like the tactile system, the movement or vestibular system develops early, enabling the infant to respond to movement of the body in space. This sense actually begins developing *in utero*. The fetus receives constant movement stimulation from the amniotic fluid as well as the mother's own body movements. The movement system helps the child orient himself in space, to know which end is up or down. It helps the child to explore the world—to crawl, walk, and run in new ways. Along with the tactile system, it is critical for development of body posture, eye movements, motor skills, spatial awareness, and balance. The movement system also plays an important role in arousal, attention, and alertness.

Another important function of the movement system is to enable the child to feel secure when moving in space.

Sammy's Fear of Movement   Almost any movement was overwhelming for Sammy. She was terrified if her feet left the ground. She startled and stiffened if moved unexpectedly. And going to the playground was completely unacceptable to her. When she was 5 years old, she began a playground desensitization program so that she could overcome the immense fear that she had developed in this environment. This system
relied on shaping principles in **Tool Sheet 13, Changing Behavior**. The program involved going to the playground and sitting in the car or on a bench while watching the other children play. This was repeated for a few weeks. Next we had her stand next to a piece of equipment, then the following week she had to sit on the swing with it not moving. Finally she learned to tolerate moving slowly on the swing and sometimes she would try the sliding board.

A secure sense of where the body is in space contributes to the development of emotional stability. This is why we often see children with anxiety who are also afraid of moving. What usually happens is that the child has an extreme sensitivity to movement then becomes anxious about situations when they move in space. Sometimes children develop phobias about the movement activity, just like Sammy did about the playground. They then strongly resist places or activities that require body movement.

Children with hypersensitivities to movement typically show an intolerance for lying on their stomach or back and they prefer upright postures like standing. They often have low muscle tone or a looseness in their muscles that contributes to a slowness in developing motor skills. Balance is often wobbly and the child often has a fear of irregular or unexpected movement.

In contrast, when the child is under-responsive to movement in space, he or she craves movement and may become very fussy and demanding unless the parents provide movement stimulation for him or her. For example, 9-year-old Amanda would come home from school each day and spend almost an hour rocking vigorously in a glider chair. If she was interrupted or prevented from doing this, she would become very irritable and impossible to be around.

> **Tip:** Find just the right amount of movement stimulation for your child. Keep track of what kind of movement—rocking, swinging, jumping, spinning, or sports activities that he likes to do. How long does he engage in these activities and at what time of day? What is your child's behavior like right after the stimulation and later in the day? Does it help or hinder your child to do that kind of movement? If the movement is detrimental to your child, meaning that it makes him hyper or it is repetitive and meaningless, redirect him to another activity each time he begins to rock, spin, or perform other movement. Or channel his repetitive movement activity to make it become meaningful. For instance, have him rock his body while looking at pictures, or have him swing and sing at the same time.

When a child is fearful of movement experiences and has a strong preference for movement activities to be near to the ground, there is often an accompanying separation anxiety disorder. The child relies heavily upon the parent to provide safety in new situations such as helping them to find a place to play where other children won't bump into them, causing them to fall. This was the case with Sammy. She disliked playing on playground equipment, and preferred standing

close by an adult when outside. Whenever possible, she preferred to play inside with small toys or looking at books, avoiding all opportunities for moving.

One often sees children like Sammy showing a fearfulness of new situations, rigidity, and a resistance to change. Sammy preferred sameness in all her routines and would become very agitated when routines varied.

When a child is under-reactive to movement stimulation, he often challenges parents by climbing onto dangerous surfaces, jumping from unsafe heights, or trying a movement activity that exceeds his motor capacity, such as climbing high on a jungle gym. Often the child who is under-reactive to movement is fearless and constantly tests limits. There is an impairment of judgment both in the body and mind. They may crave movement activities and become very upset when restrained from continuing to swing, climb, or spin. Parents often report that on days when the child is unable to engage in such movement activities, he becomes very irritable, has tantrums frequently, and has difficulty with sleep.

Below we summarize many of the typical problems of children with hyper- or hyposensitivities to movement.

Symptoms of Hyper- and Hyposensitivities to Movement
   Movement hypersensitivities

1. Easily overwhelmed by movement (i.e., car sick).
2. Strong fear of falling and of heights.
3. Does not enjoy playground equipment and avoids rough play.
4. Is anxious when feet leave ground.
5. Dislikes having head upside down.
6. Slow in learning skills such as climbing up stairs or playground equipment and relies on railing longer than other children the same age.
7. Enjoys movement which he or she initiates but does not like to be moved by others, particularly if the movement is unexpected.
8. Dislikes trying new movement activities or has difficulty learning them.

   Undersensitivity to movement

1. Craves movement and does not feel dizziness when other children do.
2. Likes to climb to high, precarious places. No sense of limits or controls.
3. Is in constant movement, rocking or running about.
4. Likes to swing very high and/or for long periods of time.
5. Frequently rides on the merry-go-round while others run around to keep the platform turning.
6. Enjoys getting into an upside-down position.

Helping Your Child with Problems Processing Movement   Movement occurs in different directions. There is forward-back movement that occurs with rocking or gliding. This tends to be calming to the nervous system. There is side-to-side movement and up-down movement (i.e., jumping or bouncing) that can be alerting or arousing to the body. And there is spinning in a circle or an orbit (when your face stays in one direction and your body moves in a circle) which tend to be highly arousing to the body. Another dimension of movement is speed or velocity. Movement can accelerate or decelerate like when a child sleds down a hill or puts the brakes on the bicycle to avoid hitting an obstacle. Finally, movement can be random or predictable in rhythm and tempo. Rocking in a rhythm is very calming and helps the child to anticipate and predict the movement pattern. Riding a roller coaster is an example of random and unpredictable movement, which is arousing.

> **Tip:** Movement experiences are more easily accepted when children can do them in activities that are meaningful to them. For example, if your child wants to learn how to do a somersault because all of his friends are learning to do this, then he will be motivated to learn how. While your child is learning to move in new ways, encourage him to actively control the movement—to decide what kind of movement it is, and how fast or how high it is.

Movement activities should involve your child's choice of activity guided by his or her own interest and skill. Play should be the medium through which movement is introduced. **Tool Sheet 3, Guidelines for Helping Children Move with Ease and Comfort**, presents a list of movement stimulation activities. An occupational therapist can help you develop a comprehensive program for your child. The activities presented in these guidelines distinguish between activities for children who are under- or oversensitive to movement. There are also some precautions offered for children who are so sensitive to movement that they show a severe, adverse reaction. If this is your child, use great caution in trying these activities. An occupational therapist can inform you what to look for and how to do movement with your child so that it is integrating, not disorganizing.

Motor Planning Problems

Motor planning problems, also known as developmental dyspraxia, are very common in children with sensory integration disorder. Children with dyspraxia have trouble with basic tasks such as learning to tie their shoes, getting dressed, getting on and off playground equipment, or learning how to sequence a series of movements like skipping or galloping. Whenever a child has motor planning problems, there is almost always a problem processing touch and/or movement, which means that these underlying sensory issues should also be addressed. By doing so, your child will have a better sense of where his body is in space and what it feels like to do certain actions.

> **Tip:** The real problem that occurs for children with motor planning difficulties is not so much in the processing of sensory input or the ability to produce the movement skill, but in the middle step—the planning of movement. Help your child by thinking out what he wishes to build, where he wants to move and how, or what the final product will be, then take the task apart into small steps.

Sammy's Motor Planning Problems   Sammy had significant motor planning problems. She had low muscle tone or floppiness to her muscles that made it difficult for her to control her movements. Often children with developmental dyspraxia are also sensitive to touch and movement or have other sensory processing issues. In Sammy's case, she had an extreme fearfulness of new movement activities along with poor balance. She fell frequently at school and avoided playground activities. She was terrified of swings, jungle gyms, and any piece of movement equipment. If she watched children running about and moving, she was overwhelmed. Sammy was a very shy and withdrawn child. This trait became even more extreme if she was asked to do things like climb onto the jungle gym. She would bite her lip, begin to tremble all over, and cry. If her mother was nearby, she would rush to her side, cling to her even when there were very appealing activities. This was especially frustrating for her parents because they wanted her to have fun like other children. A hay ride with her cousins turned out to be disastrous.

If one looked closely at how Sammy moved, you could see that her movements were stiff and awkward. As she grew older, she seemed to move almost like a robot. When she tried to do any kind of movement, she would be very slow and deliberate. If she was asked to skip across the room or try to do a jumping jack, she would have to say the movements aloud ("Arms and legs jump out, arms and legs jump in") as she moved in a jerky manner. The only way she could learn sequenced, unfamiliar movement patterns like this was through verbal and physical prompts as well as a person demonstrating what the movement looked like.

How Sammy's Motor Planning Problems Impacted Her Relationships with Peers   Sammy had a great deal of difficulty playing with other children. Her parents tried to structure play dates for her to help her learn social skills. We had to break down what she would do with friends in a very structured way. For instance, if she had a play date with another child, it only went well if there was a planned activity like making cookies or going bowling. Her mother found that she had to list in advance of the play date what would happen, in a predictable sequence. She also discovered that she needed to pop her head into Sammy's room at regular intervals to be sure that the play date was going well. Often she would find Sammy absorbed in play with her dolls while the other child did something completely different at the other end of the room. On occasion the play date would end badly with one or the other child crying, "She's not doing what I want her to do!" or "She won't share her toys!" Usually the child never wanted to return for a repeat play date, which was very painful for Sammy's parents. Sammy, on the other hand, was content to play alone and stay isolated in her own world.

When motor planning problems are present, the child experiences extreme frustration over tasks that he cannot perform. He may break toys then become very upset when he cannot fix them. Often the child relies heavily on his parents to guide him when an activity changes. Some parents find that they need to prepare their child several days in advance about upcoming events to prevent major emotional upsets. Parents often find that they need to explain everything that is going to happen, as well as giving verbal feedback while the activity is occurring. The child struggles with getting started on tasks and has difficulty knowing how to carry out the necessary steps to complete the task. Activities with sequences such as undressing and dressing are struggles for the child.

Some of the common symptoms of the child with poor motor planning are delays in dressing and fine and gross motor skills involving imitation, sequenced movements (i.e., lacing, skipping), and construction (i.e., building from a block model). The accuracy of movement is often poor, particularly skilled hand movements such as handwriting. Sometimes the child's movement is explosive or jerky, has too much or too little force, is too slow or too fast, and the aim is off. Speech articulation may be poor because this is also a planned, skilled motor activity. Nonhabitual or new tasks are very difficult for the child with poor motor planning; therefore, they prefer routines and strongly resist changes. Transitions from one activity to the next may cause behavioral upset.

> **Tip:** Establish routines for as many transitions as you can so that your child knows how to change activities without falling apart. For example, you may write and draw out the morning routine on poster boards, each one prompting where to go next. Place these in strategic places like a treasure hunt. When your child finishes the last step of the routine down at the breakfast table before the school bus arrives, he will find a surprise in his lunch box that day.

Initiating new movement sequences are often very difficult. For instance, the child may not be able to tell you what he plans to do because he lacks an internal plan. As a result, one may see the child with poor motor planning becoming very disruptive and aggressive, particularly when there is no external structure to organize him. Or the child may become passive, preferring repetition of certain favorite activities, and resisting new and different tasks. One may observe tantrums, aggressive behavior, poor play skills with peers, frustration, and a strong resistance to change. Some children become very controlling and manipulative because of their inability to control and impact their environment. Needless to say, poor self-concept is a major problem for these children. Below we list some of the common symptoms of motor control and motor planning problems observed in children.

Motor Control Problems in the Child

1. Frequently breaks toys; cannot seem to judge how hard or soft to press when handling toys.
2. Trips over obstacles or bumps into them.
3. Falls frequently (after 18 months).
4. Slumped body posture when sitting or standing.
5. Leans head on hand or arm.
6. Prefers to lie down rather than sit, or to sit rather than stand.
7. Has a loose grip on objects such as a pencil, scissors, or spoon, or grip is too tight on objects.
8. Becomes fatigued easily during physical activities.
9. Is loose jointed and floppy; may sit with legs in a W.
10. Has difficulty manipulating small objects, particularly fasteners.
11. Eats in a sloppy manner.
12. Does not use two hands for tasks that require two hands, such as holding down the paper while drawing, holding the cup while pouring.

Motor Planning Problems in the Child

1. Fear of trying new motor activities. Likes things to be the same and predictable (i.e., routines).
2. Difficulty making transitions from one activity to the next.
3. Must be prepared in advance several times before change is introduced.
4. Cannot plan sequences in activities, needing structure from an adult.
5. Easily frustrated.
6. Is very controlling of activities.
7. Difficulty playing with peers.
8. Aggressive or destructive in play.
9. Has a temper tantrum easily.
10. Did not crawl before starting to walk.
11. Difficulty with dressing and sequenced motor actions.

Teaching Your Child to Be Better at Motor Planning   Learning how to organize and plan purposeful actions is a very important skill. It impacts the ability to make transitions from one activity to the next and to move through sequences like dressing or moving through an obstacle course. It also has a lot to do with being able to organize projects that involve movement as well as organizing play. **Tool Sheet 4, Teaching Your Child to Be More Coordinated**, provides a sequence that will help your child learn this skill.

Summary

Sensory integrative disorders have a major impact on a child's capacity to tolerate a variety of sensory stimulation from others and the environment and to respond in an adaptive or flexible way to sensory information. This will pave the way for skilled and purposeful actions and interactions. Sensory integrative disorders are common among learning disabled and emotional disturbed children and may be observed as early as infancy. The touch system is important for protection and survival but it is also important for learning such things as motor skills, perception of shapes, textures, and contours of objects, and motor planning. A well-functioning touch system is essential for emotional stability. The most common types of tactile problems are tactile defensiveness and tactile hyposensitivities. Tactile defensiveness is a severe sensitivity to being touched that may be related to touch in the environment, such as from the clothing on our bodies, sitting on a chair, or tolerating the proximity of peers. It can be other-initiated, like when mom strokes her child or washes his face. It can also be self-initiated, as when the child puts a textured food into his mouth or touches a textured toy. In contrast children with tactile hyposensitivities do not experience touch unless it is very intense, which can cause the child to not react to painful experiences.

The movement or vestibular system affects body posture, muscle tone, coordination of the eyes with the body movement, and balance. This is an important system for motor planning. It helps the child to feel aroused and alert. It offers security to the body when moving in space. Problems with this system impact security of movement, perceiving body movement in space, and tolerating different kinds of movement. It helps us to maintain good posture during movement patterns, and to coordinate the two body sides for complex movements like jumping jacks.

Motor planning problems, also called developmental dyspraxia, impact the planning of skilled or nonhabitual movements. When a child has a motor planning problem, he or she usually has problems processing touch and movement. The problem can impact postural movements, like holding the body in a stable sitting position, and the ability to sequence movements, like tying shoes or skipping. Motor planning affects language skills in being able to say what you are going to do. Problems in this area impact the child's ability to build constructions like a Lego structure, to draw, and to conceptualize how to use objects symbolically.

This chapter provided ideas for parent on how to address these various problems. Below we provide the names of books that give a more complete explanation of sensory integration disorders in children and more ideas on activities to help your child.

Resources

Ayres, A. J. (1979). *Sensory integration and the child*. Los Angeles, CA: Western Psychological Services.

Wilbarger, P., & Wilbarger, J. (1991). *Sensory defensiveness in children 2–12*. Santa Barbara, CA: Avanti Education Programs.

9

The Curious, Clueless, and Disorganized Child

Tamara: The Brilliant, Curious, Clueless, and Disorganized Child

Tamara is an unusual 10 year old. She is tiny for her age, but you are drawn to her large, intelligent eyes. When she talks, you enter her vast interior world peopled with lady warriors who defend the frail and friendless or futuristic scientists who live in another galaxy light years away. She reads voraciously, often choosing books that would seem to be beyond her years. Tamara's mind is always trying to make sense of the diverse facets of her world. She is interested in the black hole theory and the history of the American civil war.

Yet this gifted, curious child has a great deal of trouble dealing with each day and particularly the demands of school. She is profoundly disorganized. Getting up is very hard because she reads at night under the covers and does not get enough sleep. Once her father has succeeded in awakening her, she cannot find anything because nothing has a place of its own. All of her belongings are strewn around the house. Her shoes are in the family room, her math homework is in the kitchen, and her homework story is still on the computer. She finally puts on clothes from the piles of laundry that litter the floor because she has never put her clean clothes away.

Breakfast is easy. She has eaten the same kind of pop tart for 4 years because it is the only breakfast food she likes. But then the real trouble begins. She has brought her book to the breakfast table and assures her parents that she simply needs to finish an exciting chapter. Everything stops. She does not eat the pop tart; she does not print her homework paper.

When there are five minutes left before the school bus arrives, her parents tell her to get ready. She becomes frustrated because she does not know where anything is and because her parents are yelling at her. Her emotional distress increases as she rushes around, gets her math homework, forgets the homework paper, cannot find her shoes, puts on old boots, and finally runs out the door carrying her jacket and eating the pop tart with jam squirting on her shirt. Often in fact she misses the school bus and has to be driven to school later by her mother.

Both mother and daughter are frustrated and upset. Occasionally Tamara's distress can descend into depression as she feels overwhelmed and incompetent. More profoundly, she worries that her parents and teachers want her to be someone she cannot become.

Tamara is a good example of a very intelligent but profoundly disorganized child with attention problems. She has extreme difficulty understanding the concept of time. She really has no idea how long anything takes. She can easily become distracted either by something external like a book or a computer game, or something internal like her dreams of a medieval super-hero. It is hard for her to get started on a project. In the classroom, she wanders around, looking at the classroom displays. When she finally settles down to work, the time is almost up. If she has a long-term assignment, she cannot begin to set small deadlines so that she will get the work in on time. If she remembers, she starts her assignment the night before it is due, stays up late, and cannot hand it in the next day.

In addition to trouble with time, Tamara has trouble with space. She has no internal sense of where things should be. She is constantly losing things, and this causes her enormous frustration. Tamara is also disorganized in terms of her body. She is unaware when she has spilled something on herself or whether her sweater is inside out. Her handwriting is so messy that she cannot read it herself! When Tamara is sitting on a sofa, it is not unusual for her to suddenly be upside down with her legs over her head.

Tamara is often frustrated and discouraged, particularly when she has experienced social ostracism because of her unorthodox ways. She wants to slip into the library and ignore the other students who are making comments about her. When her parents talk to her about how disorganized she is, Tamara wants to scream with rage and anger. Why can they not understand? She just cannot do it!

Research in the areas of attention deficit disorder, attention deficit-hyperactivity disorder, and problems of executive functioning points to neurological differences that make it difficult for a child like Tamara to focus and become organized. Chapter 6 on attention gives pertinent information on how organization and attention problems develop. However, here we are focusing on how to manage a child with these problems. Parenting a child like this is hard because you basically have to plan and organize to a degree that seems excessive and inappropriate. However, normal age guidelines do not apply for these children, who operationally are much younger than their years. As a rule of thumb it makes sense to set age expectations for focus and organization that are about a third younger than the chronological age of your child. For instance, if your child is nine you might set expectations for being orderly and independent at the level of a six year old.

Children who have extreme problems of organization and attention often have these same problems as adults. Your job as parents is to help your child learn organizational strategies that are not innate so that she can successfully navigate her world both as a child and later as an adult. Bear in mind that there are many disorganized people who have been very successful. Learning coping skills takes time, but it can be done. This chapter will help you do just this. You will benefit both your child and the adult your child becomes.

> **Tip:** Although parents may find a child's disorganization frustrating, remember that the person most distressed is the child himself. It is discouraging never to be able to find what you want or hand in the assignment the teacher is requesting. No wonder many such children give up!

Providing Structure at Home around Time and Space

When children like Tamara do not get the structure they require, they can become easily overwhelmed and emotionally dysregulated. Conversely, if the parent is too structured and appears critical of their failure to catch on, they can become easily frustrated and discouraged. Having a set routine is imperative for these children because it helps instill a rhythm to the day so that the child can develop a better sense of what needs to be done, when it needs to be done, and how it needs to be done. The *way* in which the structure is installed needs to be perceived as helpful rather than tyrannical. See **Tool Sheet 5, Learning to Pay Attention**, for a list of structures to help with attention and organization.

Waking Up

Children like Tamara often have an extremely hard time waking up and they may need their parents' help getting them going. Once your child enters elementary school, your goal should be to have her get herself up by using an alarm clock, but this may not be enough. When the alarm clock and a pat from a parent are not enough, you may have to try more extreme measures. Your goal here is to engage the nervous system and get it going so that the child will become alert. Here are some suggestions for "getting awake."

- If your child has attention deficit disorder and takes a stimulant, have him take it first thing when he wakes up.
- Showering or bathing first thing can be stimulating.
- Try eating first, dressing later.
- Listen to rousing music.
- Bring toast and juice upstairs so that your child has something in his stomach right away before he gets out of bed.
- Vigorous massage will help to awaken the nervous system.
- Gently pull your child's legs and arms to engage his muscles in traction.
- Smelling peppermint can be arousing.

As parents, you need to figure out what works best for your child, but also what works best for your whole family.

Structuring the Beginning of the Day

As a parent, the first thing that you need to figure out is how you want the day to go. What should happen at what time? You might want to refer to **Providing Structure to the Day, Tool Sheet 22**, as you plot what you want to happen, and at what time. Because these children have trouble internalizing a routine, you need to try hard to keep the same daily routine so that they can begin to internalize that structure. Here is what Tamara's schedule might look like:

6:50 a.m., Tamara wakes up with the alarm clock and a friendly pat by a parent.
7:00 a.m., her parent returns to give her a vigorous massage.
7:15 a.m., Tamara is dressed and downstairs.
7:30 a.m., Tamara has finished eating.
7:40 a.m., she has brushed her hair and brushed her teeth.
7: 50 a.m., she has her jacket on and book bag ready.
7: 55 a.m., Tamara is out the door on her way to the bus stop.

Because Tamara was so hard to wake up, her parents had to be more involved than they would typically be. Because of her disorganization, 25 minutes were allotted to getting personal hygiene taken care of and school materials packed up to go. In fact, her parents began to insist that she put her backpack by the door at night after she was finished with her homework. In order to get initial compliance with a schedule such as this, you may want to give concrete reinforcers. See **Tool Sheet 17, A Token Economy.**

> **Tip:** Times are included in this chart because we are trying to help Tamara be more conscious of time and look at a clock more often. For young children, it is helpful to have a digital clock in the kitchen.

Time Management after School

Time management at the end of the day is also important. This is what Tamara's schedule would look like:

3:00 p.m., she is home and relaxing, with a snack, reading a book, playing a computer game, etc.

4:00 p.m., she starts homework.

4:00 to 6:00 p.m., homework, with a 5-minute break after each completed assignment.

6:00 p.m., family dinner.

6:30 to 7:30 p.m., relaxing, computer, TV, phone calls, e-mail.

7:30 p.m., Tamara has a bath and heads to bed.

8:00 to 8:15 p.m., a parent reads to her.

8:15 p.m., lights out.

Most children need a break after school. They also are very hungry. Some families provide a snack that is really a mini-dinner, with items such as soup, cheese, and crackers. It is important to have some protein at this time to restore energy. Some children need a physical outlet because they have been inside all day. They need to have vigorous exercise, perhaps to be outdoors playing with friends. What your child needs as a break will very much depend on his disposition and interests.

There needs to be an expectation and agreement that homework will begin at a certain time, and it is wise to get a large amount of homework done before dinner if this is possible. There also needs to be a policy about what kind of breaks a child can take while he is doing homework. Some families adopt a rule that the child has to sit at the kitchen counter and cannot get up until he has finished everything. However, children with attention problems usually cannot sustain that kind of effort and need more frequent breaks to help them regain their focus. Breaks should not last long, or your child will be unable to turn his attention back to his work. Getting a glass of water or letting the dog out may suffice. For a very active girl or boy, it might be helpful to do a few pushups or jumping jacks during break. Sometimes it helps to have the child check in with a parent after every assignment in order to get your positive attention and support to keep going.

> **Tip:** Family dinner is very important. The goal is for all family members to eat together at the same time. Try to avoid a cafeteria approach to dinner with everyone eating different things. This is a good time for children to learn to try new foods. However, the most important thing about family dinner is communication. Here children learn to talk and be heard but also they learn to listen. Children from families who have dinner together every night show higher academic achievement and success in life.

Time Management at the End of the Day

Planning for the end of the day is also important. There should be an agreed upon time for going to bed, for head on pillow, and for lights out. Rewarding children for making these deadlines will help them begin to internalize a structure. Getting children to sleep and dealing with them when they wake in the night are dealt with in detail in Chapter 4. (See **Tool Sheet 20, Managing Your Child at Night**).

Getting Compliance with Scheduling

Many children will follow your plan after you have set out clear expectations. However, other children may need more support to internalize this structure. In order to win compliance with the schedule you have worked out, you should give some thought to positive reinforcement as a way of getting your child's attention and good will.

The strategy **Changing Behavior (Tool Sheet 13)** outlines how you can build new behaviors by using behavioral principles of positive reinforcement, creating behavioral chains, and ignoring behavior. Here is what to keep in mind.

- Being positive—With disorganized children a parent needs to stay positive. If the child is having trouble, it is because he cannot do a complex task and therefore gets overwhelmed and shuts down, with occasional doses of oppositional behavior thrown in. By reinforcing what a child is doing right, you show him that you see that he is trying, and what is more that he can be successful. Tamara's mother tried very hard to figure out a positive way of addressing the issue of getting organized with her daughter. Initially she said, "Tamara, you are such a pig. Your room is a mess and the wet towels you leave around the house are getting moldy." This did not work. Next she experimented with a more validating approach, which resulted in better compliance. She said, "Tamara, I know how hard it is for you to keep your room tidy. This week let's just focus on keeping the wet towels hung up in the bathroom. I don't expect you to be perfect, but it would really help me if you did this."
- Chaining—No, we do not recommend chaining your child to the desk! We use chaining to refer to building chains of linked behaviors. Gradually, as your child becomes committed to getting more organized, you can begin to encourage chains of behaviors rather than individual behaviors. Here you move from reinforcing specific behaviors, such as brushing teeth, to reinforcing "chunks" of behaviors. A chunk of dressing behaviors may include clothes, teeth, and hair.
- Ignoring behavior—Sometimes you want to ignore behavior in order to discourage it, a process called putting on extinction in psychological jargon. Ignore inappropriate or ineffective behaviors such as complaining about how much one does not want to get up or complaining that you never have the right breakfast food. Then you reinforce the right behaviors such as getting up and eating breakfast.
- Natural consequences—When we are thinking about positive reinforcement, natural consequences are the most powerful thing you can do. For instance, if you are ready for bed early, you get an extra long story time. If you get to the kitchen on time in the morning, you get pancakes rather than cereal because your father has time to cook a breakfast.
- A token economy—When you are trying to teach a string of behaviors or your child is not responding to natural consequences, you may want to consider using a structured token economy system (**Tool Sheet 17**). In a token economy, you give a child a concrete reward, such as a sticker or a poker chip, every time the child performs the desired behavior. Tamara's daily schedule could easily be converted into a token system. Simply give her a poker chip or a check on a chart every time she completes each step of her schedule.

> **Tip:** In a token economy system, you can give extra weight or double rewards for the behaviors that are particularly hard or important, such as finishing homework before dinner.

Work with your child to determine what would be a good reinforcer or reward. A good reinforcer is something that the child likes a great deal and cannot get easily. Once something becomes a reinforcer, the only way to get the reward is by earning it through the system. For instance, let's say your child loves to rent movies, and you make this a reward (or reinforcer). Then you won't be able to rent a movie just for the fun of it; it has to be earned. In the case of a young child, you might want to consider a grab bag filled with small treats such as a beautiful pencil, a bouncing ball, or baseball cards. For every one to three poker chips that the child earns, he wins a pick from the bag. There are a few cardinal principles that you want to keep in mind when you are doing a token economy system:

1. Do not make it hard to get rewards. Young children need to get a reward every day and sometimes the poker chips themselves are not powerful enough. We want children to buy into the system and follow its rules. Therefore they need to get rewards often.
2. The reward should be what the child wants the most—candy or a skate board. However, the parents control the currency; that is, how many chips are necessary to get the reward. If you aren't keen on a trip to a fast food restaurant, you require a large number of chips to earn this particular reward. If you love going to movies, require a small number of chips to earn the reward.
3. Change your system of rewards frequently, usually once every 10 to 14 days so that interest remains high.
4. Do not take away the poker chips when your child has done something wrong. Have a different punishment, but do not undermine the reward system.
5. You can weight reinforcers; for instance, doing homework before dinner might get you double the reinforcement that you would get for completing the same work after dinner.
6. Often when you have more than one child, your other children will want in on this system because they see their sibling getting something that they do not have. This is not a problem. They can earn rewards too, but for different things. A young child might earn a reward for going to the potty. An older child might earn a reward for practicing the piano.
7. Once you have a reward system, you cannot get the reward without earning it; that is, you cannot go to a movie unless you have earned the points.

Is a Token Economy System Bribery?   As parents, you may feel ambivalent about using concrete rewards or reinforcers for engaging in behavior that is normally expected of everyone. Some parents may therefore feel that giving their child a concrete reward for doing something like brushing his teeth is bribing him and thus teaching the wrong values. Our response is that bribery refers to an act that is either illegal or immoral. When we use reinforcement, we are instilling structure in children who are by nature somewhat chaotic. The rewards are helpful because we are asking them to learn to do something that they have trouble learning to do innately. When they have learned the complex behavior, you will note that your children will no longer expect to be rewarded for it. You can move on to a new behavior that is hard and where they need help. Remember, most adults would not go to work unless they were paid. For children, learning these difficult life skills definitely feels like work!

Learning to Manage Belongings and Space

Because finding and organizing belongings are so hard for them, these children need to have far fewer things than another child might manage.

- Space stations—The parent needs to manage the child's space and get the child to help maintain the system. Toys need to be containable, or the child will become disorganized. Together with your child, identify which few toys are kept in the bedroom. It is unrealistic to expect disorganized children to put away puzzles with every piece in place. However, they might be able to stack puzzles on a shelf and put Legos in a bin. The fewer the toys, the greater the organization and calm.
- Clothes—Don't expect these children to put away their clean clothes, because the result will be a wasteland of dirty and clean clothes all mixed up on the floor. The bedroom should have a bin for dirty clothes because it increases the likelihood that some of the dirty clothes will make it to the hamper. Likewise, have a simple system for clothes, either easily opened drawers at the child's height or open shelving. Some children benefit a great deal from having clothes selected and laid out for them the night before so that it is easy to get dressed in the morning. If this works for a fire fighter, chances are it will work for your child.
- Distractions—Because children like Tamara often get distracted in their rooms and have trouble getting ready in the morning or going to sleep at night, minimize what will distract them. Televisions and computers are usually too tempting and should therefore be in another part of the house, rather than in your child's bedroom. Limit the number of toys in the bedroom for the same reason.
- Few responsibilities yield successful bedroom organization—Although children like Tamara have trouble maintaining a system, that does not mean that they should have no responsibility for their rooms. They can certainly be taught that they have to make their bed and pick up their clothes and put them in the bin. Again, natural consequences can help to teach this skill. If they don't make their bed in the morning, they may be asked to make it before they can sit down to dinner. The key requirement is to keep positive and not overwhelm the child with too many responsibilities.
- Parent supervision—If parents are patrolling the room daily and demanding that things be picked up, it will lead to frustration on the part of both parent and child. Consider having a weekly room clean up that has to be done before the child gets his allowance.
- Other spaces in the home—In addition to the child's bedroom, try to designate other spaces for other things. When children come home from school, they need a place near the door where they can leave shoes, coat, and backpack. You should also designate a place for doing homework, although this varies greatly with the individual child.

Helping Your Child with Homework

Getting organized to help your child do homework is a major challenge. With your lovable but disorganized child, always remember that the person most bothered by his lack of organization is the child himself. He cannot help it that order does not come naturally. Here is how you can help him.

Figuring Out Where to Do Homework Some children with attention problems like to work near their parent so that they can check in when they have a problem or when they have completed an assignment. Other children benefit from a quiet desk in a quiet place. Still others work best on the floor listening to music. For some children as young as nine or ten, it is organizing to do all of their written homework on the computer. Ideally, children will do their work in one area because then all their materials will be in one place. Having one place to work also facilitates having a homework rhythm where the child goes to the same place at the same time every day.

Homework Materials and Systems Young children are constantly being asked to do projects that require art supplies. It is good if you can have some commonly needed materials already in stock so that you don't need to run out to the store at homework time. Many families benefit from the equivalent of a fishing tackle box which has school supplies such as scissors, markers, paper clips, a stapler, scotch tape, a ruler, and pencil sharpener. The child, with parental assistance, makes sure that the box is put back in its designated spot, ready for the next day.

The computer is becoming an indispensable homework tool, particularly for disorganized children. Routinely, children are being taught word processing skills as early as the third grade. Spatially challenged children like Tamara may find that learning to type is difficult, and it will take them more drill and practice to learn touch typing. However, learning to type correctly will be an enormous help in the long run. Children from elementary school on can often benefit from having an Alphasmart or other portable device for writing down assignments and doing homework. In the higher grades, teachers increasingly are posting assignments on the Internet. The advantage of a computer, of course, is that everything stays in one place, and for the disorganized child this is a huge boon. The following is a list of materials and systems that will be helpful for your child:

The Tool Box Get a fishing tackle box or some other utility case for holding essential school supplies. We want all materials in one place with the capability of moving them from room to room. Include the following:

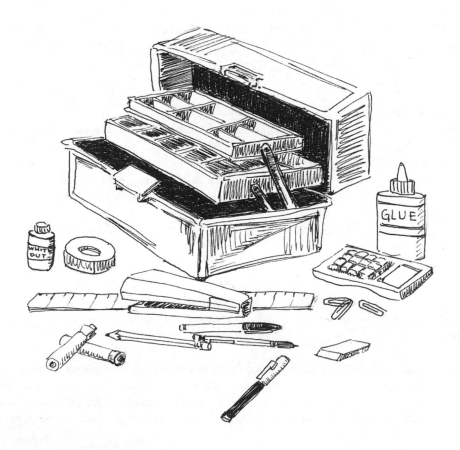

- Markers
- Colored pencils
- Crayons
- Paper clips
- A stapler
- Scotch tape
- A ruler or tape measure
- A pencil sharpener
- Pens
- Pencils
- An eraser
- White-out
- Rubber cement
- Glue
- Reinforcements
- Staple remover
- Highlighters
- Hole punch
- Post-its
- Calculator

At Home Reference Material   You will probably need a designated shelf for reference material, although increasingly your child will be going online to search for research information. Remember, online research is easy, but not always reliable. Consider having the following resources:

- A dictionary
- A current atlas
- A thesaurus
- A computer

The Backpack   Consider the size of your child and the number of essential books and materials that he or she has to take to school. You may want a bag on wheels. Remember, the larger the bag, the more your child will put in it and the heavier it will be. You may want to put a luggage tag on the backpack with a list of commonly assigned books and the day when that homework is assigned. Your child can check that list to make sure he has packed what he needs.

The Binder or Notebook System
- Your child will need a big binder with pockets and separators by subject, or smaller binders in different colors for each subject.
- You will need a pad with three-holed paper. For some children, all assignments are written on the same pad and later the paper is put into the appropriate section of the binder.
- A pencil case is needed with pencils, pens, a six inch ruler, eraser, and calculator.
- Two large, clear plastic folders in different colors are necessary with an elastic band to close them.
    - Folder one (red indicating STOP) where the student puts everything that is handed back to him—papers, tests, quizzes, finished study guides, etc. These can be filed at one's leisure, but in the meantime, nothing is lost.
    - Folder two (green indicating GO back to school) where the student puts everything related to that night's homework—study guides to be filled out, finished

assignments, etc. Next day after everything is handed in, this should be empty. The child can look and immediately see if he has remembered to hand in his homework.

The Assignment Book   It is important to expect your child to make some effort to write down homework assignments from the earliest grades of school in order to establish a habit of recording expectations. How one does this depends on the child's age:

- Early grade school—there is usually a hand-out to be filled in, such as a list of spelling words and the requirement that you write a sentence using them. Likewise there might be a sheet of math problems. Put these sheets in the green folder.
- Older grade school—Once the teacher starts to write assignments on the board, the child needs a book to write down what he has to do. Ideally, this book should have three holes punched in it and it should fit into the binder. Some children like a small book like an adult pocket calendar, that fits in a pouch of the backpack. Each subject needs to be indicated to remind the child that he has homework in every subject.

Books   Some disorganized children are constantly losing their books. Or a small child may not be able to carry all of his books. In both cases, you may want to buy a duplicate of particularly large texts so that it is not necessary to transport all of the books to and from school each day. This can be expensive. However, if your child has an Individualized Educational Plan, your school system may supply the duplicate set.

Paper   Many children put three-holed, lined paper in their binders in each section and take notes daily that are put back in that section. This is less likely to happen with the disorganized child. Consider getting your child a pad with three holes already punched in it. Throughout the day, your child can take notes in all subjects in the same pad, on different sheets of paper. Over the weekend, the pages can be put in the appropriate section of the binder. In the meantime, all notes stay in the pad and nothing is lost.

Homework and Time Management

Another major ingredient to successful homework is managing time effectively.

When in the day? You need to plan with your child when to do homework. Ideally, homework should be started after a break from the school day, but a large part of it should be finished before dinner.

What is due when? With an older child, it may be helpful to have a large calendar on the wall indicating when long-term projects are due. The parent can then help his child record mini-deadlines for the different components of the project. Of course, putting up such a calendar does not mean that the child will look at it, but it is a start at

helping your child understand when there are tests. You may want to review the calendar with your child or help record events using different colors for tests, quizzes, homework sheets, projects, and essays.

How to stay focused? With many disorganized children, problems with attention can make homework a protracted experience. It is alarming to parents when they behold the slowness with which the child approaches his backpack and the delays that occur between sitting down at the table and getting out the first assignment. Once the child is finally started, the parent again may be dismayed to see that instead of starting to write the second spelling sentence, your child has wandered off to play with his cat or he is fiddling with pencils and paper clips rather than writing. When you observe this kind of drift, it may be helpful to teach your child to play Beat the Clock. For a more comprehensive discussion of attention issues, see Chapter 6 and also review **Tool Sheet 5, Learning to Pay Attention**.

> **Tip:** Beat the Clock—The child estimates how long an assignment will take and how long he can stay focused. With these two factors in mind, parent and child estimate how much he can accomplish in a specific time. The child then sets the kitchen timer and tries to meet his own deadline. Give a cheer or small reward when the child finishes within the time estimate.

For example, Tamara had success playing Beat the Clock. At ten, she felt that she could concentrate for only 10 minutes on a grammar exercise, but she could do the creative writing assignment for 30 minutes. She started by setting a time to see if she could complete half of her grammar assignment in a 10-minute burst. She then took a quick break doing jumping jacks, before working for another 10-minute burst to finish the assignment. When she had completed the whole grammar assignment, she took a 10-minute break and played a computer game. This was a little risky because it was hard for her to limit this break to 10 minutes. However, she began to realize that she was getting her homework done more quickly, and she enjoyed the games so much that she powered through the boring work to get her reward. The goal here is to learn to focus for a specified length of time. Some children will initially only be able to focus for 5 minutes. However, with practice, they will find that they can stay with a task for longer periods. Another goal is to help your child become aware of when she is concentrating and when her mind is drifting. By working in spurts, you seek to make work time more efficient and have a higher degree of focus.

Parent Review   Whether or not parents check that homework has been done is a controversial subject. Your role will be influenced by both your child and the teacher. Some teachers are adamant that the parents have nothing to do with homework. They feel that children should learn to bear the consequences for unfinished and poorly done work and they want to enforce these standards in the classroom. Other teachers want parents to be more involved. With extremely disorganized children like Tamara, parents need to be more hands-on than they otherwise would be, at least in the early grades. After all, this is a very intelligent child who often cannot manifest her ability because she loses things or simply never realizes that she had an assignment. If it is determined that reviewing homework is a good idea, the parent can help in several ways.

- Help the child plan what he will do and when he will do it.
- Check the assignment book to determine that nothing has been forgotten. In some schools, you can even check online to verify the assignments.

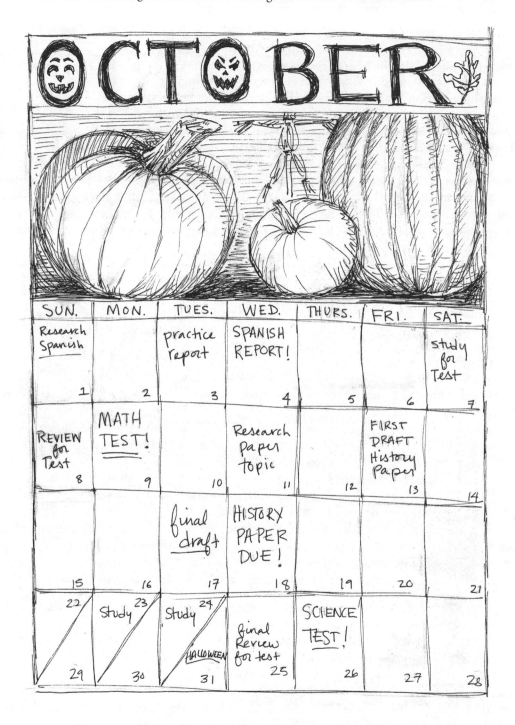

SUN.	MON.	TUES.	WED.	THURS.	FRI.	SAT.
Research Spanish 1	2	practice report 3	SPANISH REPORT! 4	5	6	study for Test 7
REVIEW for Test 8	MATH TEST! 9	10	Research paper topic 11	12	FIRST DRAFT History Paper 13	14
15	16	final draft 17	HISTORY PAPER DUE! 18	19	20	21
22 29	Study 23 30	Study 24 HALLOWEEN 31	final Review for test 25	SCIENCE TEST! 26	27	28

- It is critical that this review be upbeat with lots of positive reinforcement and validation of the child. If the child has forgotten something, it should be pointed out that he remembered other things. If he is daydreaming, it should be pointed out that he has already knocked out a lot of his work, or at least he did yesterday. If he is cranky and does not want to work, the parent can remind him of the positive natural consequences for finishing his work, such as seeing a favorite television program.

With children like Tamara, the parent needs to be a cheerleader rather than a critical score keeper. Validation **Tool Sheet 10** reminds you how to do this. Your role in homework is not to do the work for your child. Rather, you are helping your child know what he has to do by providing a system so that the work once done is not lost. Once your child has learned this system, he has expanded the skills that he needs to be independent.

Helping Your Child Learn to Study

As your child moves through school, there are new challenges that parents face. Of course, we want our child to read, do math calculations, and write. However, as children advance in age, the new basic skill that they need to learn is how to study. James Zull has written an illuminating book entitled, *The Art of Changing the Brain* (2002). In this book, he discusses the fact that all learning is hard wired into specific cells in the brain. In other words, as we learn, we are actually changing the structure of the brain by expanding nerve cells and adding connections between these cells. In a real sense, learning is physical. For instance, in 15 minutes of repeating vocabulary words and their meanings, you are actually causing a new branch or dendrite to grow on a cell. So what do you as parents need to know about the brain in order to get these cells to grow?

Consider the Senses   It is helpful to know that all of our senses are involved in learning. The more you know about what are the strongest ways your child learns, the better you can help.

- Is your child a visual learner? Does she need to see information written down in order to fully comprehend it? Some children learn best when complex information is converted to charts or other diagrams. Some visual children have powerful visual memories, and they study best by looking at a textbook and remembering where on the page they saw a certain term or fact.
- On the other hand, does your child do better when he hears information? These children often pick up a great deal of data by listening to what the teacher is saying, what parents are saying, what the television is saying. They also learn best by talking to themselves or others because they understand their own thinking best when they hear it. Sometimes reading a book out loud helps the child because she is hearing what she is reading.
- Another group of children benefit from doing things with their hands. These children may need to write or draw in order to retain information. For example, some young children learn their letters not by seeing them or hearing them, but by making them out of play dough, or drawing them in the sand.
- Often children are helped in learning by moving their whole body. These are the children who walk around the room as they try to memorize a poem for class. Another child may need to learn a poem to the rhythm of doing jumping jacks. Perhaps the child can learn his multiplication tables by doing a somersault every time he gets ten problems correct.

In fact, for most children it is vitally important to enhance learning by engaging all of these modalities—seeing, hearing, touching, and moving.

Emotions and Learning   You need to know that there is a large emotional component to learning. People learn best when it is pleasurable and shut down when they are frustrated or get overwhelmed. Often the support of another person makes learning enjoyable. This is why young children may want a parent present when they do homework or older children may want to work in a study group. Giving your child supportive comments and encouragement will also

help him relax and engage. If we talk to our children in a positive manner, recalling their successes, they relax and open up. If we criticize them and remind them of their failures, they tend to tighten up, grow anxious, and become less available for learning. As a parent you can make learning a pleasure every day as you snuggle with your child to read a story, play a letter game to name the letters, or count change together so your child has enough money for an ice-cream cone. With older children, you can encourage emotional connectedness when you cut out an article about something they are studying or take them to see something of interest. The more interested and curious you are, the more your child will be emotionally engaged and therefore become interested and curious himself.

Taking Action   Getting your child to act in a particular way may lead to better learning. In other words, sitting passively in front of a book or homework sheet is not as effective as making review lists, filling out study guides, writing an essay, doing a lab report, building a diorama, writing a poem, going to see an exhibit, chanting out the answers to questions, explaining a concept to a friend, or drawing a map.

Repetition Is Key   To really learn material you must go over it multiple times. Remember when we said that all learning is physical. Repeated trials will build longer cell arms and stronger links between cells. The more important and repetitious the signal, the more we learn. This is the reason it is so valuable to put facts on file cards and go over them several times. As you flip through the spelling words, or vocabulary words, or math facts, or historical terms, you are sending repeated signals to the brain and strengthening nerve connections. In this way you are learning more. Often parents can make games that have relevance for their children.

For example, one skillful parent wanted her daughter to learn Hindi. She therefore constructed a game like Concentration, where she made two cards with the same Hindi word on them. She then spread all of the cards face down on the table. Each player was allowed to turn over two cards at a time. If they turned over a pair of matching cards, they kept them. The daughter loved this game and learned a large number of words. Note that this game had many components conducive to learning. It was action oriented, it was using sight and hearing, and it was also played in the context of a loving, supportive relationship.

> **Tip:** Not everyone has the same skill at memory. However, if you get organized and plan for numerous repetitions, every child can learn what he needs to know. Note that it is important when you are doing repetitions to simply reinforce success, not errors. If we stress what the child did wrong, we may actually be reinforcing faulty learning.

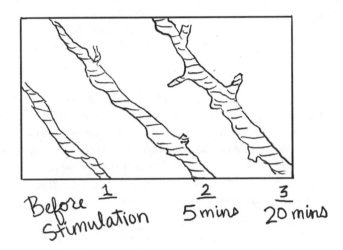

Before Stimulation 1   2   3
              5 mins 20 mins

Link New Information to Known Information   It is helpful to tie new learning to knowledge that the child already has. For instance, in learning about the characteristics of mammals, you can use what you know about your own body and then figure out how a whale is like you. Memory tricks often make use of this. For instance, if you have to learn the names of the Great Lakes, you remember a familiar word "HOMES," which stands for Huron, Ontario, Michigan, Erie, and Superior.

As a parent, you may be more aware of what your child knows than he is. Sometimes a child's personal experience can lead him to understand complex principles. For example, James Zull describes a young woman struggling in an environmental science class. Her teacher was talking about how different chemicals discharged into rivers by factories hurt wildlife. She was having trouble grasping the chemical interactions that were taking place. Suddenly, the student recalled getting two ducklings for Easter which she put in a large bucket of water. One of her older brothers decided to play a trick on her. He put dishwasher soap into the water and the ducks sank. She rescued her ducks, but while she was sitting in class, she had the flash of insight that the detergent had dissolved the oil on the ducks' feathers that kept them afloat. Now she knew why chemicals hurt wildlife. She remembered this story because it was emotionally intense. She cared about the ducklings and in the process learned chemistry and gained new insight into water pollution.

Learning Often Occurs by Metaphor   Metaphor expands our experience by relating the unknown to the known. An example of this is a communication skill that we teach to children; namely, the ice-cream sandwich. Here, the chocolate of the cookie relates to positive things that you say to someone. The vanilla ice cream is saying how you feel and asking for what you want. You finish with more chocolate, positive comments. Ideally, the metaphor of the ice-cream sandwich helps the child remember an important piece of new information. A foreign language teacher had success using a metaphor to teach the concept of the subjunctive case. He likened the subjunctive to a shadow. A shadow has meaning, but it is somewhat elusive; there, but not totally clear.

Try to think of metaphors or similes that have personal relevance to your child. For instance, your child might delight in eating cherries but hate having to spit out the pits. Is this like learning to play the violin, where hearing yourself play is delightful, but practicing the scales is unpleasant? Sometimes you are simply reminding your child of his own experience and how it applies to a new situation. For instance, when your child says that he does not want to invite a certain person in his class to his birthday party, you might remind him about how he felt when another child excluded him.

Encourage Your Child to Think   Thinking is hard and takes time, but you want to teach your child that you value his using his head. Your goal is to help your child understand that learning is a reciprocal process. The goal is for him to actually have a conversation with his teacher or his book. You can encourage your child to mark up books he is reading (or write on post-its that he puts on the page). Urge your child to underline what he thinks is important, put question marks for things that make no sense, write * on the page when he gets a creative idea, or what we call a creative burst, write "ha" when he finds something funny.

> **Tip:** A creative burst refers to an insight, new idea, or disagreement that pops into a child's head. Capture this idea by a * in the margin or put the idea on a post-it right on the page. The point of a creative burst is to have an interaction between the child and what he is reading. Your child is responding with his own idea to question what is said or add another thought. Interaction shows thinking!

For example, one can see how this creative thinking might work for a child reading *Robin Hood*. Suddenly he thinks that Robin is like Luke Skywalker in Star Wars. He comments that Robin and Luke are trying to restore power to people who care about their subjects and want to protect them. This would be a creative burst that should be written in the margin or on the post-it. Tell him what a creative thinker he is. Thinking takes time.

You can help your child think is several ways:

- Ask him to tell you what he is thinking about. The more the child tries to articulate what is on his mind, the more his thinking will become clear.
- Help your child draw a map of his ideas to aid in the thinking process. Many schools have pictorial outlines that help children organize ideas when they are writing an essay. For instance, you might have a tree where the trunk is the main idea, the branches are the different supporting ideas, and the leaves are the specific facts that back up the child's thinking.

- Get your child to tell you everything that he knows about a given topic. This is basically asking your child to brainstorm. You may help by writing a word for every idea your child says.

An example is brainstorming ideas about the causes of the civil war:

railroads	immigrants	territorial expansion	learning to hunt	France
tobacco	cotton	the Bible	underground railroad	
England	horses	plantations	cities	
Dred Scott	heroic ideal	*Uncle Tom's Cabin*	slaves	

1. Organizing ideas into topics: when all the ideas are written down, you ask your child what ideas go together. Your child then uses a colored marker to underline the words that he feels are related to each other. Each cluster of ideas has a different color: Economic causes in yellow (railroads, immigrants, territorial expansion, tobacco); idealistic causes in purple (*Uncle Tom's Cabin*, Dred Scott, the Bible, underground railroad, slaves); international causes in blue (England, France); cultural causes in green (learning to hunt, slaves, plantations, cities, heroic ideal).
2. Ordering the topics: finally, you ask which idea should go first, which second, etc. Your child orders the categories. Now you have an outline! All the child has to do is try to figure out how to articulate the central idea, which becomes the thesis statement.

Helping Your Disorganized Child Cope with Social Issues

Children such as Tamara are at enormous risk for social difficulties. Her problems processing information that make it difficult to see that there is a specific bin for Legos also makes it hard for her to read social cues. Because she has trouble reading social cues, she finds it hard to perceive what other children are thinking about her. Should a child on a climber shout at her to get out of the way, Tamara may feel seriously offended, whereas another child would realize that the other child is swinging in her direction and needs space. Her attention problems lead her to talk "at" other children rather than tune in and listen to them. Often she violates the space of others by getting too near or talking too loudly. She may do things that other children feel are "weird," such as laugh in too loud a voice, or lean out of her chair and put her head on the floor. She frequently makes silly jokes that contain bathroom humor. While this is appropriate for a 6 year old, other 10 year olds find this odd. Tamara's messy appearance and frequent crankiness can also turn off other children. When she invites another child to play, she may suddenly refuse to play outdoors even though the other child came over expressly to play on her climber.

Several things are happening for Tamara that affect her social life. First of all, she is caught up in her own interests and finds it hard to figure out or respect the other child's preferences. Second, while she was initially happy with the idea of having a play date, the actual play date itself might be overwhelming. She may find herself excited and silly, then wildly out of control. This may feel uncomfortable to Tamara, who is happiest alone reading a book or playing a computer game. In fact, being with other children can be frustrating because it demands so much interaction and negotiation. Solitary play is her way of feeling centered and calm.

The children who are able to tolerate Tamara's eccentricities are in for a treat. She has a tremendous imagination, a wide-ranging curiosity, great analytic thinking skills, and a fierce loyalty. She is also remarkably nonjudgmental of other people.

A parent can help a child like Tamara by bringing structure to her social life, but it is hard to know how much to push. It is clear that after a long day at school trying to meet the demands of teachers and get along with other children on the play ground, your child may need to be alone to regroup. Here are some things you can try to help your child adjust socially.

Set Up Play Dates   Setting up play dates on weekends may help. The cardinal rule here is to keep them short and sweet, perhaps one to one and a half hours long. You need to put some thought into the play date because children like Tamara may have trouble figuring out what to do with a friend and retreat to solitary pursuits. Before the play date, remind your child to put away any toys that she is not comfortable sharing with her friend. Also remind her that her friend has come to play and she cannot go off and leave her friend by herself. During the play date, the parent should be prepared to generate an activity if conflict develops because Tamara refuses to do something that her friend wants to do. A trip to the park or making chocolate pudding may save the day and refocus the children. During the play date, the parent has the advantage of watching the play unfold and in the process can gain greater understanding of her child.

Reframing or Changing How a Child Thinks About Something   Observing what gets your child upset may give you an idea about how to be helpful. Sometimes parents are useful in reframing for a child what has happened. By reframing, we mean explaining a situation from another point of view.

For example, imagine that Tamara is upset because her friend had insisted on playing dolls all afternoon while she wanted to build with Legos. Later, the parent might point out that her friend was not playing dolls because she was selfish, which was Tamara's perception. Rather the friend is finding dolls interesting on account of her new baby brother. Here the parent is suggesting an alternate explanation for the friend's behavior and helping Tamara to empathize with her friend.

Structured Activities   Putting your child in structured school extracurricular activities may be helpful if it is not too overwhelming. In Tamara's case, she had success in her elementary school years by participating in a school Geography Bee. This program attracted intelligent and quirky children who liked learning the names of rivers and capitals and mountains. Tamara studied with her mother and enjoyed developing her expertise. Tamara experienced great success in this activity as she advanced to the finals. In the process, she earned the respect of her classmates.

Sometimes it is helpful to plan an after-school activity with another child as a way of promoting a friendship. Maybe another child wants to take swimming lessons with your child. Group activities, such as the Cub Scouts or Brownies, may work because they are structured and give a sense of belonging. Here the crucial variables should be your child's interests, the availability of alternative activities, and your ability to get the child to the activity.

Networking   Some parents are fortunate to be surrounded by family and old friends. However, other families are new to a community and benefit a great deal from a community of friends raising their children together. Because of the irritability and unpredictability of these disorganized children, they will do best when they are surrounded by a community of adults and children who know them and appreciate them. These long-term relationships are almost like sibling relationships. Obviously, the key ingredient is the relationship between the parents. In a sense, it is this tight community that together raises these children.

Learning Another Point of View   In addition to structuring play dates or other activities, the parents' role is also to help children like Tamara appreciate another person's point of view. One way that you can work on this is by reading stories and then discussing the characters with your child. Why did Peter Pan want to go to Neverland? What was Wendy feeling when she left home? What do you think that her parents were feeling? Why did she return home? What would you have done?

Social Tips   Parents can help their child by giving objective feedback about what might help them get along with other children. Mary was upset because she moved to a new city and was wearing clothes that the other children laughed at. Her mother visited the school, checked out the other kids, and immediately went out to buy clothes that would help her daughter fit in.

Communication Skills   Parents can also help children get along by helping them plan what they might say to another child. Mary had trouble on the playground because she had a tendency to get mad at other children who did not do what she liked. Her mother taught her to do an ice-cream sandwich (**Tool Sheet 23**) to tell a girl to stop chasing her. It went something like this: "Susan, I really like having you as a friend

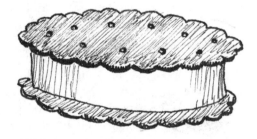

but it upsets me when you chase me so I want you to stop. Will you come over to my house after school some time?"

When occasionally your child slips up and does something egregious to another child, you can encourage her to make a repair (refer to **Teaching Consequences and Repair, Tool Sheet 14**). For instance, if Mary hits Susan in her frustration, she might draw her a special picture and tell her that she is sorry.

The important thing here is to have empathy for your child as he learns to empathize with others. His disorganization is going to make him somewhat odd and other children initially may not get what he is about. When your child feels rejected, be sympathetic even when his actions have been ill advised and rightfully earned the wrath of another child (see **Validation, Tool Sheet 10**). Remember, even if you cannot sympathize with your child's actions, you can always validate her feelings; for example, "I know that you are tired of playing with Susan, but her mother has been delayed. What could we do that would feel comfortable for you but not make Susan feel left out? Do you want to watch a video together?"

If these social problems are pronounced in your child, you may want to get the help of a mental health professional. A social skills group can be a helpful way of teaching social skills in a group setting. The advantage here is that the therapist can see problems unfold and give immediate feedback to the child about what might be a better strategy.

Working with the School "Tamara, I have already given the instructions for this exercise two times. Who do you think you are that I should have to repeat them just for you? Tamara, if you cared about your work, you would not be so messy! Tamara, don't tell me that you forgot your homework again! Tamara, how many times do I have to tell you to show your work in math?"

Understandably, teachers are frustrated by disorganized children like Tamara. However, years of similar comments may have a corrosive effect on a child's self-esteem. Very intelligent children, such as Tamara, learn to question their competence because both adults and children find them exasperating. Teachers can help these children in a variety of ways.

- These children need many reminders because they do not understand instructions the first time they are given. If you sit near a child and can touch him on the shoulder it may help to get his attention.
- Place the disorganized student next to someone who is focused so that he can see what he is supposed to be doing, even if he missed the oral instruction.
- Encourage variety in the type of product you require from different children. Can the child show what he knows by drawing a picture rather than writing a paragraph? Some children grasp math easily, but they have trouble doing large numbers of problems. Can they be allowed to do every other problem instead? Another child in an in-school gifted program was encouraged to do research papers on topics of interest. This 10-year-old child grew to hate school because of the volume of work required in addition to his regular assignments. This problem would have been eliminated if this very bright child had been allowed to read on topics of interest and then make an oral report of his findings to the teacher.
- Use a variety of learning tools. Access to a computer can be invaluable for these disorganized children with fine motor problems. Encourage these children to learn touch typing from the summer of third grade or fourth grade. For a child having trouble doing math, graph paper can be invaluable in helping them align columns correctly. As they get older, the calculator is a great help because it allows them to think through the steps of a problem and not get distracted by making errors in calculating. For a young, restless child, having a floor seat with back support might enable him to sit through circle time.

- Structured homework time in school. Disorganized children are helped when they can do most of their work during assigned periods where there is a resource teacher available if they need help. Some children need the quiet of a carrel or a silent library to do their work. Avoid isolating them at a desk in the corner of the room as this increases the sense of being different from the other children.

In elementary school these children may appear not to be working to their capacity. Be patient. With time, their output will reflect their thinking but it may take years. The issue is to help these children feel able and productive now! Many disorganized children do in fact give up because they never can meet the expectations of their teachers or their parents. Their emotions overwhelm them and they may act up: "You think I am bad? I'll show you bad!" They then pick fights, distract others, and become bullies. A little sense of humor and acceptance that disorganized children are simply developing at a different pace will help teachers validate their ideas and their curiosity.

Summary

Certain children are born with neurological wiring that makes it hard for them to get into a rhythm of focus and organization. Parents can help these children in a variety of ways. We have already discussed in Chapter 6 that many of these children have attention problems and we have focused on tools to help in this area. This chapter shows that one can help children be successful by providing structure to their day, by figuring out how to be successful with homework and studying, by helping them navigate friendships, and by mediating between them and their teachers. As the child grows older, he will learn his own coping methods to augment the ones that you have taught him. The key is to be patient and not expect these children to be sleek, efficient machines. Allow them to set their own goals and reach them in their own way, even if the solution is not always elegant. These children often have unique and creative insights into their world and compassion for others who are not neat, tidy, and organized. They have much to teach us and they will make an enormous contribution to our world when they have grown up.

10
Depression
Trying to Halt a Downward Slide

Most people get depressed from time to time. Disappointing things happen and we respond by feeling discouraged. In the majority of children, these "down" feelings are transient, and before you know it, they are back to being happy and engaged. Sometimes these negative moods become locked in, and the child is overcome by persistent sadness and hopelessness. In this chapter, we will look at three ways in which children deal with depression: by withdrawing, by becoming irritable and negative, and by a rollercoaster of up and down moods.

Some children who are sad become withdrawn from the interests, toys, or activities that used to be sources of pleasure. This withdrawal may also extend to not wanting to be with friends. Often these sad children say disparaging things about themselves, commenting that nobody likes them or they are stupid in school. Even as they put themselves down, they may try to avoid taking responsibility for their actions. What is going wrong is usually the fault of someone else. These withdrawn children are frustrating to their parents because of their marked sadness, passivity, and lack of interest or enthusiasm.

Other depressed children may behave in an altogether different manner. Rather than withdrawing, they are exceedingly intense and reactive. These children are characterized by a high degree of irritability, with frequent outbursts of anger. They often are impulsive and have trouble focusing because of their intense negative feelings.

Depression can manifest itself in a third way. These children are the hardest to diagnose because of the variability of their behavior. They are markedly uneven, at times happy, creative, and imaginative, and at other times they are sad or defiant. In addition they share many symptoms of attention deficit and hyperactivity disorder, including impulsivity and distractibility, as well as traits of oppositional defiant children, who are argumentative and uncooperative. Some of these children talk in a fast and unstoppable manner that may veer off in unexpected directions. Although they have a lot to say, they do not listen well and are often unable to read nonverbal cues. They also have trouble knowing what they feel or why they feel a certain way. These children exhibit the behavioral pattern of bipolar depression. However, one must be cautious as this diagnosis is frequently overused and misused. The fact that your child has variability in mood usually does not mean that he has bipolar illness. A child psychologist or psychiatrist will help make the proper diagnosis.

Childhood depression is pervasive. The National Institute of Mental Health (NIMH) estimates that in the United States there are 1.5 million children under the age of 15 who are severely depressed. Even though it is prevalent, the good news is that we can change the long-term outcome for your child with proper diagnosis and intervention.

What Causes Depression?
The cause of a depression can vary. In some cases, there is an identifiable influence from the environment that causes a child to close down. Common environmental stressors are when parents get divorced, when there is a death in the family, or when a child is bullied in the classroom.

In these cases, the child is responding to a marked change in his world that he cannot control, and this helplessness leads to negative and discouraged feelings. Another common environmental cause of depression is when there is illness in the family. For example, there is a particularly high correlation of depressed children having a depressed parent. When the parent is ill, it is not surprising that he is not able to give the warmth and support that children need to flourish. Parents may or may not be aware of these environmental stressors.

In other cases, depression results from primarily internal causes, which are not obvious to the outside observer. In these cases, a child may become overwhelmed by despairing thoughts or worries that often show a distorted understanding of the world. A child may worry that a healthy parent might die or believe that his anger at his sister is the reason that she develops diabetes. The first clue that these internal worries are taking place may be reflected in a change in behavior, such as a problem sleeping or refusal to go to school. It is important to encourage your child to share these scary thoughts and show him that you appreciate how upsetting these ideas are for him.

Current research is seeking to gain more insight into the different types of depression and how to treat them. Ellen Leibenluft's research at NIMH focuses on two groups of children under the age of 12 who show extreme signs of mood disorder (March 2006 presentation to the American Psychiatric Association at Shepherd Pratt). She is finding that they have different characteristics. One group consists of children who exhibit signs of mood dysregulation. They are withdrawn or angry at least half the day on most days and show marked irritability and distractibility. Often they become very intense, acting out in an angry or inappropriate manner. Leibenluft's second group consists of children who fit the criteria of bipolar depression. At times they are very sad but at other times they seem happy but agitated. They can be very talkative, often speaking in a rushed manner that may or may not slip off topic. These children may have a diminished need for sleep and get up in the middle of the night to play with toys. In addition, this group of children seems to have difficulty shifting attention as the events in their environment change. They are not reading and reacting to social cues in the way that others do. They are not anticipating consequences for their actions and therefore appear to have trouble inhibiting their actions when it is appropriate to do so. Current research is exploring whether there are brain differences between these two groups of children.

In Leibenluft's bipolar population, there is often a family history of mood disorder. Other researchers have noted a genetic predisposition to depression. Stanley Greenspan (2002) notes that depression is a familial disorder whereby certain biological factors make one vulnerable to extreme emotional dysregulation.

> **Tip:** Genetic factors do not directly cause depression. They make one vulnerable to developing depression.

In trying to gauge the severity of the depression, parents should figure out how long their child's distressed periods last, how frequently they recur, and what settings appear to trigger the depression. Is he this way only at home, or is he also withdrawn or angry at school? Is this a child who used to like to play with neighborhood children and now wants to stay at home? Is he acting depressed with all of his caregivers—parents, babysitter, grandparents, etc.? The more pervasive the behavior, the more cause there is for concern.

Three Portraits of Depressed Children

We will look at three individual children who represent the three groups of depressed children mentioned above: the withdrawn child, the angry child, and the behaviorally inconsistent child who switches between agitated and depressed moods. For each group of children we will consider strategies that you as parents can use to deal with these difficult and often intense behaviors. We hope that seeing the ways in which these parents cope with their depressed children will encourage you to expand your own parenting skills.

The Depressed Child Who Withdraws

Fatima: The Depressed Child Who Withdraws

First, let us consider Fatima. She is a beautiful child with straight black hair and large brown eyes. She has two older brothers, ages 6 and 8. Her parents became concerned about her behavior when she was four and a half years old. Fatima at this time had been attending nursery school for one and a half years. Initially school had gone well. She was engaged in the classroom activities and enjoyed running around outdoors and playing on the swings. In a fall teacher-parent conference, her teacher described her as a leader and pointed out that she played well with both boys and girls. However, after Christmas of her pre-kindergarten year, Fatima's behavior showed a marked change. She began to refuse to go to school and did not want to see children for play dates. During the school day, she refused to participate in group activities and spent much of her time crouched under a table. At circle time, she was quiet and refused to answer questions. After school her babysitter reported that she was listless and tired, but thought she was reacting to the loss of her afternoon nap. However, her parents noticed other changes. When they were home, Fatima was becoming irritable and oppositional. When her parents asked her to do something like put on her shoes, she would growl at them or simply not respond. When her parents disciplined her by putting her in her room, she would slam the door, fall on the floor, and scream. She confided in her mother, "Mommy, I'm not having a good life."

Fatima's parents were very concerned by their daughter's behavior and recognized that she was unhappy. They were willing to make whatever changes were necessary to restore to Fatima the playfulness and energy that seemed to have disappeared. As her parents described their family life, it became evident that Fatima's distress coincided with her mother returning to school four days a week. Fatima had always been a sensitive child who was attuned to the mood of everyone in the family. Now her mother's mood was changing as she tried to meet the demands of family and school. As she rushed to get her children to school and make her first class, she had little patience for their delays or silliness. Fatima picked up on this tension. She also missed the cuddly times that she used to have with her mother when she came home for lunch. Meanwhile, the behavior of her older brothers also changed. They seemed to be noisier and wilder than ever, particularly when their parents came home. The babysitter reported that they were teasing Fatima more and, when she cried, they called her a "cry baby."

What to Do to Help Fatima? Fatima's parents felt that the change in the family structure brought about by the return to school was a major factor in Fatima's depression. They therefore began to consider ways of helping Fatima feel more supported and safe (see Appendix 2, **Tool Sheet 22, Providing Structure to the Day**).

> **Tip:** Time is a critical factor in family life. When children are very sensitive, they can easily become disturbed by changes in routine. They need a predictable schedule that allows time with their parents to ground them for the day. Imagine your child as a battery that needs to be plugged in periodically in order to run effectively. You need to schedule your day to include this recharging time with your child.

Fatima's parents changed their schedules so that they got up earlier in the morning. Because Fatima was an early riser, her parents told her that when she heard the 6:30 a.m. alarm, she could come into bed with them and simply hang out with one or both parents for 30 minutes before the boys had to get up.

As part of their new routine, Fatima's mother or father spent at least 15 minutes of this time in child-centered time (see **Tool Sheet 11**). The central idea of child-centered time is that you give focused attention to what your child is doing. The child initiates an activity and the parent describes what the child is doing, almost as though a mirror is reflecting him. Fatima always brought a favorite stuffed animal into her parents' room. She would then tell her parents stories about her animal. The parents would listen intently and occasionally interrupt to summarize the story and ask if they had heard correctly. As she was cuddled in bed, a parent would sometimes simply describe Fatima and tell her what she had done the day before and what she was going to do that day.

Fatima knew that when the second alarm went off at 7:00 a.m., they would have to go and wake her older brothers. She liked being the first one up and felt particularly proud of getting dressed and running downstairs before the boys. Fatima loved these quiet, slow-to-get-started mornings, and felt ready when it was time to go to school. Separation from her parents was no longer so difficult.

In addition to getting up earlier to have special time in bed with her child, Fatima's mother changed her schedule so that one day a week she could rotate picking up a different child in turn and taking that child out for lunch or a snack. Gradually Fatima's symptoms disappeared, and she returned to the vibrant and engaged child she had been. Her older brothers also benefited from this one-on-one time and they became less wild and more manageable.

Fatima's case illustrates a number of characteristics of depressed children. She was one of those children who fit into the withdrawn category. When her parents began to see that they had a problem, Fatima was depressed in all settings: home, school, and with friends. She also was depressed for at least half of most days. In Fatima's case, her mother's return to school was the stressor that pushed her into depression. Fatima will have to be watched to see whether this slip into depression becomes a pattern or whether this was an isolated case brought on by a major change in her family life.

What to Do with a Depressed and Withdrawn Child

Validation The first and most important intervention for any child is validation (**Tool Sheet 10**). It is important for parents to be positive, showing your child that you see his strengths and appreciate him. When a child becomes depressed, you need to try to understand what he is feeling. *Do not* tell him what he should be feeling. Accept how he is feeling and tell him that you understand that at times he is frustrated, sad, angry, etc.

Validation is the most important of all of our tools. Validation reassures your child that you are on his side, that he is a worthwhile and cherished individual. Occasionally your child may act in an ill-advised manner. When this happens, try to express your understanding for what he was feeling that led him to act in an unacceptable way. You can always validate how your child feels, even if you disagree with a specific action.

In the case of Fatima, her parents are validating her when they are doing child-centered time and cuddling with her in the morning. They are also validating her by showing they understand how she is feeling and know what frustrates, worries, or discourages her. This is not to say that the parents would agree that these irritations *should* be frustrating her. It is simply to say that they are trying to understand her view of the world and accept that this is how she feels. It is important to remember that children often are not aware of what they are feeling, and in fact they may not have the language to describe what is going on. As a parent, you can help them articulate how they feel and give them the words that they need.

Getting a Move on At the same time that you validate your child, you need to ask for small behavior changes. In particular, you want your child to start *being active* rather than withdrawing. The theory behind this strategy is that by doing activities that are pleasurable, your child may actually change his mood. You can help you child by trying to figure out what activities might be attractive and fun. Every child is different. **Tool Sheet 12**, Having Fun, is designed to get you thinking about activities your child might like. The more interesting the activity is, the more the activity may distract your child from whatever is bothering him. Action becomes distraction (see **Distraction, Tool Sheet 6**). In addition, pleasurable activities have the chance of helping a child feel competent.

As you try to assess what will work, consider a variety of options. Exercise and movement are often useful in changing mood. For a young child, it is often helpful to go to the playground where there are swings and climbing opportunities. For older children, some type of sport may be beneficial, although some children flourish doing more individual activities such as bike riding, playing on a trampoline, or dancing. By stimulating the movement receptors in the body and brain, one actually improves mood by elevating arousal levels that lead

to a state of emotional well-being. The combination of a physical activity with an activity that focuses on the senses is particularly helpful. Music and dancing are helpful because the deep bass or interesting melody will actually pull your child into a changed emotional state. The same is true of art projects with lots of color and texture. There is a reason why children (and parents) often like to rough house. If you are wrestling or engaged in a pillow fight, it enhances the physical and emotional arousal level in a pleasurable way.

Some children are easily overwhelmed by physical activity. You may find that when they are withdrawn, they can be pulled back by a *solitary activity* which seems within their control. If your child loves making model airplanes, you can help him by providing the equipment. Reading would also qualify as a solitary activity that may enhance your child's pleasure and thereby move him from depression to a happier state.

Developing Social Skills: Connecting with Others   If your child has withdrawn from others, you may want to find a structured activity that will ensure that she *interacts with other children* on a regular basis. A reading club or Scouts might work because both have clear expectations about what the child should do and what is going to happen. Or it might be good simply to know that Karen is coming over every Wednesday and she and Fatima are going to play with their dolls. Sometimes it makes a difference with *whom* the child might do an activity. In other words, who might be the carrot who would get your child to try something new? If you think it might be helpful to get your child outside to the neighborhood pool, try setting up a weekly swim date with a good friend. Or if your child insists on staying inside, try having someone he loves, such as a grandfather, come over periodically to work on the electric train. This might progress to going to the store for train materials or taking a trip on a train.

Assess What Might Be a Stressor That Is Depressing Your Child   Getting your child engaged in pleasurable activities is a good way to start dealing with depression. You may also want to make other structural changes in his life that will improve his emotional regulation. Fatima's parents were particularly adept at making changes in the *daily schedule* that helped their daughter. Consider the following questions as you try to figure out what environmental factors might be having a negative impact on your child's mood:

- Is your child eating in a healthy way throughout the day, or does her blood sugar decline rapidly, making her more irritable and vulnerable to depression?
- Do you need to add a snack or small meal at a certain time to keep his blood sugar even or increase the amount of protein he is getting?
- How much sleep is your child getting, enough or too much?
- Is this child getting enough stimulation throughout his day or is he overwhelmed? Should there be more or fewer activities in the afternoons?
- Does he need to be involved in activities that give him more exercise?
- Does your child need to have "his own thing" that defines who he is and gives him a sense of control?
- What is the quality of family time? Is there calm, centered family time where the child feels seen and heard?
- Are meal times an occasion of family closeness or chaos?
- Are there ways to facilitate more connections with other children? Does he need to spend more or less time with other children?

The Depressed Child Who Is Angry and Irritable

Fatima is a child who becomes withdrawn when depressed. Susannah, in contrast, is a child whose depression is expressed through anger and other irritable, disorganized behavior.

Susannah: The Angry and Reactive Depressed Child

Susannah is the oldest child in her family and has long, blond, curly hair and a lanky build, with long arms and legs. She loves to dress up in coordinated outfits, and her favorite color is pink, although purple is a close second. In pre-kindergarten at age three, Susannah was popular with the other children because she was attractive and had a lot of good ideas. When she was happy, her classmates wanted to be with her. However, when she was unhappy, she could be extremely negative towards the other children. On her fourth birthday, her mother brought cupcakes to school and attached a birthday balloon to the tray. Susannah immediately focused on the balloon and started to play with it. The other children of course wanted a turn, but Susannah only allowed certain friends to bob it up and down in the air. When Mary asked for her turn, Susannah told her that she could not touch the balloon because she was "a mean girl." When the teacher asked her to make sure everyone had a turn, Susannah started to scream that it was her birthday and she could do what she wanted. Her mother had to take the balloon out to the car.

This intense irritability and desire for control continued as Susannah attended elementary school. At times Susannah would become frustrated and refuse to do an activity "because I don't want to and it's dumb." Socially, Susannah became a queen of clubs and did not hesitate to say that only select friends could join, and no one else was invited. At home, she woke up in a cheerful mood. However, she was very clingy to her mother and became distraught when her mother left the house. In addition, Susannah did not like going out of the house for any reason, whether it was a play date or an errand with her mother.

As she moved into second grade she began to have nightly temper tantrums about homework. If her mother did something she did not like, Susannah would become wild and hit or kick her mother. Susannah was frightened by many things. At one point she said, "I get scared when there is a shadow that is not me and not my sister." Her behavior outside of the family could get out of hand. At a family wedding, she was wild and goofy, running around and knocking into people. When her sister spilled a drink on her, she became inconsolable, crawling under a table and refusing to talk for over an hour. Her behavior was draining the whole family. At one point her mother commented, "Susannah sucks the life out of me."

What to Do with a Depressed, Intense, Irritable Child   Susannah's parents demonstrated skill in managing their intense, reactive, and depressed daughter. Many of the parenting skills that were helpful to Fatima were also helpful in this case. The parents made frequent use of **Tool Sheet 10, Validation,** by showing that they understood Susannah's intense feelings. Her mother tried to make room for child-centered time (**Tool Sheet 11**). When she was able to spend time on the floor intently paying attention to her daughter, Susannah seemed calmer and less

oppositional. Adjusting the daily schedule (see **Providing Structure to the Day, Tool Sheet 22**) was critical for Susannah. Her mother noticed that when she had an activity after school, she melted down when she came home. Therefore, her mother stopped after-school activities except for an occasional play date. Susannah therefore had down time playing with her dolls and her dog. This allowed her to calm down and return to a state of even regulation. She was therefore focused and steady when it was time for homework.

In addition to validation, child-centered time, and adjusting the daily schedule, the family had Susannah tutored so that she could more easily master the early reading skills that had been frustrating to her and had added to her depression. Often enhancing school competence helps children feel more confident and lightens their mood. Susannah also benefited from play therapy. As she played with dolls, she was encouraged to use feeling words. Gradually, she began to use these feeling words to describe herself. She then progressed to being able to talk with her mother about what made her feel sad and what made her feel happy. Susannah came to believe that her mother would support her and understand her. In turn, her mother was relieved to find that there was an effective way of dealing with this wild, unpredictable child. When a child is totally shut down in depression, consultation with a child psychiatrist is important to see whether or not medication might be helpful.

Positive Reinforcement   In addition to the interventions described above, there are certain other skills that are needed for children like Susannah who are rebellious and constantly testing limits. Although these children are disruptive, they need to feel supported rather than criticized and attacked. Even a mild comment with a slightly negative slant can disorganize these children and send them into a tantrum. Because of this, one wants to encourage positive behaviors with positive reinforcement.

> **Tip:** Figure out what your child is doing right rather than repeatedly stressing what he is doing wrong.

In Susannah's case, her parents emphasized what a good story teller she was and had her dictate stories that they typed up and sent to her grandparents.

Shaping   In addition to reinforcement, there are times when you want your child to develop new skills and behaviors. In this case you may need to shape your child's behavior in a new, desired direction. For instance, initially Susannah stamped her foot and refused to do her homework. Her parents realized that they needed to change this behavior and get her to do her homework. Their first approach was to ask her about homework and praise her if she could remember anything that had been assigned. They then sat with her and helped her to get out the materials that she needed and list what had to be done. In this early stage, they sat with her the entire time and praised her as she finished each assignment. However, gradually they started getting up and doing other things in the kitchen. They encouraged her to sing out when she finished an assignment. Eventually, she did her work independently and simply checked in when she was finished.

Chaining   When you link describing the assignment, getting out the materials, and starting the work, you have a chain of behaviors. The parents' job is to grow the chain by adding more links, in this case getting her to do more assignments without parental intervention.

Ignoring   Because Susannah was so demanding, she initially screamed and yelled abusive comments about school and her parents. Her parents responded by explaining that nothing could happen while she was yelling and it hurt their ears. They left the room (see **Observing Limits, Tool Sheet 15**). After she stopped screaming, they returned to the room and complimented her for getting herself in control. Be mindful that if you start paying attention to a child's screaming (even parental screaming is considered paying attention), you are actually reinforcing the screaming and it is more likely to recur.

Natural Consequences   At times, hard-to-manage children do not respond well to compliments and need a stronger reinforcement to meet their goal. In most cases, one does well to use natural consequences (see **Teaching Consequences and Repair, Tool Sheet 14**). The goal here is to reward the child for doing what is expected in a natural, common sense way. If Susannah is able to finish her homework by 7:30 p.m., she might have time to watch a video. Otherwise she will need to go upstairs and get ready for bed by 8:00 p.m. If Susannah can help her mother by emptying the dishwasher, her mother would have the time to drive her to her friend's house. It is helpful to explain  this in advance to your child so that he knows what the incentive might be and can plan for it.

A Token Economy   Sometimes when a parent is trying to teach a series of skills, praise alone does not work. You also may have trouble thinking of an appropriate natural consequence. For example, you might want your child to get ready for school in a more independent way or you want your child to focus on practicing the piano. In this case consider a token economy system (see **Tool Sheet 17**). In essence, here you are creating a stronger reward by expanding the possible reinforcers. The key to a token economy is to manage expectations and change reinforcers frequently.

> **Tip:** If you use concrete reinforcers such as a grab bag, toy, or treat, you need to change the reinforcer every 10 days or so to prevent your child from becoming bored. Some rewards, such as money or credit chips, are less boring because they can be used for different things.

In the case of Susannah, her parents gave rewards when she finished her homework by dinner (one poker chip), and when she showed "serious focus" with no screaming or abusive language (a second poker chip).

Time Out   If positive reinforcement or a token economy is not solving your problem, it may be necessary to work on more negative ways of controlling behavior; namely an aversive consequence or punishment. However, remember that because depressed children are very reactive, this may backfire and cause an increase in negative behavior. We recommend trying a one, two, three warning system similar to that described in Thomas Phelan's *One, Two Three Magic* (1995). Our system is described in **Tool Sheet 16, Time Out**. The emphasis in our system is on step two.

In time out the parents' goal is to identify a behavior that they want to eliminate, which we call an outlaw behavior. In Susannah's case this might be screaming and calling her mother abusive names. It is usually better to explain a limit (in this case no bad words) in terms of what the parent needs rather than what the child needs (**Observing Limits, Tool Sheet 15**). For another child, the outlaw behavior might be pinching.

Once you have identified the outlaw behavior, the parent then tells the child that she has a plan. When the parent firmly says "One," it is a warning that Susannah is arguing or using bad language. If the behavior happens again, or "One" has no effect, the parent says "Two" in a firm manner. At this point Susannah is expected to leave the room and get herself calm. The bonus is that she can come back when she is ready to be cooperative. Should the arguing and bad language recur, the parent says "Three" in a way that is final. This is a signal that the child needs to go to a designated time-out spot. She must stay in time out until the parent says that it is time to come back. Usually children stay for one minute for each year, but if the parent needs to calm down as well, the child may need to stay longer. If your child refuses to go to time out, leave the room yourself if that is possible. Withdraw any attention from your child until the time out is over.

Tip: Cultivate a "hairy eyeball" look and tone. Every parent needs a voice and expression which means I AM SERIOUS. This needs to be a firm voice, not a scary voice. When you give your child the "hairy eyeball," it means pay attention now and I am prepared to do what it takes to make you mind. There is no need for shouting, just firmness and clarity.

With a depressed child, one's goal is not only to change behavior but also to change emotional state. We want the child to learn how to calm himself down and feel happier. Because of this, we consider "Two" to be the critical step. You and your child need to take some time to figure out what might work at step two: "What would make you feel better when you are angry or feel that life is unfair? It is really hard to calm down. We have to be creative and figure out what might work for you. Let's brainstorm together." A variety of ideas are summarized on **Tool Sheet 1, Self-Soothing**. In addition to things that the child can do, the parent also may want to help her child figure out a special place to which she can go when she is angry or frustrated or sad. A classic example of this is the card table fort, a table covered by a blanket with comfort objects inside, such as a soft blanket, a stuffed animal, or a drawing pad. However, some children need to be active in order to let off steam and prefer running around the yard or jumping on a trampoline. The more that you can work with your child to find a way to regroup, the more that he will think that you are respecting his difficulties and trying to help him rather than punish him.

The Depressed Child at Risk for Bipolar Disorder   The third group of depressed children that we are considering are those with bipolar disorder. Stanley Greenspan and Ira Glovinski (2002) have written a helpful book about what they call bipolar patterns. They point out that for children under the age of 12, bipolarity is a controversial diagnosis. These researchers see a biological pattern of vulnerability that may lead to bipolarity in early adolescence if a child is in a stressful environment. Ellen Leibenluft's research suggests that children meeting criteria for bipolarity appear to have unique brain structure that makes it harder for them to inhibit actions and to shift their thinking in response to changing outside reinforcers. For instance, healthy children are wired to pick up on environmental cues that allow them to seek positive reinforcement and avoid punishment. If they know that their teacher will keep them in at recess if they are making a lot of noise, most children will quiet down and not lose recess time. Children with bipolarity are not as sensitive to these outside reinforcers and often get stuck in negative feelings and negative behavior even when it leads to punishing consequences.

The following are the key criteria that researchers have identified in their study of bipolar vulnerability.

Factors Showing Vulnerability to Bipolar Depression
- All of these children show extreme emotional dysregulation, which means that they are emotionally intense and react quickly to what happens around them. Their moods are up and down.
- Sometimes the intensity leads to total engagement in an activity, so much so that they can stay up late at night doing what interests them.
- These children have an early history of being extremely sensitive to and reactive to outside stimuli. This sensitivity has been described in Chapter 8, which deals with children who have trouble with sensory overload.
- They have trouble with social interactions and their intensity makes it hard for parents to calm them or get them to behave appropriately.
- These children also often show constricted emotions and have trouble understanding and expressing how they feel.
- Their thinking tends to be "all-or-nothing," with difficulty understanding nuance.
- They are not as sensitive to outside reinforcers as other children.

Marilyn: A Child at Risk for Bipolar Disorder

Looking at Marilyn's behavior in childhood shows her vulnerability to bipolar depression. At eight, she was always a little awkward and big for her age. Her uncle joked that with luck she would play for the Mystics. Marilyn had wonderful qualities. She loved being read to and developed into an avid reader on her own. She also loved information. She read biographies of famous people, such as Madame Curie, and boasted that she was going to be famous herself some day. She loved listening to music and dancing as well as playing basketball with her brother.

From the time that she could talk, Marilyn was exceptionally verbal; however, she was also extraordinarily irritable and argumentative. She resented having any demands made upon her. When she was in preschool, this seemed rather typical of a child who wanted to be "the boss" of her world. However, as she got older, she remained irritable and negative.

In first and second grades, Marilyn did minimal work and was always one of the last to finish, if indeed she was able to complete the task. She had enormous trouble focusing on tasks. She didn't care if she finished her work and complained that most assignments were stupid. However, her trouble with work was most clearly seen at home when she had to do homework. There her frustration rapidly escalated to anger. Homework became a battle scene.

With her school attention problems, low threshold for frustration, and dislike of being told what to do, Marilyn showed characteristics of an emotionally intense, dysregulated child with oppositional and ADHD traits. It was in her interpersonal interactions and thinking that Marilyn showed qualities that would eventually lead to a bipolar diagnosis.

From her earliest years, Marilyn had difficulty forming relationships with other people. For instance, she had a beloved babysitter whom she had had since birth who was responsible for supervising homework. She loved this woman, who was exceptionally warm and funny. However, Marilyn hated being forced to do homework and at one point told her mother that the babysitter had taken her allowance money. Marilyn clearly wanted the babysitter to back off and give her an easier time. She was appalled when her mother told her that if the babysitter had stolen, she would be fired. All of a sudden, Marilyn changed her story because she really cared for the woman and knew that she needed a job. Amazingly enough, she found her allowance money. However, she continued to be enraged that the babysitter was asking her to do her homework.

By fifth grade, Marilyn had made one good friend in her class. She and her friend liked to write fantasy stories on the Web. However, when they played it was rarely collaboratively. Each girl simply made up her own story and then they read them to each other. When she was at school, she tended to say off-putting things. What she thought of as "joking" with others in a friendly way, the other children perceived as mean, derogatory comments. For instance, when a girl in summer camp commented that she did not like the lunch food, Marilyn said, "You want your mommy!" If other people reacted negatively to what she said, she refused to stop, saying, "I should be able to talk about anything I want to talk about. This is America."

In addition to her verbally aggressive, argumentative style, Marilyn demonstrated extremely black and white thinking, with others usually being in the wrong and her being in the right. When there was a problem, it was because someone else had made a mistake, never Marilyn.

Her problem in taking another point of view was seen one year at her mother's birthday. Marilyn decided to give her mother a present she knew she would love; namely, allowing mom to watch Marilyn as she wrote one of her fantasy stories. When it was suggested that

perhaps Marilyn might get her mother something else that would be special for her, Marilyn was unable to think of anything other than things that she herself would like. Occasionally Marilyn would be overcome with a sense of loneliness and an awareness that she did not have many friends. She also began to worry a great deal about her parents dying and leaving her alone.

As Marilyn moved into middle school, she became increasingly intense and judgmental in her opinions. She openly criticized teachers for assignments that were "stupid" or for opinions that were too liberal. Her language became increasingly studded with expletives. Intellectually, despite her intelligence and curiosity, Marilyn found it hard to organize her thinking into an essay or a formal presentation. As the demands for expository writing increased, her writing appeared disjointed and undeveloped as though she could not keep her thoughts together. As her comfort level with teachers and students began to decline, she sought solace in reading fantasy books and playing online computer games. Here at least she had a role and relationships prescribed by the game. In this setting, she was socially comfortable.

The first clue to the bipolar diagnosis was the intense negative mood that Marilyn showed from her earliest years. She was often irritable and agitated and had trouble focusing. She became frustrated easily, and when frustrated became angry and abusive. What distinguished her from other depressed children was the rigidity of her thinking, her trouble relating to others and these highly intense times of activity. She also could become intensely engaged, staying up all right reading or doing computer games. In terms of thinking, Marilyn passionately expressed ideas but showed limited ability to back up her point of view. She would often go off on tangents, but basically kept repeating ideas and provocative phrases. She would disparage others, but be unable to meet their arguments. Despite a wonderful vocabulary, she had trouble organizing complex ideas. Socially, Marilyn had enormous difficulty because it was so hard for her to understand and empathize with another person's point of view. She therefore said things that were upsetting to others, but failed to process how others were responding to her. At school, she had friends who shared her interest in fantasy and computers. She loved it when they all were playing the same online computer games, but she rarely saw them outside of school.

What to Do to Manage a Child at Risk for Bipolar Disorder   The task of parenting a child like Marilyn is daunting. Although Marilyn had good periods when she could be funny and charming, these good periods were invariability followed by difficult periods characterized by irritability, argumentativeness, and lack of cooperation. As she grew older, it became clearer that her emotional dysregulation was limiting her both intellectually and socially. In her case, irritability led to negative thinking. However, she did not have the dejected, hopeless quality typical of other depressed children. Because of this it took a while before the bipolar disorder diagnosis was ultimately made. By adolescence, there were increasingly episodes of the more obvious signs of depression.

Her parents ceaselessly tried to address Marilyn's needs. Over time they tried many different types of interventions. Because of her difficulties with handwriting and expressing complex ideas, they provided tutoring help. She was enrolled in a social skills program to help her listen better to other children. Her parents tried a token reinforcement (see **A Token Economy, Tool Sheet 17**) system to lower her resistance to homework. She could earn points by starting homework before dinner and finishing each subject in 20 minutes or less. She worked with a therapist to gain more understanding of her feelings so that she could develop more effective problem-solving strategies. She and her family also worked with a family therapist to deal with conflicts and gain more compliance around homework and chores. These interventions were all constructive in helping Marilyn deal more effectively with her family  and her world. However, they did not erase all of the behavioral manifestations of what came to be seen as bipolar disorder.

Addressing Sensory Regulation Issues   In devising a strategy for helping your child with this kind of extreme emotional intensity and rigidity, it may be helpful to go back and reconsider the different patterns of vulnerability outlined by Greenspan and Glovinsky (2002). One of the first indications of this behavioral pattern is that these children from their earliest years are alert and intensely reactive to sensory input. Parents need to figure out the unique sensory pattern of their child in order to make sure that they take in information in the right doses.

> **Tip:** Most children with bipolar illness have a sensory profile called sensory modulation disorder. They react either by becoming easily overwhelmed and hyper-stimulated by sensory input or they are chronically unresponsive and passive. These children are unpredictable in the way that they process their world. They can get upset easily although often one can't identify what set them off.

Chapter 9 shows how children vary enormously in terms of their reaction to touch, sound, taste, and smell. What is comforting and what is irritating? How much visual stimulation is absorbing and at what point does it get overwhelming? After figuring out your child's unique sensory system, devise a plan that takes advantage of his strengths and weaknesses:

- Figure out good self-calming activities of the type summarized in **Tool Sheet 1, Self-Soothing**.
- What is the optimal number of activities for the child balancing a need for engagement with an awareness of when one is overwhelmed?
- Give the child a "head's up" about what is going to happen by posting the daily and weekly schedules.
- Make sure pleasurable activities happen frequently.

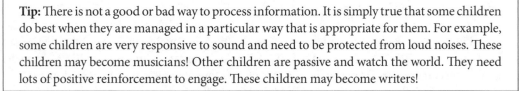

Tip: There is not a good or bad way to process information. It is simply true that some children do best when they are managed in a particular way that is appropriate for them. For example, some children are very responsive to sound and need to be protected from loud noises. These children may become musicians! Other children are passive and watch the world. They need lots of positive reinforcement to engage. These children may become writers!

Addressing a Child's Difficulty in Communicating Using an Ice-Cream Sandwich Another aspect of emotionally vulnerable and depressed children is their difficulty in reading social cues and making friends. One way of addressing social problems is by teaching better ways of communication.

The first step of any communication is to figure out what you want to have happen. Understanding your goal is useful for parent and child alike. A quick and handy communication style is the **Ice-Cream Sandwich, Tool Sheet 23**. This is a great skill to teach a young child who is getting into fights and not using his words. In essence, the structure of an ice-cream sandwich is two positive statements with a request sandwiched in between. The theory behind this is that you are more likely to get positive attention when you yourself are positive.

For example, Marilyn's parents found that when she was absorbed in writing, it was very hard to get her attention. She had trouble focusing on what her parents were saying and what they needed her to do. In this instance, their goal was for her to get ready for church in a timely manner. The ice-cream sandwich might go like this: "I can see that you are really enjoying writing a story (a positive statement). We need to leave in ten minutes, so you need to stop working and put on your shoes (the ask). I am sure that we will have time for more writing after church and I am eager to read your story (a positive)."

This skill is readily adaptable to a child. They can learn the ice-cream sandwich and use it themselves when they are having trouble with a friend (or a parent for that matter). For instance, imagine that Marilyn wants her friend Alice to join her basketball team. You could teach Marilyn to do an ice-cream sandwich, which might be as follows: "Alice, I really enjoy playing this computer game with you. I think that we would also have fun playing basketball and I am on a great team, The Goddesses, which I think you would like. Will you sign up? Then we can play basketball on Saturday and come back after the game to play on the computer."

Communication Skills: Having GREAT FUN Communicating   Using an acronym can be a helpful way to teach communication skills. This will help both parent and child remember the series of steps that will make you a successful communicator. The central concepts for successful communication are embedded in the acronym GREAT. This is a complex skill that you can teach to older, school-aged children. The best way to teach it is by using it. This has an added advantage in that effective communications lead children to be more cooperative and less reactive.

Let us look at the components of Having GREAT FUN Communicating.

- G—What is your goal? In this case her parents want Marilyn to go to bed earlier.
- R—Review the situation: "Marilyn, you are spending too much time playing on the computer and as a result you are staying up much too late. It is hard getting you up in the morning."
- E—Express how you feel: "Marilyn, I need to get to sleep by 10:00 p.m. or I cannot function in the morning. I therefore need to know that you are off the computer by 9:30 p.m. and have turned out your light."
- A—Ask for what you want: "You need to get off the computer at 9:30 and put the modem in my room so that I know you are not tempted to use it."
- T—Think about why the other person might do it your way: "If you can limit your use of the computer, I think that you will get more sleep and that everything will be less frustrating for you. You are such a good kid and I understand that the computer is a passion. I am glad that you like computer games … you might even design one as a career."

How we do a GREAT is with FUN!

- F—You need to be fair. If Marilyn's brother is having an overnight and she wants something special, you might let her stay up a little later.
- U—Understanding. Listen to what Marilyn is saying. If she is anxious about something such as a test, let her stay up a little later to study. If she has been invited to a friend's house, let her stay up a little later. The key is letting her know that you hear what she is saying.
- N—Negotiate. You and your child need to learn to meet each other half way. For instance, perhaps Marilyn wants to stay up late because she wants a sleep over. You want to encourage her friendships. Therefore, you reach a compromise. She and her friend can stay up until 10:30, but the next night she must go to bed at 9:30 and cannot stay up late watching a movie.

Addressing Difficulty in Understanding How One Feels   Another characteristic of the depressed child can be constricted emotion. In other words, these children do not appear to be in touch with how they are feeling. There are many ways in which parents can help their children to identify their feelings. When you empathize with your child, you are suggesting how he is feeling and why he feels that way. You may not be right, but at least you are giving your child something to react to. It is important to be somewhat tentative, because of course the child is the ultimate authority on how he feels. As you talk about feelings in this comfortable way, your child may tune in more to how he is actually feeling. It is important to tie feelings to what the child is actually sensing in his body. For instance, how do "sad" and "angry" feel different? It may be that getting tearful is an early alert that you are feeling sad but it might be a sign that you are tired. Is feeling red in the face an early sign that you are angry?

Once your child knows what he is feeling, you can begin to consciously change negative feelings to positive feelings. Many of our tools address this. When one is feeling agitated, **Tool Sheet 1, Self-Soothing**, can be helpful. For instance, your child might find it soothing to play with his dog. When your child is focused on depressing thoughts, try **Tool Sheet 6, Distraction**. For example, if your child is depressed as the weekend looms before him, consider going to a funny movie. **Tool Sheet 12, Having Fun**, suggests activities you might encourage your child to do or do as a family, such as going bowling or playing miniature golf. As a parent, you are going to rely on your knowledge of your child to figure out what activities might help him change his feelings. Your choice of actions will be based on your child's unique nature and circumstances.

Marilyn was helped enormously by her ability to speak with her father. He was the one person who was always there, who listened to her. When she was with him, he was very validating (**Validation, Tool Sheet 10**). It was particularly comforting for her to know that if school was terrible, she could call him during the day. He told her that he understood that she sometimes felt irritable or discouraged because he had had similar problems when he was young. Marilyn and her father enjoyed going horseback riding together. When her father was not there, Marilyn found music very comforting. When she was angry, wild dancing was a release. When she felt sad, certain rock music made her feel better.

Addressing Inflexible Thinking   Finally, how do we help a child who has black and white thinking and has difficulty taking into account another person's perspective? Marilyn, at ten, had an emerging capacity to think through complex situations but her low threshold for frustration made that difficult. In general, the calmer the child, the more clearly he thinks. If your child is screaming at you or refusing to talk, it may be helpful to just take a break and talk about the issue later. If there is a major problem to confront, try to pick a moment when your child is calm and therefore able to think.

After your child is calm, you want to encourage him to use problem-solving skills. Here are the steps to lead him through:

1. What is the problem?
2. What are the alternatives to the problem?
3. What are the pros and cons of each alternative?
4. Which one will I choose and why?

In Marilyn's case, you are actually trying to get her to appreciate that there is more than one way of doing something. Children who are depressed are often too agitated to think clearly; however, that does not mean that you don't want them to try. As a parent, you need to model a calm approach to a problem. For example, Marilyn got a report card revealing that she had not handed in any of her writing assignments. That is a problem! Marilyn explained the situation by telling her parents that her hand hurt when she wrote and she hated her teacher. Her parents responded that it would be a pity if she had to go to summer school! Together father and daughter brainstormed and assessed alternative courses of action:

- Do the homework on the bus on the way to school
- Not do the homework
- Do the homework before dinner and earn television time after dinner
- Get dad to sit down with you and help you focus on homework
- Plan on going to summer school

The next step was to think about the pros and cons of each alternative. Marilyn ended up doing most of her homework on the bus. For a depressed child, it is hard to know that there are alternatives and that there might be a hopeful outcome. Using problem-solving skills is therefore very important.

For many children, the rigid thinking inherent in depression is most clearly seen in the child's difficulty taking another person's perspective. If you help your child in a slow and steady manner, you will get results in his ability to understand where other people are coming from. Try looking at perspective taking in a story. For a young child you could tell the story of *The Hare and the Tortoise*. How did the tortoise feel when the hare was boasting about what a fast runner he was? What might the tortoise have been thinking as he started out on the race and saw the hare disappear over the horizon? What was the hare's reason for taking a nap? How did he feel when he woke up? What did the tortoise think at the end of the race?

Remember, parents, that just sitting around the dinner table is an opportunity for children to listen to others and hear what they are doing, what they are feeling, and why they feel that way. Encourage your children to listen to each other and say things that are supportive. Listening to your family members is the best way to learn to understand and appreciate others.

> **Tip:** Empathy may develop in children from their first year to their eighth year. Some older children continue to have trouble taking another person's point of view, but they can learn to do this. The more you talk about different points of view, the more your child will begin to tune in. Be patient and children will gradually learn to take another perspective and appreciate why different people have different opinions.

Summary

In conclusion, we have looked at three different children who are struggling with depression. Fatima was depressed because of a sudden change of circumstance with her mother returning to work. Her depression took the form of a withdrawal. The solution to her depression was relatively simple, with a major change in scheduling that allowed more time with her mother and other pleasurable activities.

Susannah was depressed from her earliest years. The cause of Susannah's depression was primarily biological. She was irritable and agitated as an infant and this pattern continued with more angry, agitated behavior as she grew older. She was easily overstimulated by circumstances that would not have bothered another child. Here, what worked was simplifying her world so that she was not easily overstimulated. In addition, she needed to recognize when she was irritable and upset and then use strategies to soothe and distract herself. She also needed her parents to set clear limits. At first, they tried many ways of encouraging positive behavior. When that did not always work, Susannah's parents had to clearly observe their own limits and give consequences for negative or destructive behavior. As the family structure became clearer, Susannah settled down and did what was expected of her. She became much happier and less depressed. Her parents had figured out what she needed, and she responded well.

With Marilyn, the cause of the depression was again largely biological. She had a family history of bipolar disorder that made her vulnerable to depression. Her case is particularly interesting because it shows how hard it is to diagnose this disorder. Initially, the professionals working with her felt that she had ADHD. As she grew older and refused to do school work or participate in family and school activities, she met criteria for oppositional defiant disorder. The key elements in her eventual diagnosis of bipolar disorder lay in her ability to engage intensely in activity for a long period of time (often through the night) and in her black and white thinking, particularly her inability to anticipate consequences for her actions. She also had difficulty understanding how she felt and how others felt. What helped Marilyn were parents who validated her and understood what she was going through. These parents also worked hard to help her learn the tools to calm herself, communicate with others, and solve problems more effectively.

11

The Perils of Parenting a Hard-to-Manage Child
Spending Time with Your Child to Make Things Better

Becky's Mother: A Parent Overwhelmed by Her Child

"It drives me crazy that Becky can't play by herself. Here she is, 7 years old, and all she wants to do is watch TV. I find myself screaming at her half the time, 'Can't you do anything else besides watch TV! Get off the sofa!' When she was little, she followed me around the house constantly. She was welded to my side. I could barely breathe without her touching me somewhere. I was constantly peeling her off of my body. Sometimes I didn't want to be touched by anybody because I was so sick of her lying all over me. Her idea of fun was to jump on the sofa and throw the cushions around. Other times she went outside and threw the gravel in our driveway against the retaining wall. I thought that she must have had some serious learning problems because her play was so repetitive. What I found the most annoying is that she liked to climb all over me, shoving her feet on my stomach. The whole time she would be laughing, and it made me angry that she would laugh while she was hurting me.

"Now that she is older I am even more discouraged because she does not do what she is supposed to do. Sometimes she will read for school but it's like pulling teeth. I try to interest her in things like art projects, puzzles, and board games, but she's not interested. Now and then she'll ride bikes with the other kids, but what she likes to do most is roam around the neighborhood or play rough with our family dog, pulling at his hair until he bites her. Now she's in second grade and has no friends except one neighbor girl who bosses her around. I don't want my child to be left out, rejected, or bullied by other kids, but most of all, I have no idea what to do with her when we spend time together. Honestly, I need a major vacation from this kid of mine. She's hard to parent and I need a break!"

This parent's story is a familiar one to many parents with hard-to-manage children. Many parents find themselves at a breaking point, completely at a loss about what to do with their child. Some of the child's behaviors are intolerable. Living with a difficult child day-to-day can be so overwhelming that you may even have thoughts of walking out the door to escape from your own child. Some parents may think, "I don't like my own child. There is nothing here I enjoy." It is an extremely hard place to be in when one feels this way. Not only that, but some parents find themselves screaming at their child all the time. One mother said, "This is not who I want to be and how I want to parent. My child has made me become a wicked witch! I happened to walk in front of the bathroom mirror when I was screaming at her and I couldn't believe what had become of me."

At the root of the problem is your child's unique wiring. The children we have described in this book are often intense, irritable, disorganized, moody, and reactive. They have trouble achieving and maintaining a calm, relaxed state. Easy going, they are not!!! We refer to them as dysregulated, because they have trouble getting comfortable, steady, and rolling with the

punches. The simplest thing can set them off into screaming or withdrawing; it may take quite a while for them to calm down. These children are hard to parent because of their sensitivities. When left to their own devices, they may be clueless what to do and end up bothering you by following you around the house, asking for things they cannot have, playing in a destructive way, or vegging out in front of the television. Just a few minutes of being around this can have a devastating effect on your relationship with your child.

In this book we have looked at many reasons children have trouble managing day-to-day tasks, interactions with others, and play. Some children are intense and overly active. They seek physical games and can't sit still for quiet play. They crave intensity and often settle for getting an angry response rather than no response. Other children are sensitive to sensory stimulation and may become agitated by the noise made by vacuum cleaners and kitchen appliances. They become overwhelmed when they are bathed or dressed and even react to a comforting touch by their parents or an accidental touch from other children. When overwhelmed, they may withdraw or become aggressive. Some children are watchers who would rather observe other children than participate in play themselves. They may have difficulty thinking of play ideas and resist trying anything new. Other children have mood disorders that make them inflexible and intolerant of change. When they feel anxious because they cannot cope with the demands made on them or they are angry that they don't get what they want, they will react by exploding in a temper outburst. These are some of the things that make parenting extremely difficult.

These unique temperamental characteristics affect how your child can interact with his world and also how you interact with him. It can be extremely frustrating to you as a parent because you cannot get him to behave appropriately. You may even feel that you cannot form a basic connection with your child. Likewise, your child does not know how to connect with you. He may find it hard to develop a calm and comfortable attachment to anyone.

> **Tip:** With these hard to manage children, irritability can be like a virus that infects the entire family. Child-centered time can be the vaccine that leads the family to health.

It is not surprising that these intense, reactive children often get parents to react in an intense manner. It is as though there is a virus running through the whole family. Everyone becomes a little intense and out of control. Faced with a challenging child, you may react in ways that inadvertently are not so helpful. Typically, parents end up either under or overstimulating their child. For example, if your child acts like he doesn't want to play with you, you may turn your back on him. Most parents respond to irritating behavior by giving up or getting angry. Then when their child is calm and happy, they may tend to leave him alone so as not to "rock the boat." Or in the case of the highly distractible child who constantly seeks novelty, you may inadvertently exacerbate the problem by presenting too many activities to your child in order to keep him happy. If you feel like the circus clown or entertainment committee around your child, you are probably doing too much of the work. Under- or overstimulating a child is understandable, but it is not very effective.

It is important to recognize the personal stress that coping with a difficult child places on everyone in your family. Because you have little sleep, you may have reduced patience. Because babysitters also cannot cope with the child's moodiness or reactivity, you may feel trapped without relief. Marital tension may be heightened as you feel overwhelmed by the problems of the fussy and difficult child. You may end up making accommodations that interfere with your own lives, such as allowing your child to sleep in your bed so that everyone can get some rest. In some cases, the father may become peripheral to the family, working long hours to avoid a hectic home life and a constantly screaming infant. The danger of child abuse is real.

An adequate support system is necessary to help your family cope with a difficult situation. Yet, where are you going to find it? More and more, parents are finding that they have no extended family in their geographic area and, as a result, have no one to help them or to provide respite. Parent-child groups are usually a good alternative support for many families; however, many out-of-control children cannot tolerate being in a group situation, thus removing this option for parents. As the child grows older, parents find that their child doesn't get invited to birthday parties or other child-friendly activities because he is disruptive. Often these types of activities are too stimulating for the child who has problems of self-regulation. As a result, you may feel even more isolated and removed from the typical activities other parents engage

in with their children. Sometimes when you persevere in taking your child to parties or other gatherings, you may feel stigmatized by other parents because of your child's "out-of-control" behavior. It is not uncommon for grandparents or relatives to point a disapproving eye towards the parents without any understanding of what it is like to parent a very difficult child.

The experience of depression is very real for many parents who struggle to cope with the demands of parenting a fussy baby or angry, uncooperative child. Many mothers feel inadequate when normal parenting skills do not seem to work. First-time parents often confuse their child's temperamental difficulties with their own inexperience. This exacerbates their feelings of depression or helplessness. These feelings are compounded when the infant or child rejects being held and cuddled because of hypersensitivities to touch. Sometimes the parent may herself have similar hypersensitivities, which compound her inability to respond to her child in a sensitive way. One's sense of competence begins to erode.

How to Work with Your Child to Make Things Change

One of the best ways to help your child learn to be calm, organized, and emotionally healthy is to help him to interact and play more effectively with you. Children learn the main emotional messages of life through play interactions with the people who mean the most to them—mainly you! Dr. Stanley Greenspan, a child psychiatrist, has popularized the importance of playing with your child in order to help him become more related and engaged. He has called this approach "Floor Time." Others in the field have termed it "Watch, Wait, and Wonder." Whatever you call this "special time" with your child, it is a time to focus on what your child is doing and to join in his play. By your mere presence, you will positively affect your child's development in many ways.

We feel that daily child-centered time is the single most powerful tool for improving the parent–child relationship and helping your child to develop good feelings about himself and a sense of mastery. In child-centered time, your child initiates all interactions. This helps your child to figure out what he wants to do and how he is going to play with you and the toys. It requires the child to form thoughts in his head, plan motor sequences, and organize his actions. Meanwhile, as you watch your child play, your job is to try to discover what it is that your child is seeking and needing from you and the environment. Does your child need you to be calm and quiet, boisterous and energetic, adding creative ideas, or simply watching and admiring him? In this process, you will find that you gradually become more attuned to your child's needs, how your child wishes to communicate and interact, as well as the quality of your relationship with your child.

Child-centered time focuses on improving the developmental capacities of your child within the context of his relationship with you. You want to help your child become more engaged and interactive, more attached to you, to communicate using gestures and words, to be motivated and intentional in play ideas, and to organize symbolic play. Here's how to do it.

How to Do Child-Centered Time

First, set aside *15 to 20 minutes every day* during which you can provide focused, nonjudgmental attention for your child. Be sure the answering machine is on, that there is nothing cooking on the stove, and there are no other interruptions that interfere with your time with your child. If this seems too long, do it for a shorter time. The most important thing is to do it daily.

Tell your child that it is "special time" so that he knows that this is a time designated for him to play with you.

This is not a teaching time so it is best to select materials that are more *open ended* in nature. For example, dolls, cars, buckets, houses, blocks, toy airplanes, and other such objects lend themselves to multiple ways of playing, whereas puzzles, board games, and highly structured activities have only one way to play with them. You want games or materials that let your child use his imagination. There is no right or wrong way to play with the toys. The major goal is that your child should become engaged in something that interests him.

> **Tip:** Some parents have difficulty allowing their child to take the lead or may realize that they are overstimulating (e.g., too verbal, too active). The way to know if you are doing this is to think about how much work you are doing when you play with your child. Are you organizing and entertaining your child 90% of the time? It should feel like an 80–20 balance (your child doing 80% of the work). You can videotape your play and watch what it looks like. If you are too active in your child's play, pause and ask yourself these questions: "What is he doing or trying to tell me?" or "Am I following his play topic when he has changed focus to something else?"

Watch your child carefully and see what he seeks during the play. For example, if your child likes to throw things, pick things that are safe to throw and that can be used in an imaginative way. Older children can tell you what they want to do during their time with you.

Your child is the *initiator* of all play and you are the interested observer and facilitator. Your child needs to form the initial idea in his head so that he can launch his ideas into actions. You respond to his idea by describing what he is doing and if appropriate, elaborating and expanding upon what he is doing in whatever way that he seeks or needs from you. The important concept here is to give space to the child to think his own thoughts. You do not want to "one up" him. You want him to know that you see him. By describing what he is doing, you are acting like a mirror for him. For some children this is the first time that they perceive that you are really interested in them and appreciate them. It just shows how imperceptive some children can be!

> **Tip:** Some parents cannot see the value of doing child-centered time, particularly when the child is demanding and won't listen to limits. They may say things like "Won't this make him even more demanding of me if I give him more time?" If your child can learn how to exert control in a healthy, adaptive way while getting his emotional needs for attention met during "special time," then it will make accepting limits easier at other times of the day.

In general the role of the parent is to be unintrusive and nondirective. At times, however, you may want to *shape the child's play* so that it is more productive. This may be necessary when the child seems to have gotten stuck in repetitive play and is becoming bored by the exercise.

For example, one of Becky's favorite things to do was to throw her body against the sofa cushions or her mother's own body. Her parents got the idea to fill a wading pool with plastic balls. Becky immediately seized this opportunity to throw the balls every which way, making a huge mess. A friend suggested that they enclose the wading pool using a large pup tent. This worked like a charm. When Becky became exuberant, throwing the balls about, they were contained in one place. Her parents had made an adaptation that better allowed Becky to do what she wanted to do!

However, Becky's play often got stuck in sensory seeking kinds of behavior. She liked to bury herself in the balls and throw the balls, but there was little variation from this. After days of observing and describing Becky burying herself in the balls and tossing the balls, her mother decided to intervene to see if she could help Becky develop her play in a richer way and bring more imagination into her activity. One day her mother started tossing the balls about, matching her energy. Becky said, "What are you doing?" Her mother responded to Becky, "Look! It's a big storm!" This fueled Becky's imagination. She stopped, looked at her mother and said, "We'd better get really quiet. There could also be a monster!" Becky then submerged her body in the ball pit, and lay quietly for the "monster or storm to pass."

> **Tip:** Some parents have difficulty letting their child take the lead in play. They may have difficulty resisting the temptation to teach their child new skills, particularly when they are worried about lags in development. The conceptual underpinnings of child-centered time is in the knowledge that play is the medium by which a child learns and that children learn best when actively engaged in the presence of a loving parent. As the child becomes the initiator of interactions, self-motivation improves. You will notice that your child becomes more of an active participant in interactions with others. He will be more interested in exploring his world. This is an ideal approach for children with limited interests and sensory, emotional, or learning needs.

Parents need to *go slowly*. "Watch, wait, and wonder" what your child is seeking and needing from you. This allows your child the time to process and organize his ideas. Often adults do not realize that children need more time to process information than we do. Children, especially ones who might be experiencing learning, sensory, attention, or mood regulation problems, need more time to organize their thoughts and actions. This means that when you play with your child, it may feel "slow-paced." Many children need time to register and process sensory input, to organize ideas, repeat actions until they are mastered, and to respond to whatever you

might introduce into the play. In other instances, a child with a high activity level or inattention may move quickly from one toy to the next, abandoning ideas mid-stream because he can't stay with anything very long. By commenting on what he is doing, you will give him the feedback that will sustain his play for a longer time.

> **Tip:** Some parents view development in their child as something that should be taught. It is often hard to stop the urge to teach skills or direct play. If you are a "natural-born teacher," you may have many good things to offer your child, but there are certain things that cannot be taught explicitly. Going back to the goals of child-centered time, it is important to understand the process and why this is different than a teaching time.

Sometimes You Can Help Your Child Communicate More Clearly. Often one reason a child's play becomes so repetitive is that his language or ideas are not well developed. Suppose your child's gestures, words, or ideas are hard to understand. Describe what your child is doing and pause to indicate that you are confused. By asking for clarification, you may in fact help your child be clearer about what he wants to happen and in the process enrich the play.

For example, Becky went through a long period when she made wild gestures and roared like a lion. She got louder and louder. Her mother asked in an animated way, "Yes, I wonder what the lion wants?!" Becky then had to think about what the lion might want rather than simply roar. She was delighted and reported, "The lion is hungry and wants to eat mommy." Becky's mom reflected that it sounded like the lion wanted to have mommy for lunch. "Yes, a mommy sandwich." Becky then looked at her mother and said, "Not really. They want a peanut butter and jelly sandwich." Her mother's question got Becky thinking and made her play richer. Becky's mother felt that she was connected in an intimate way with her child and was aware that she was helping Becky become more focused and expressive.

Set Out Clear Rules. Before you start, make sure that breakable objects have been put away. Then explain the rules. Nothing should be broken, the room should not be damaged, and no one is allowed to hurt anyone else. Otherwise, avoid prohibitions such as telling a child not to touch something. Also ignore interruptions. Let the answering machine deal with the telephone, do not answer it. Some children get rambunctious during play with their moms and dads. A rule of "inside voices" is important.

Organize the play area to *make toys and materials available that promote sensorimotor development and emotional themes* in a safe way. If he has tactile hypersensitivities, put out textured toys and heavy objects. If your child has feeding problems, put out dolls and feeding utensils and mediums such as corn, dried beans, or water.

In general, the *toys should be childproof and developmentally appropriate.* Following is a list of age-appropriate toys.

6 to 12 months
    Blocks
    Dolls and stuffed animals
    Koosh balls
    Noise makers
    Cloth books
    Activity centers
Toddlers
    Toy telephones
    Cradle with doll
    Toy trains and cars
    Blocks
    Dolls
    Connecting blocks
    Action figures
    Doll house
    Cars, planes, and trains
School-aged children
    Board games and card games
    Jigsaws
    Rubbing your child's back while you watch sports
    Throwing a ball around
    Listening to your child read
    Dancing with your child
    Helping gather materials for a school project
    Cooking

> **Tip:** Daily child-centered time is for children of all ages. The goal is to focus on the here and now and be totally attuned to your child. For an older child, this could happen when you are watching the news together. Be an active listener to your child! Show that you hear what he says and that you notice what he does.

Try to *avoid praising your child* during "special time." Instead, try to mirror your child so that he can learn that you see him. By describing what your child is doing, you are showing your child that you are paying attention to him. By waiting for him to initiate the play, you are showing him that you know that he has ideas and that you are interested in his ideas. You are comfortable giving him the time he needs to do what he wants to do. In this way, your child feels seen for who he is and what he is doing.

You may want to keep *a journal* as a way of tracking your child's development. This may help you focus on your child. However, not keeping a journal is also fine. Sometimes you just want to play and not "over think" it. Here are some things that you can notice if you want to make a journal:

- What did you observe today about your child?
- What did he play with?
- What play ideas did he express to you?
- What was the pace and tempo of the play?
- Did he talk about particular things as he played?
- Did he repeat certain ideas?
- What did he want you to be like during the play?
- Did he want you to play a particular role, to just watch and admire him, or did he want you to come up with ideas?
- What was your experience like to play with your child?
- What kinds of feelings did you have as you played?
- Were you having fun or did you feel bored at times?
- Notice if you experienced feelings of stress, depression, not knowing what to do, or feelings of displeasure as you played with your child.
- After the "special time," reflect upon any connections you might have with your own past. For example, how did your parents play with you?
- Did you have any particular memories that got stirred up as you played with your child?
- Notice if there are any changes in your family's dynamics as a result of your doing "special time" with your child.

Tip: Parents with mild to moderate depression may find it hard to engage with their children. They are tired and this is just one more thing being asked of them. Sometimes mothers are experiencing postpartum "blues" and don't want to do anything. However, in truth, these parents often find unexpected benefits to doing "child-centered time." Once a depressed parent begins to see progress in her child's behaviors, she often feels improved self-esteem and effectiveness as a parent. If you recognize that you are feeling depressed, it is important to nurture yourself. Take breaks, have lunch with a loving friend, or do something soothing. A good therapist can help you explore these feelings and give you the support that you need. Sometimes medication is necessary to break the cycle if your depression doesn't improve over time. However, child-centered time may actually energize you and make you happier.

Both parents or other caregivers should take turns doing child-centered time with your children. You may notice that how your child plays with each of you is different. This is normal. Your child has a different relationship with each of you and it will be expressed in many ways, including how he plays with you. Sometimes one parent is resistant to doing the play and this may place a strain on the person who does get involved in this process. Therefore, it is important that you both try to be involved in child-centered time.

Parent quote: "I used to carry my 18-month-old all day long. She breast fed at least 12 times each day. I even slept with her with my breast in her mouth through the night. The special time helped me to realize that she could be alone without needing me all the time. I could see that she was ready to separate from me by the way she played, like hide and seek and wanting me to stay in one place while she moved away, then returning to my side. One day I suddenly took a look at my family and thought how my other child was missing out on what he needed and how I never spent any time with my husband any more. I began to feel like a person again. The therapy helped sort out what our family needed."

What You and Your Child Will Get Out of Child-Centered Time   Here are some of the rewards for engaging in child-centered time.

- You provide your child with focused, nonjudgmental attention. The message that this sends is that you admire his competence. Whatever he expresses is important to you. Nonjudgmental attention tells your child that you are listening to him. It paves the way for your child to come to you to tell you what is on his mind.
- Child-centered time helps a child to become an initiator. Some children with motor planning problems or severe sensory or attention problems cannot get started without help. The child-centered time will eventually help your child to figure out how to get started in play. Remember that this is the most important step in the motor planning process—getting started!
- The open-ended and self-directed nature of child-centered time helps your child learn to engage in a variety of activities. Playing in the presence of a caring adult intensifies his interests, his curiosity, and his willingness to try new things. Once your child learns to be self-directed and motivated in play, this power to engage should translate to other areas in his life—becoming more independent in areas such as reading or school work or sports.

Parent quote: "I used to hate spending time with my child and couldn't wait to get away from him, all that fussing and crying. I went back to work to get away from him and dreaded coming home at night. I hate to say this but I didn't like my own child. I thought he was a monster, and I was becoming one too, the way I screamed at him all the time. Now we have so much fun together and I realize that my reactions to his crying just set him off even more. Now I really miss him when I'm away from him. I feel like I got my baby back."

- Child-centered time leads to a sense of mastery, which in turn leads to a greater sense of competence. You may find that your child starts taking more initiative to get dressed or be ready for school on time.
- By following the pace and timing of your child's play, you will promote sustained and focused attention. Children learn best when they stay with a task and can do many different things with one toy.
- Child-centered time will promote your child's creativity. Children who spend time playing on their own tend to develop into more divergent thinkers as they grow older.
- You will help to develop your child's communication skills. When your child is less specific in his gestures or words, simply reflect back, "Tell me more. What is it that you want or are telling me?" You want your child to refine his signal giving or language so that it is clear what he wants to express. Many children cannot express details about their thoughts or feelings. Ask your child "What else can you tell me about this?" or say comments like, "What is Superman feeling as he jumps off the roof?" These questions

will help your child define his ideas in more specific ways and also develop his language skills.

- Your child will enhance his sensorimotor skills through play. Watch what your child seeks and needs in play. Does he crash and bang into things? Is he interested in fingering soft textures? Does he need toys that swing or move or does he need highly visual toys with windows and openings to look through? By providing materials that give the sensory input that your child needs, you will help develop sensorimotor skills.
- Child-centered time will help broaden the repertoire of interactions that you and your child have with one another. Often parents and their children develop routines or scripts that are limited in range and variety. For example, you may have a "get ready to go out" script or "it's homework time" routine that defines how you interact with your child. Child-centered time allows you to have more opportunities to interact with your child in new and more varied ways. Together you may be the construction team for a spaceship, with your child the designer and you placing blocks where he directs you. Or you may both learn to dance hip hop together, you following your child's lead.
- Child-centered time helps you expand your relationship with your child to develop a secure and joyful attachment with one another. Often the relationship you have with your child is altered when your child has trouble controlling himself. An overly clingy child or a constantly irritable child will affect not only the way the two of you interact day in, day out, but will impact how you perceive and feel about one another. Child-centered time helps to reset the way your relationship has developed and allows space for a healthier way of being together. The clingy child may still want to sit by your side, but your calm presence and nonjudgmental stance allows him the security to move away and explore when he is ready.

What You Will Notice in Yourself From Doing Child-Centered Time   Here are some things that you may notice change in yourself as a result of doing the child-centered time with your child:

- It may be easier to read your child's cues and what he wants. As you give more time for your child to express himself, you may find that you give space to speculating what your child is telling you. Instead of jumping to a conclusion or anticipating your child's needs, you listen and wait, wondering "what is it you are telling me?"
- You may find that you are becoming more responsive or attuned to your child and more comfortable allowing him to take the lead in the interaction. It will help to unburden you so that you don't feel that you always have to do everything for your child.
- Many parents report that by doing child-centered time, they feel a greater sense of competence. They often state that they feel that they are more of a facilitator rather than a director of their child's activity.
- Some parents state that they don't enjoy their irritable child. Child-centered time helps you to take pleasure in your child and to put the fun back in your relationship.
- Because you are letting your child take the lead in the play, you will find that you begin to appreciate your child's intrinsic drive for mastery—what he can do himself and what skills are internally wired to help him learn.
- Sometimes child-centered time elicits uncomfortable feelings or strong reactions in parents. Reflect on what the play is eliciting in your. Try to understand these reactions and what they might mean for you and your relationship with your child. The important thing is that you are giving your child focused, nonjudgmental attention and the joy of interacting with you.

- You may find that your image of yourself and your child changes to that of a "competent parent and a competent child." Through child-centered time, parents who have felt overwhelmed by their children's difficulties may begin to acquire new ways of interacting and enjoying their child at home. If this is done regularly, children become less demanding and less negative because they know that they can count on time with their parents. If parents take notes on what their child is doing, they will have an invaluable developmental history of their child.

Parent quote: "I was afraid that my child would hit or bite me. I was scared to even go to sleep at night for fear that he might attack me. Imagine that! A big woman like me afraid of a 5 year old. It took me a long time to get used to him playing like he does, wanting to pull and push on things the way he does, but now I understand that he needs to do this because of his tactile defensiveness, his high need for physical contact, and his getting overstimulated so easily. Once I relaxed about him needing that rough kind of play, I started to think of ways to do it with him that felt OK for both of us. It seemed amazing to me when he stopped the hitting and biting. We're both a lot happier now."

Modifications in Child-Centered Time for Different Family and Child Needs   It is very useful to practice child-centered time with whoever the important caregivers are in the child's life. For example, if a grandmother is the primary caregiver, she should be involved in this activity as well as the biological parent. When possible, both parents should participate so that each can explore the uniqueness of their relationship with their child. Sometimes there is a competition between mother and father, one feeling that they know what is best for the child and that the other should do it their way. Child-centered time helps parents to allow one another to find the way that they interact best with their child and to permit differences in parenting styles. Each parent should take a turn practicing child-centered time with their child while the other is an observer of the process. Often this way of working helps each parent to see how their relationship with their child is unique.

There are many modifications that can be made in the child-centered time. The entire family may participate in doing it. In a two-parents, two-children family, one parent may be "assigned" to one child, while the other parent focuses on play with the other child in the family. It is preferable to focus on one child at a time to gain the most impact from this technique.

Parent quote: "My child was so developmentally delayed that I couldn't let up for a single minute. I did therapy with him all day long. Even when he was feeding, I used to stretch his heel cords so that I could fit everything in that he needed. After doing child-centered time, I realized what a relief it was not to be his therapist. Only I could be his mom. No one else could be this for my child. I also discovered that all the early intervention services that were supposed to be 'family-centered' were not really 'family-centered.' The special time that I learned helped me figure out that no one in our family was happy. We just drove from one therapy appointment to the next, doing things all day long for Asher. Nancy, our older daughter, was always left out. Now we spend time together as a family, having fun, and Asher is making all kinds of progress that no other therapy could have done for him. I think what did it for him is that he's finally motivated to move and learn. And I'm happy as a mom and that's good for the whole family."

Does Child-Centered Time Actually Work?

Here are some things that research has shown change as a result of doing child-centered time.

- Children show more organized and secure attachment relationships.
- Children show greater gains in cognitive development and mood regulation.

- Mothers tend to feel greater parenting satisfaction and competence and a decrease in depression.
- Parents feel less overall stress.
- Children develop better attention and are less irritable.

The reason that child-centered time is so powerful is that it addresses the underpinnings of self-regulation. It helps the child be better at organizing attention, tolerating distress, mastering sensory experiences, and developing social skills. The research also shows that working on improving the parent–child relationship may prevent long-term emotional and behavioral problems in children at risk.

How to Do Child-Centered Time: A Summary

Here are some instructions that will help you to learn child-centered time. We also provide you with information on how to do child-centered time in **Tool Sheet 11, Child-Centered Time**.

1. Set aside 15 to 20 minutes each day when there are no interruptions. Be sure to do the play during a time when you and your child are well rested and you don't have other things to worry about like something cooking on the stove or the doorbell ringing. Take the telephone off the hook or put the answering machine on. Be sure that your child's physical needs are met, such as toileting, feeding, etc., so that you won't need to stop the play to take care of these needs. Put things out of reach that you don't want your child playing with (e.g., business papers, fragile objects). Use an area that is childproof where there are no prohibitions or limits that you might have to set.

2. If you can, put out two sets of toys so that you can join in play with your child (i.e., two toy telephones, action figures or dolls, several trucks and blocks). Select toys that allow your child to explore and try new things that are more open ended in nature. Avoid toys that require teaching or that are highly structured like board games, puzzles, or coloring.

3. Let your child know that he or she is getting "special time" with you. For a young child, get on the floor with him or her unless it is uncomfortable for you to get down to and up from the floor. Try to stay close to your child so that he or she can see your face and you can see what he or she is doing. For an older child you may simply join in an activity he finds engaging. With passive children who like television, you might start by watching television or a video with him. Verbalize what you are noticing or thinking. You might also wonder aloud what he is thinking about.

4. Let your child take the lead and initiate what happens. Anything that your child does is OK except hurting himself or you or destroying toys and materials. If your child wants to throw toys, put out soft things that are OK to throw like foam balls or bean bags. Play with your child however she or he wants to play. Discover what she or he wants from you during this time. Does she want you to admire her? To imitate him? Try out what you think he wants from you and watch his reaction. See if your child starts to notice you and begin to interact more. Respond to what your child is doing, but don't take over the play.

5. Watch, wait, and wonder what your child is doing. Think about what your child is getting out of doing a particular activity. Enter her world and reflect on what her

experience of it and you might be. Observing your child is the first step to providing a foundation of good listening.

6. Watch what your child seeks in play with you and try to pick materials each play time that allow for those kinds of interactions. For example, if your child likes to bang and push toys, pick things that are OK to bang and push.

7. Avoid cleaning up toys that your child seems to be finished with until special time is over. Your child may return to those toys to play some more. Only clean up if your child is becoming overstimulated by the materials and needs less stimulation.

8. Talk with your child about what he's doing without leading the play or guiding what should happen next. For example, you may describe what she did (What a big bounce you made with that ball! Look how you like to run!). With older children, you can ask questions about what is happening (How come the baby doll is crying? What is the monster thinking of doing now?). It's useful to help your child bridge play ideas, particularly if your child does something, then moves onto the next play topic, leaving a play idea hanging. (What happened to the dinosaur? I thought he wanted some food to eat.)

9. Have fun! This is very important! Try to enjoy playing with your child during "special time." If you find it boring, find the balance that will make the play fun and interesting for both of you.

10. Remember that "special time" is not a teaching time. Try to avoid praising your child or setting limits while you play. You want the motivation and pleasure of doing things together and exploring the world to come from within the child rather than because you are encouraging it through praise or reinforcement. There is no right or wrong way to play with toys.

11. When "special time" is over, make it clear to your child that it is time to end. If your child shows frustration because it is difficult to end "special time," empathize with him and help him express his frustration (e.g., "Wouldn't it be wonderful if we could do this all day long! I wish we could, but now it's time to stop and do something else"). If your child should become tired during the play time, end it earlier. Clean up the toys and transition to something else like a snack, reading a book, or some other activity.

12. Try to do "special time" every day, particularly during times when there are other stressors in the child's or family's life.

13. If there are other siblings, try to set aside time for focused interaction with them as well.

14. Take at least 20 minutes each day for yourself to rest, relax, and do something just for you. Activities like catching up on household chores, food shopping, and other work don't count as time for yourself. This is your time to restore yourself.

Being a "Good Enough" Parent

The child psychologist Donald W. Winnicott is famous for assuring parents that they do not need to be perfect, they simply need to be "good enough." Nowhere is this more important than in dealing with children who are intense and have trouble controlling their emotions. These children are by definition hard to parent. Their behavior tends to run in extremes. They can accelerate in their emotions and behavior or withdraw and shut down. In the face of these extremes, parents try many tactics and they are often going to feel that they are making things worse rather than better. Not to worry!! If you cannot figure out what will help on a given occasion, there will surely be another situation where you can try a new approach. You do not have to get it right, you simply have to keep trying to understand your child and figure out what strategies are effective.

The techniques that we have described in this book appear simple, but in fact they are hard to master. You do not need to be an expert, just keep working on it and you will become more skillful. Raising a child is a long process and you are not in it alone. Teachers, friends, family, neighbors, and coaches all have a hand in raising your child. You just need to be a good enough parent to figure out what is working well for your child and what is not. Where he has strengths, play to them. Where he has weaknesses, try to figure out what will help. Sometimes you will get it right. At other moments you may misunderstand what is going on and be positively unhelpful. In the long run, anyone reading this book is on the path to expanding his skills to help children.

Difficult children will often overwhelm the adults who are with them. As parents, we need to practice the skills that we are teaching our children. Just as children need structure in their lives, so do parents. When we eat right, get the sleep we need, exercise, and look after our own health issues, we will have the energy to cope with our children. Flight attendants remind us of this every time we get on an airplane. Adults are instructed to put on their oxygen masks first, before they help their children. Similarly, unless we look after ourselves, we will not have the energy and endurance to help our children. Are you eating three healthy meals a day? Do you do some sort of aerobic exercise at least four times a week? Are you getting 8 hours of sleep (including imperative naps)?

At times children will drive us around the bend. Then the issue is, how can we regain our cool? We have found that exercises in meditation and mindfulness can be invaluable in helping parents keep themselves in a calm and reasonable state. You may find that the tools mentioned in **Tool Sheet 8, Mindfulness: Stilling the Mind**, are helpful to you. In particular, you are urged to try mindful breathing. Here the goal is to calm yourself by breathing deeply and thinking only about your breath. Try sitting upright, closing your eyes, and breathing in for three counts and out for three counts. Feel your abdomen contract as you breathe in and expand as you breathe out. Focus your attention on the air as it enters and moves deep into your body and then as it is  expelled from your body. As other thoughts come into your mind, and they will, note them, then usher them out. You might imagine that your mind is a nonstick pan—simply let the worries slide off. Or imagine that your worries have been placed on an airport conveyor belt. Watch as they come off the belt and are put in long-term storage. It is perfectly normal to get distracted. Congratulate yourself on noticing the distraction and then refocus on counting the breath as it enters and leaves your body.

There are times when parents find their own emotions escalating when their child is upset and not responding to what they have been asked to do. This is frustrating! You have tried mindful breathing and you are still feeling upset. One powerful skill to use at this time is to distract yourself from what is happening (see **Tool Sheet 6, Distraction**). You want to concentrate with all your awareness on something other than your child. You will know what it is that is most distracting for you—a good detective story, watching television news, practicing your golf swing, watching baseball, or running. The aim behind distraction is simply to have your mind become absorbed with something other than what is happening with your child so that you can calm down, think, and plan more effectively.

There are other times when a child is grating and you are simply worn out. At these times you need to consider self-calming techniques that will take away tension or stress. Again, what you choose will vary from person to person (see **Tool Sheet 1, Self-Soothing**). Consider all of the five senses as you try to figure out what will be restorative. What is visually restful, what smells give you a sense of well-being? Do you need a massage or a warm bath? What music would calm or reinvigorate you? Would a cup of tea taste good?

> **Tip:** Raising a child who is intense and reactive or shut-down and withdrawn is exhausting. You need to train a babysitter to look after your child so that you can get breaks. Don't make the mistake of thinking you are the only one who can care for your child.

Although emotionally dysregulated children may appear younger than their years at certain times, remember that they will mature. Time is in your favor. The intensity of these children may lead to your child developing into an adult with strong feelings. These adults often have a great passion for life and a drive that makes them successful once they know how to harness it. As a parent you need to practice radical acceptance that your child is the way he is. If your child knows that you accept him the way he is and appreciate him, he will come to accept and appreciate himself and in the process his behavior will improve.

Summary

This chapter explores the heavy toll that having a hard-to-control child takes on a family. These children are exhausting and parents inevitably will begin to question their competence. Parents do not need to be perfect; they simply need to be good enough. In this chapter we have stressed that the first requirement for parents is to take care of themselves. If they are not emotionally calm and intellectually focused, they will not be able to handle their difficult child. It is important to always keep in mind that parents are encouraged to use child-centered time as a tool for maintaining and developing their close relationship with their child. This is particularly true in cases where parent–child interactions may have been derailed. It is an ideal way for parents to come to appreciate their child for his own uniqueness. In the process, it is a catalyst for development, expanding your child's curiosity, motivation, attention, language, and creativity. Taken together with the other skills offered in this book, child-centered time can make an enormous difference in the parent–child relationship.

12
The Toolbox

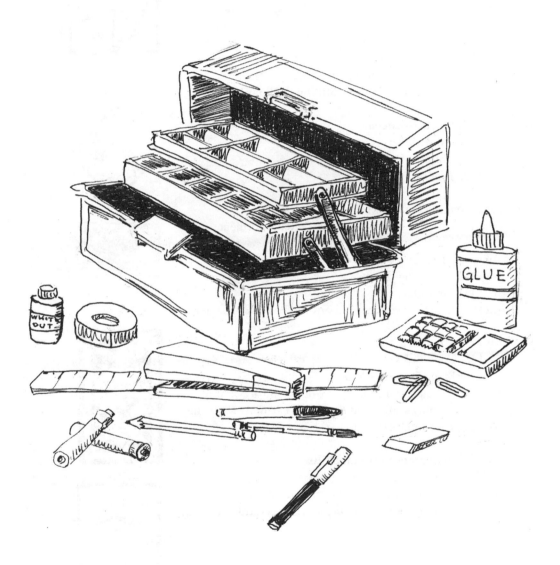

CONTENTS

Tools for Teaching Children to Calm Down

Tool 1. Self-Soothing

Activities that Are Mentally Soothing   What does your child like to do that is calming? The activities might include playing with Legos or dolls, reading, video games, etc. Bear in mind that to be soothing, the task should not be too demanding or frustrating. Make a poster or chart with your child, listing his favorite activities. Pictures or line drawings may need to accompany the list. Refer to this with your child, updating it periodically. Indicate which activities are best at certain times of the day or for certain settings.

Activities Involving the Sense of Touch

1. Often children are soothed through the sense of touch. A soft or silky object, such as a favorite stuffed animal or blanket, can be very comforting.
2. Water is a calming agent. Playing in a warm bath can be helpful, as can playing in the sink with water and bubbles. Swimming can also be very relaxing.
3. Children need loving touch. Snuggling with a parent is always good, be it before going to sleep or while watching a movie. If a child is upset, a back pat or hug may help them feel better. Pay attention to whether your child needs firm or lighter types of touch and where on the body he is more apt to accept touch. Usually the back, palms, and soles of the feet are accepting of touch. If your child cannot tolerate direct contact, place a soft pillow between you and your child. Some children find comfort in wrapping themselves up in a quilt or blanket, or climbing under a bean bag chair.
4. Patting or holding a pet can help a child to relax.
5. Traction is very organizing for many children. You can grasp your child's ankles and stretch him long while he lies on his back. The same technique can be done with the wrists, extending the arms overhead while you "stretch" your child. Teach your child to take each finger or toe and pull on them, one at a time. Massaging and pulling on the ears is often soothing. Traction can also be done with a chin-up bar attached to your door jamb that your child can hang from it.

Activities Using Sound

6. Music can wind kids up but it can also slow them down. Encourage your child to identify music that is calming.
7. Some children calm down when they hear a systematic relaxation tape. You might want to record **Tool Sheet 9, Systematic Relaxation**, or adapt it to your child.
8. Some children find it soothing to listen to a story tape. It is most relaxing if it is a well-known story.

9. Sometimes children need sounds screened out. The quietness of wearing heavy ear phones that screen out all sounds may help your child.

10. Listening to a pet purr or breathe can be very calming.

Activities Using Vision

11. Some children find it comforting to watch a familiar television show or video.

12. For some children it is relaxing to look through a family photo album.

13. Younger children may like to leaf through picture books, whereas older children may find it soothing to read a favorite story.

14. Watching a simple visual phenomenon like bubbles floating up in a bubble column, goldfish swimming in a tank, or gazing at glow-in-the-dark stars on the bedroom ceiling are very soothing.

15. Dimming the lights can be very effective in calming your child.

16. Sitting in enclosed spaces like a pup tent limits visual distractions and calms many children. Having a flashlight in this enclosed space may enhance the coziness and feeling of security.

Activities Using the Sense of Smell

17. Children draw comfort from familiar, significant smells. One child will be soothed by the smell of his mother's shampoo, or soap or perfume. Another child may relax to cooking smells such as cinnamon or a spice. Consider incense sticks or scented candles. Lavender and vanilla are particularly soothing, whereas peppermint and pine are alerting.

Activities Using Taste and Texture

18. Given the concern about childhood obesity, we don't want to rely solely on food for self-soothing, but occasionally on a cold winter day, a cup of hot chocolate with a marshmallow might be truly mood changing.
19. Some children relax while eating crunchy snacks like large pretzels, potato chips, carrot sticks, or apples. These food textures provide heavy work for the mouth.

Activities Involving Movement

20. Movement can be very soothing, particularly when a child is frustrated or angry. In essence, large motor activities help the child, "blow off steam." Many children are comforted by repetitive back-and-forth rocking motions, such as being in a swing or rocking chair.
21. Some children find spinning to be organizing. One can purchase a toy like a small merry-go-round, called a Dizzy Disc J or Sit 'n' Spin. (Order through Abilitations; 1 (800) 850-8602.)
22. Other children find it soothing to jump up and down. Trampolines facilitate this, as do spring balls that a child can sit and hop on.
23. Gross motor activities such as running, throwing balls, or shooting baskets can be particularly soothing. A child may try running around his house several times or running up and down the stairs of his apartment building.

Activities Using the Hands

24. Drawing and coloring are very restful for some children.
25. Other children like to do craft projects that focus their attention on something that is pleasurable, away from something that is frustrating. Beading or building model airplanes might work. The repetition and rhythm of knitting and weaving also soothe.
26. The hands have important pressure points on them that calm the entire body. Teach your child to clasp his hands together, palm to palm, pressing the thumb web spaces against one another. Massage the web space and pull on each finger. Do this slowly.
27. Playing a musical instrument like the piano or a string instrument provides calming input to the hands.
28. Working with clay, Model Magic, or Sculpey is very grounding. Immersing the hands in sand, dried beans, or wet sand provides deep pressure to the hands and calms the entire body.

Activities Involving Deep Breathing

29. Deep breathing activities are very soothing. Yoga encourages breathing with movement. There are some child yoga videotapes that teach children the moves and positions.
30. Blow toys or musical instruments requiring breathing help to vibrate the airway and encourage deep, calming air intake.
31. Some children need extra body feedback to learn to breathe deeply. Place a heavy bean bag animal on your child's abdomen while he lies on his back. Watch the rise and fall of the toy animal lying on the stomach.

Activities that Use Creativity and Imagination

32. Children benefit from simply "zoning out" into an imaginary world of their own making. It is a delight to hear your child muttering to himself as he plays with a stick or a pillow, knowing that he is engrossed in his own fantasy life.

33. Creating the time and space to allow your child to dream up what he would like to do or play with is very important for overall life satisfaction and relaxation. Often a child's life becomes so overscheduled that there is no time to do whatever makes his heart sing.

Tool 2. Activities for Problems of Touch

I. Activities for the Tactually Sensitive Child

1. Encourage tactile exploration of attractive materials that your child likes. Provide opportunities at home that will make your child want to touch things. Set up enclosed areas like an inner tube, a wading pool filled with dried corn, or a fort behind the sofa. Fill these areas with heavy objects like large bean bag animals, flashlights, and stress balls. Set out objects that vibrate, like a battery-operated pillow or a toy lady bug. Use materials that provide deep pressure on large body surfaces, such as large blocks, body pillows, and bean bag chairs.

2. Help your child tolerate physical contact games. Encourage games with high contact with other people that allow your child to withdraw in socially acceptable ways. For example, play a game called "earthquake." Your child lies under pillows. He keeps his body very still until signaled by you to start the "earthquake," wiggling the pillows until they fall over. Playing inside a large refrigerator box or a pup tent filled with soft pillows or climbing through large rubber tubes can be an engaging way to get contact from the environment. You can make a "people sandwich" by having your child lie underneath a soft comforter with other children. Use materials that offer resistance like a large stretchy tubing that you can push and pull on. These games do not provide direct physical contact between children but allow them safe physical boundaries that help them tolerate being in close proximity with one another without actually touching.

3. Use interesting objects that entice the child to touch them. A trick that often works for children with tactile sensitivities is to use highly appealing visual activities that provide touch, such as putting stickers on body parts. Playing dress-up or playing with small toys in a sand box are ways to incorporate the tactile and visual senses. You can also use the auditory channel in the same way. For example, taking a stick and pulling it over a grate to make a noise or holding a vibrating ball that makes a humming noise are ways to combine sound with touch.

4. Combine movement and touch in games. Use movement coupled with touch for children who enjoy movement. For example, give your child a carpet ride by pulling him down the hallway while he lies prone on a beach towel. Or rock your child back and forth with one adult holding each end of the blanket, then gently swing your child so that he lands safely on the sofa cushions situated on the floor.

5. Introduce rough textures to help desensitize the body. Scratchy textures such as bristle blocks or sandpaper are sometimes appealing to children with touch sensitivities

because the texture gives more input than a smooth texture. Similarly playing at the beach or in a sand box or tub of dried corn or rice helps desensitize children.

6. Use toys that offer deep pressure and resistance. Toys that offer resistance such as pulling putty, clay, or Model Magic help provide heavy deep pressure to the skin and joints. Have your child pull on a rubber hoop. Bury hands inside a bin of dried beans to find small objects. Knead bread.

7. Touch your child where you know he can tolerate it. When you touch your child use firm, sustained contact, first touching mainly on your child's back, abdomen, and pelvis. If you need to brush your child's hair or wash his face, place one hand on his back while you do this.

8. Use firm pressure and massage to relax your child and allow him to tolerate physical contact: At nighttime, give your child a "massage" using a squeeze, release type of touch rather than a stroking motion. If your child still objects, try just resting your hand on his back, thigh, or forearm without moving it. That way you still have some contact with him but without the aversive response. Read to your child, listen to music together, or tell him a story while you do this. If the only contact that your child can tolerate is his back or side of his body leaning against you, then that is where you start to offer contact.

9. Put something soft and inviting between you and your child if he can't tolerate direct contact. When it is impossible to touch your child directly, it is often useful to begin with games like the "hot dog" where you wrap your child up in a soft comforter, then massage his back with a large ball, rolling it up and down the back in different ways (e.g., light tapping, firm rub) to provide "toppings" on the hot dog. You can take a pillow and squeeze it around your child's back when you give him a hug (a pillow hug).

10. Daily care tips: at tooth-brushing time, use an electric toothbrush or rub the gums with a Nuk toothbrush to help desensitize the inside of the mouth. If your child objects strongly to being dressed, place one hand on his arm, leg, or back and hold it still while

you pull his shirt or pants onto his body. At bath time, avoid wiping because this often sets off a defensive reaction. Try to scrub vigorously or dab with the wash cloth, whichever your child tolerates best. Likewise, drying the body often works best when using a warm towel from the dryer, wrapping your child loosely with the towel, then patting dry through the towel. If getting into the bathtub is difficult for your child to tolerate, wrap him loosely in a towel then help him to submerge into the water.

11. Let your child lead. Always let your child initiate the touch on his own terms. Avoid being judgmental about how much or how long he plays with textured toys or engages in tactile activities or contact with others. His nervous system will be the guide.

12. What to do if your child becomes overwhelmed and nothing is working: Sometimes children are so severely defensive to touch that it is necessary to take action to help him overcome his defensiveness. This should only be done under the guidance of an occupational therapist who can observe his responses and help you know exactly how to do the technique. For example, Pat Wilbarger (Wilbarger & Wilbarger, 1991) has developed a brushing technique that involves rubbing the extremities, back, hands, and feet with a surgical brush in a systematic way.

13. Be sensitive to the emotional meanings of touch. Because of the intimate link between touch and emotions, all tactile activities should be introduced in a nurturing, caring way. Watch for any negative responses that your child feels. Sometimes children attach a negative meaning to a particular activity. For example, some children start to gag just seeing a food texture that bothers their mouth. A child who is sensitive may think that other children are hurting him when he is randomly touched or bumped on the playground. Help your child to understand what really happened, separating out his body reactions and feelings from the actual event.

14. Watch for sensory overload. Keep a log of behaviors that occur when you try introducing tactile activities. Watch for any changes in your child's sleep patterns or activity level. Tactile stimulation affects the nervous system for at least 30 minutes but sometimes hours after the touch has stopped. The lingering sensation may feel tingly or itchy. Watch for unusual behaviors such as self-abuse, rapid breathing, sweating or flushing, destructiveness, problems sleeping, or extreme restlessness. These are symptoms of overarousal of the autonomic nervous system. If your child experiences negative effects from tactile stimulation, rock your child slowly, apply firm pressure on the back and abdomen, and present a visually interesting task for him to focus on while listening to relaxing music.

II. Activities for Children Who Are Undersensitive to Touch

1. Help your child feel his body when he is touched. Registering touch is the central issue for children who are undersensitive to touch. In essence, they are touched but don't feel it. If your child has this problem, you will need to provide tactile experiences that force your child to attend to the fact that he is receiving touch. The stimulation needs to be done by combining touch with another sensory channel—movement, auditory, or visual. For example, one activity may be wrapping your child's hand up in resistive

putty, then waiting for your child to look at his hand and figure out what to do about it. You may wrap your child up in a large piece of paper to be a "hot dog" instead of using a blanket so that the noise of the paper orients him to the touch.

2. Make the touch experience intense: vibration and traction are helpful. Some children like hanging from a suspended bar, or they like to touch a toy that vibrates in their hands. You can gently pull on your child's ankles or wrists while he lies down to "stretch" him or shake his trunk gently in a "wiggly worm" game.

3. Help keep your child from hurting himself. If your child has self-abusive behaviors such as hitting his head or biting his hand, institute a daily regime, several times a day whereby you apply light touch, stroking the  areas that are affected (e.g., bit, hit, etc.) This provides a different kind of sensory feedback to the body part rather than the repeated stimulation that your child might do. If your child hits his head, be sure to provide input to both the face and hand. Make it a routine that is fun that the child can anticipate. You might use moist tissues or a paintbrush dipped in water to stroke your child's face or massage lotion on the face and hands. When abusive behaviors are present, it is very important to come up with a systematic plan for addressing these problems.

4. It's not always a simple problem of undersensitivity. The child who is underreactive to touch often has sensitivities to touch as well. You may need to do activities that we suggest in the first section of this tool sheet.

Tool 3. Guidelines for Helping Children Move with Ease and Comfort

1. Use a slow, gradual approach if your child is fearful of movement. This child responds best when rocked in a forward-backward or side-to-side movement. You can try spinning as long as the face is always in one direction (not a circular spin). Often children with this problem do best if movement is coupled with firm, deep pressure to help to organize the movement experience through the sense of touch. The child needs a very gradual approach, starting with activities that are close to the ground.

2. Movement should have a purpose. Without a reason to move, movement stimulation can be extremely disorganizing. Always come up with a goal like swinging over to knock over a tower of blocks.

3. Incorporate vision with movement: encourage your child to look at a target while he is moving. For example, the lights may be dimmed while your child navigates through a tunnel on a scooter board with his flashlight. Perhaps have your child ride on a swing while holding a toy fishing rod to pick up magnetic toys on the floor. Or go "grocery shopping," planting empty boxes and cans around the room for him to pick up while he rides about on his tricycle.

4. Vary movement in direction, arc, speed, and velocity. Try to vary the movement that your child likes to do so that it occurs in all different planes of movement (forward-backward, side-side, up-down) and with the body in different positions (head upright, body tilting sideways, or body upside down). Vary the speed, direction, timing, and predictability.

5. Precautions: As with any sensory stimulation, the child's responses should be watched carefully to ensure that the activity is perceived as pleasurable. Watch for any signs such as panting, flushing or pallor, sweating, nausea or yawning, severe dizziness, or

loss of balance. You might not see these responses right away while you are doing the movement stimulation. Some children actually become disorganized in their behavior or show these body signs later in the day or after they have had even a slight amount of movement like a ride home in the car. It shows that the movement system has reached its maximum level of tolerance.

6. What should you do if your child reacts in an adverse way to the movement stimulation? If your child shows some of these signs of overstimulation from movement, encourage him to engage in slow rocking in a chair or on your lap. Try to apply firm pressure on the abdomen with your hands or with a soft pillow or large bean bag animal. Also engage your child in cognitive games such as counting or singing. This will help your child to regroup if the input has been too intense.

7. Controlling movement stimulation in the out-of-control child. The child who is under-sensitive to movement often craves spinning and seeks fast-moving, rough kinds of games. This type of child may disorganize very rapidly and without warning. Movement stimulation needs to be carefully directed so that it is purposeful and with a goal. That way the child is less apt to get wild and out of control. If the activity is set up in advance, the child learns to control the sensory stimulation and how it will happen. Movement stimulation activities that are intense and stimulating should be coupled with calming ones. For example, if your child likes to spin or roll down ramps, be sure that he has a visual target to look at to focus the eyes. Or you can help control the movement so that it is rhythmic and steady like bouncing on a trampoline to a drum beat. Use linear movement activities (e.g., forward-backward and head-to-toe rocking, swinging) to calm your child. You can use a hammock swing, a rocking chair, or a glider chair to accomplish these movements. Swinging your child in a soft blanket filled with pillows is another way to calm your child.

Tool 4. Teaching Your Child to be More Coordinated

1. Getting a plan for coordination. The first step in motor planning is to determine what your child needs to accomplish. He may need to visualize a skill in order to know what it looks like. For example, he might picture what it looks like to hit a baseball across the field.

2. Combine movement stimulation with the motor plan. Give your child sensory feedback so that he can remember the motor plan. If your child is learning how to do a somersault, you may guide him into the position, telling him to tuck his head, as you move him through the somersault. The child needs to link the feeling of enacting the motion with the actions that lead to task completion. As you move your child through the actions, describe what is happening so that you connect the plan with the movements.

3. Add variety to the motor plan. Vary tasks in many ways so that your child has to adapt. Your child can hold onto a hula hoop while sitting on the scooter board. Or he can ride down a ramp or push the scooter board inside a tunnel. Each of these variations of the same action will help your child to conceptualize new ways to do a task.

4. Help your child make choices in activities by modeling how. Many children with motor planning problems cannot choose a motor task because they don't have a concept of what to do. Select a simple planning task, and then model how to do it.

5. Getting motivated: before your child can plan what he wants to do, he must be motivated to do the task. It is important to find activities that excite your child and hold his interest and involvement. Once you have him engaged in an idea, help him picture or conceptualize what needs to happen to complete the task. Together consider details of the task to help your child elaborate on his ideas. "Picture what the bridge is going to look like. How do you want it to look? Let's make a picture. Is this a draw bridge, a suspension bridge, or a foot bridge? Can boats go under it or cars and trains ride over it?"

6. Select activities that offer sensory feedback. For example, if an obstacle course is used, the child may crawl through an opening in a large box. He can pull himself on the scooter board by holding a resistive rope. Each of these steps in the sequence has distinctly different sensory inputs that help him mark each event in time and space.

7. Plan activities with other kids. Plan activities that challenge your child's motor planning with other children so that they can model how the task is done. Their ideas will fertilize his own imagination, and he will be motivated to continue playing.

8. Putting the plan into action and make corrections along the way. What is usually the most difficult part of executing the plan is being able to change the plan if a problem comes up along the way. What helps the child to plan a smooth execution is learning how to self-correct. For example, when the pitcher throws a curve ball, your child needs to be ready to adjust his bat to make contact with the ball.

9. Using the "little voice in the head" to guide the plan: we all do self-talk to help us as we move through tasks. To teach your child how to do this, you can articulate what he is doing as he does it. This helps your child link the language with the motor actions. You can offer verbal commands or prompts while he engages in a task to help organize the sequence.

10. Create spatial markers to help keep the sequence. You can help your child by creating "space stations" to indicate the different steps of what he is doing. Organize them from left to right, putting the different materials in the correct sequence on pieces of colored construction paper. You might even go so far as to number the stations and begin with green (Go) and end with red (Stop).

11. Fine-tuning the plan: once your child has consolidated how to do a plan of actions, he should be able to enact the sequence and work on refinements in the task. Fine-tune the task by adding "a fly in the ointment," so to speak. For example, if your child now knows how to tie shoes, teach him some new knots to learn. Make a lanyard out of gimp, or teach other sequencing tasks like weaving a potholder. Vary speed, direction, accuracy requirements, complexity, or any other variables that can challenge your child to get better and better at the skill.

12. Practice, practice, practice! Practice and repetition will help consolidate the skill and enable your child to generalize it to other situations and tasks. Do at least three repetitions of any plan so that it carves a path in the brain for motor memory and recall.

Tool 5. Learning to Pay Attention

1. Modify the environment to focus your child.
   - Organize toys and work objects in clearly defined bins.
   - Limit the number of toys or objects available at any one time.
   - Use enclosed spaces such as a pup tent filled with soft pillows.
   - Encourage seating along a wall or by a corner of the room.
   - A portable fold-up cardboard "cubicle" can be constructed and placed on your child's desk for quiet focused work.
   - Allow your child to sit in a bean bag chair for reading activities.
   - Sit on a soft inflatable cushion at circle time or at the desk.
   - Seat your child next to a quiet, organized child.
2. Encourage recreational activities that organize the body and mind.
   - Enroll your child in karate, gymnastics, horseback riding, wrestling, or other high-contact sports.
   - Encourage movement on playground equipment in the afternoon.
   - Avoid vigorous movement activities after dinner. Instead encourage slow rhythmic movement, such as rocking in a chair.
3. Use organizing auditory stimulation.
   - Play Gregorian chants, Mozart, and music with female vocalists as background music. Some children respond well to New Age music or relaxing music tapes with environmental sounds like waterfalls.
   - Some children need to wear headsets that muffle or screen out noise.
4. Organize visual input for better processing.
   - Highlight important visual information with bold colors or place boundaries around content that you want your child to focus on.
   - Keep objects in organized locations. Put labels on where they go so that your child can return things to the proper location.
   - At school, encourage homework assignments to be listed in a box on the blackboard.
5. Teach your child the difference between being alert and being calm and organized.
   - What time of day is your child's most alert period? Try to do things that require quiet concentration during those times.

- Some children need to move around frequently. Giving your child a "job" such as carrying a heavy box down to another teacher's room or the task of helping to move furniture in between activities can be very organizing.
- Before a focused cognitive activity like homework, do activities that provide body movement for 5 minutes. Squeeze resistive toys or stress pulls, play with clay or Sculpey. Bury hands and feet in a bin of dried beans. Have a small snack of crunchy hard foods (hard pretzels, rice cakes, ice chips, carrot sticks, apples).
- Before bedtime, do a relaxing, calming routine, which might include a warm bath, back massage and pressure to the palm, especially the web space of the thumb.
- Do forward-backward rocking while reading, looking at pictures, or listening to rhythmic soft music.
- Some children like to lie under a heavy quilt or wrap inside a sleeping bag.
- Make a calm-down corner in your home for your child to go to. This should be a dimly lit, semienclosed place (behind the sofa, under a card table covered with a blanket or a pup tent).
- Talk to your child about how his "engine is running"—high, medium, or low, and what he needs to get his engine in the right place for homework, sleep, or playtime.
- Label when your child is calm and focused—"your engine is running at the right speed right now."

6. Teach your child to use self-talk skills. There is a little "voice in the head" that most of us use to guide our actions. Start by narrating what your child is doing, then ask him to talk through the steps of the task.
7. Teach your child to visualize the final product.
   - Visualization can be done in motor activities very easily. "Picture the ball flying over and landing in the basket." "Now do it."
   - Try to show your child what the final product will look like. "This is what we are going to make, now I will show you how to do it."
8. Speak to your child in telegrams when you want him to listen. Give instructions in attention-grabbing ways by using short commands with one small message at a time. Be sure to get his attention by touching his arm and getting him to look at you before you deliver your message.
9. Teach him organizational skills.
   - Use pictures or photographs of the sequence that will happen.
   - Teach him to have "check-ins" with you at certain points in the task to reinforce completion of steps. This may be accomplished by using a chart of the various steps in a task.
   - Give your child simple chores to complete and reinforce him with praise and checkmarks on a chart, etc. for completing them.
   - Use a picture board of activities for the day. Your child can check off as things happen or refer to the board about what will happen next.

10. Be consistent in rules, routines, and transitions.
    - Give your child advance notice of things both verbally and in picture or written form if possible.
    - Use calendars and timers to help your child anticipate the beginning and end of things.
    - Work on flexibility gradually within routines, changing just one thing at a time.

Tool 6. Distraction

Distraction is an important tool to use when one is trying to refocus a child's attention from thoughts and feelings that are destructive and ineffective. In addition, distraction can be useful in actually changing mood. As you refocus your child's attention, you will change the way he feels. The child learns that when he is feeling sad, or irritable, or anxious, he can do things that make him feel better. Gradually, the child learns that he can distract himself without the help of mom or dad.

Distraction for Babies with the Parent as Teacher

- Play a music box or CD or sing a calm song.
- Present a favorite toy.
- Touch your child gently with a favorite stuffed animal or blanket.
- Play peek-a-boo.
- Point to something that is visually interesting.
- Show your child a favorite picture book.

Distraction for Toddlers   Now we are trying to get the child to distract himself. We need to observe his behavior and note the activities that he most enjoys. These activities are the ones that have the greatest likelihood of distracting him when he is distressed. Gradually ask him what he might do to feel better and guide him to these tasks. Congratulate him on learning a way to calm down and enjoy himself.

- Running around the yard or up and down the hall three times.
- Riding a bike or jumping on a trampoline.
- Doing a puzzle or playing with blocks.
- Doing imaginative play with dolls or blocks or sticks.
- Looking at picture books or drawing.
- Playing with stuffed animals or dolls.
- Listening to a book on tape or listening to or playing music.
- Watching a favorite video or playing a simple computer game.
- Playing with the dog.
- Digging in the sandbox.

Distractions for School-Aged Children   Now your child can begin to understand the rationale for distraction. He can learn that what we do and think will affect our moods. Ideally a distraction will be active because physically doing something helps us to reorient our thoughts and our feelings. When you are feeling depressed, physical exercise is particularly important as a mood changer. For those who are feeling anxious and agitated, a repetitive activity like knitting can be soothing. If you choose to use music or movies as a distraction, be careful that you are not enhancing the mood you are trying to change. If your child is sad, do not listen to Eric Cobain. Pick something that is life embracing, like the score to the movie *Rocky*. If you are anxious, do not watch a scary movie. Pick distractions that encourage the mood you are trying to achieve.

- Playing with Legos or completing a jigsaw puzzle.
- Imaginative play with dolls or Play-mobile figures.
- Reading or listening to a book on tape.
- Listening to music.
- Riding a skate board or bicycle.
- Dancing or doing gymnastics.
- Playing ball.
- Doing an art project.
- Cooking.
- Sewing, knitting, embroidering.
- Video games.
- Movies.

Tool 7. Positive Self-Talk

Sometimes our children think in a way that is going to get them in trouble. They may get discouraged by things they cannot control, such as worrying a parent will die. Or they may begin to think in a negative manner and feel helpless to improve their lives. You can help your child think more positively and in turn feel more hopeful.

What you think affects how you feel, which affects what you do and this has consequences.

The following example looks at what happens when a child has been called to the principal's office, what he thinks will affect how he feels and what he does.

Trigger	Thought	Feeling	Action	Consequence
I am called to the principal's office.	I have done something bad.	Angry	I refuse to go.	Principal thinks I am a trouble maker.
I am called to the principal's office.	I might be getting an award.	Happy	I bounce off to the office.	Principal thinks I am a great kid and competent!
I am called to the principal's office.	My mother has died.	Scared	I start crying and sob as I walk to the office.	Principal calls the nurse.
I am called to the principal's office.	He has the test results.	Anxious	I go but am quiet and withdrawn.	Principal thinks something bad happening at home.

Help your child move from negative self-talk to positive self-talk. Instead of: "I am so stupid, I don't know the answer to this question." Try: "I don't know the answer to this question, but I bet I know the answer to some of the other questions."

Or, instead of: "My parents are so mean, they never let me do anything." Try: "I need to really explain to my parents why this is so important to me and how I will be safe."

This example will show you visually how what we think affects how we feel and what we do. In this case, the child is responding when the teachers asks him to take out his book to read.

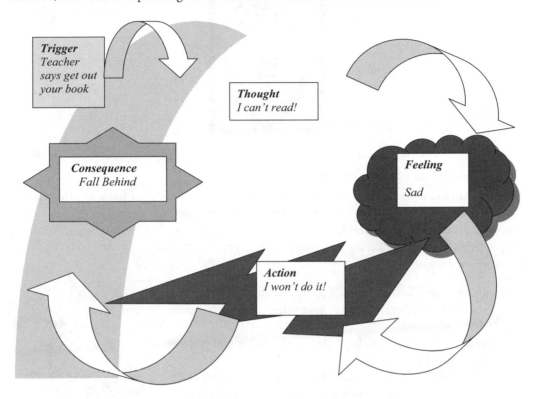

Trigger
Teacher says get out your book

Thought
I can't read!

Feeling
Sad

Consequence
Fall Behind

Action
I won't do it!

As a teacher and a parent, you can help this child use positive self talk to change the way he feels. Instead of "I can't read," try "I am getting better at reading." This will change his feeling from sad to hopeful. As a consequence, he will move from avoidance to trying.

Model positive thinking in your own life. You might catch yourself saying, "How stupid that I forgot the milk when I was at the store!" Then correct yourself and say, "I must be more tired than I realized. I forgot to buy the milk. Tonight I'll go to bed earlier."

Tool 8. Mindfulness: Stilling the Mind

The tradition of mindfulness is an ancient one. People have long sought to escape the frustrations of the day by focusing on one single thing, to the exclusion of everything else. For some people mindfulness is inextricably bound up with an awareness of a spiritual being. For other people, mindfulness is a path for restoring calm and peace to the body and inner self. Try some of the following with your child.

1. For an infant, hold your child so that he can feel your heart beat and your breathing. Try humming a calm, repetitive pattern of sound.
2. Slowly rub your child's back. Ask him to relax and just pay attention to your hand.
3. With an older child, breathe with him. Ask him to pay attention to his breathing. Then ask him to count to three as he breathes in and count to three as he breathes out: *one, … two, … three.*
4. Sing a calming song together or find a joyous piece of music.
5. Ring a bell. Listen to the sound. Remind your child to be in the moment. Use this in a variety of ways. Let the sound soothe you, let the sound give you space to focus on what needs to happen now.
6. Say a prayer together.
7. Give your child an image to think about that has meaning for him and invokes a state of peace and contentment. Examples might include sitting on the beach listening to the waves, scoring a goal in a soccer game, or patting his dog. Have him describe the image to you with as many details as possible. He might want to draw a picture of that image to hang by his bed.
8. Draw with your child, or build with Legos, just thinking about that moment and that activity.
9. Together, make a list of all the things that you are grateful for. Then slowly think about each one so that you bring it alive in your mind. Keep the list by your bed to look at just before you go to sleep.

10. Do a walking meditation where you look at the beauty of nature. Take a walk and pause to look at a caterpillar, or touch a leaf or smell a flower or the scent of pine. Be mindful of just that moment and put other thoughts out of your mind.

11. Instruct your child to feel like a "ball of love" or a "beam of sunshine." Feel the positive energy in yourself. Each time you breathe in, feel that energy get bigger and bigger. Lead your child in slow, exaggerated breathing.

12. Instruct your child to feel like the bud of a flower. Start sitting on the floor, bent over with the arms hugging the legs. Gradually lift up the head, open the arms, and rise as the bud begins to open. Imagine that the flower feels the warmth of the sun and captures the energy of the sun. What thoughts are you thinking as you open to the sun?

Tool 9. Systematic Relaxation: Stilling the Body

Find a quiet place to practice. Set aside 15 minutes to do this. A good time to do progressive relaxation is before bed time or whenever you feel tense or stressed. Here are instructions to do progressive relaxation with your child.

1. The Starting Position

   Lie on a soft comforter on your bed on your back. Let yourself sink into the comforter. Close your eyes and start to take deep breaths. Count slowly to three as you take in a deep breath, pause and hold your breath for a moment, then let the breath out slowly to the count of three.

2. Toes

   Let's start by relaxing your toes. Pretend that you are barefoot and standing in thick mud. Take your toes and squish them into the mud for 5 seconds. Relax your toes. Do it again and count to five. Relax your toes a little more each time.

3. Legs

   Now let's relax your legs. Float your legs up into the air; hold them there while you pretend a slow turtle is walking under your legs. Let your legs drop like they are very heavy. Do it again. This time drop your legs as if they were pieces of limp spaghetti.

4. Stomach

   Now that your legs are relaxed, take some deep breaths again. Let's relax your stomach. Pretend that a baby elephant is going to step on your stomach. Pull it in and make your stomach hard. Count to three while you hold your breath. Now relax and let your breath out slowly. Let's do it again.

5. Back

   Lift your arms as if you were holding onto two overhanging straps from a swing. Make your arms and back stiff. If a strong breeze blew you, you would stay strong and still. Hold it for 5 seconds. Now let your arms drop like wet noodles. Try it again. Now rest your hands on your lap.

6. Shoulders

   Stretch your arms up in the air, reaching for the sky. Keep your arms up there, spreading your fingers and holding them there for 5 seconds. Now let them drop to your sides. Take a deep breath and do the whole thing again.

7. Arms

   Pretend you have a squishy ball in each hand. Squeeze the balls as hard as you can for 5 seconds. Now pretend that the balls drop to the floor as you relax your hands. Try it again.

8. Neck

   Let's relax your neck. Pretend that you are a turtle on a rock by a peaceful pond. The sun is shining and you feel safe and warm. Bring your neck into your shell. Hold it there for 5 seconds, and then stretch your head out of your shell. Take a deep breath. Do it again.

9. Jaw

   Now it's time to relax your face. Smile as big as you can. Make the corners of your lips touch your ears. Hold it for 5 seconds. Let your smile go back to normal. Do another big stretchy smile and hold it. Now relax. Now pretend you have a big piece of bubble gum in your mouth that is hard to chew. Bite down hard on it. As hard as you can. Now relax. Open your mouth as wide as possible. Pretend that you are trying to swallow an elephant. Hold this for 5 seconds. Now slowly close your mouth.

10. Nose

   Let's relax your nose. Pretend that there is a fly on your nose and you can't use your hands to push it off. Wiggle your nose to shoo it away. Move it from side to side. Stop and relax as if the fly had gone away.

11. Eyes

   Close your eyes as tight as you can, as if you were watching a scary movie and didn't want to see it. Hold it for 5 seconds. Now relax and open your eyes if you want to. Try it again.

12. Forehead

   Now wrinkle up your forehead like you are very surprised about something. Pull your eyebrows up towards your head. Hold it for 5 seconds. Let your eyebrows drop down to a relaxed place. Do it again.

13. Ending up completely relaxed

   Pretend you are lying in a beautiful rainbow of colors. There are balloons in the rainbow. Bat the balloons softly with your hands. Roll a little in the rainbow. Let your body feel completely relaxed. Take some slow deep breaths with me. With each exhalation, say the word "relax." This is how your body feels when you are relaxed.

Tools for Building Self-Esteem

Tool 10. Validation

We need to constantly tell children that we are on their side and we see their strengths and their good sense. This is particularly true when there is conflict and children are behaving in an ill advised manner. Validation is the way that we underline what the child is doing right and show them that we believe in them. Remember, you may not be able to validate a particular action by a child, but you can always validate that you understand how they are feeling. Validation is a useful tool to get the child to calm down and start to think about his actions.

How to Validate

1. Find something good in the situation. The child's intent may be right, but in practice things did not work out as expected. You may not agree with the thought, or action, but on some level you understand what your child was thinking or trying to accomplish. For example, "I know that you wanted to do well on the science test, and studied, even though it was the wrong chapter."
2. You validate how the child is feeling. It is important to accept the reality of the child's emotions. How the child feels is how he feels, even if the parent does not feel the same way. For example, "You are feeling very frustrated that you got an F on that science test." If you first show that you understand how he is feeling, you can later discuss what he can do to improve the situation. Your child must first get calm, so he can begin to think about what he needs to do.
3. Be concrete and stick to the specifics. "When we talk about osmosis, I know that you understand it. It may be that the question on the test was confusing." Avoid escalating the discussion with judgmental words such as "Responsibility," "Self Discipline," "Appropriate," "Mature." These words will simply disorganize your child and make him more upset.
4. Be available when the child wants to talk, and avoid lecturing when the child is shut down and does not want to listen.
5. Listen. Repeat what the child has said to show that you are hearing it accurately. Be responsive so that your child knows that you are interested and hearing what he is saying.
6. Articulate underlying thoughts or feelings and try to join with your child: "I bet it was humiliating when the teacher told everyone your grade. That would have made me very angry." Be willing to back off when the child tells you that you are absolutely wrong, that is not what he was feeling.
7. Put the situation in context. "It was really important to talk with your friend Steven when his girlfriend broke up with him. I understand that there was a lot on your mind the night before your science test."

8. Normalize. "Many kids have failed a subject in sixth grade, and gone on to have a great high school career. I remember when I failed a statistics test in college." "It is upsetting not to be invited to that birthday party. I felt horrible when my friend Margot did not invite me to her anniversary party."

9. Radical acceptance. Try not to preach or be judgmental. Respect the developmental stage of your child and interact with your child at that level. Always remember that the goal is to get your child thinking of consequences and problem solving at the level at which he is developmentally capable. You are going to be there if the child wants help.

10. Never trap a child. Avoid giving ultimatums or delivering extreme consequences when you are caught up in the emotion of the situation. When in doubt, defer discussion to a later time.

Tool 11. Child-Centered Time

The goal of child-centered time is to help the child feel connected and understood by the parent. This is a form of play, where the parent gives control to the child and does what the child asks. The parent also describes what is happening so that the child knows that the parent sees him and appreciates him.

1. Your goal is to be with the child in a predictable manner so that your child knows that he will always have your undivided attention. While ideally one would like the floor time session to be 20 or 30 minutes a day, this may be hard to achieve. The important thing is to have floor time daily, even if you only have 5 to 10 minutes for some sessions.
2. Both parents should aim to have daily child-centered time with their child.
3. Let the child direct the play. You offer no ideas. If your child wants you to do something, try to oblige.
4. Describe what is happening, rather like Howard Cosell narrating a football game. See how your child reacts to this. Most children like it because they feel seen. You are holding up a verbal mirror to your child. However, if your child feels that you are being too weird, you can tone it down. Remember that although initially this may feel uncomfortable to the parent, the child will usually love the verbal attention.
5. During child-centered time, you take no telephone calls and try not to attend to other members of the family.

6. All children need some kind of one-on-one time. As children get older, child-centered time may consist of lying next to a child in bed at the end of the day and listening to him talk about anything that is on his mind. Here instead of narrating, you simply repeat what he has said to show that you heard him. For some children, this focused time can consist of simply rubbing your child's back for 5 minutes and not talking at all. The hallmark of child-centered time is that you are absolutely present for your child.

Tool 12. Having Fun

Exercise is a good mood stabilizer. Consider activities that get your child moving, including:

1. Organized sports, such as baseball and basketball
2. Martial arts, such as Tae Kwon Do and Judo
3. Dance (including ballet, jazz, hip hop)
4. Walking and climbing
5. Biking and skate boarding
6. Swimming and boating
7. Gymnastics and tumbling

Family adventures have the potential of creating a sense of closeness and support, hopefully in an undemanding way. Family adventures are a way of defining your uniqueness as a family.

1. Outdoor adventures of camping, boating, hiking, or leaf viewing
2. A mini-vacation of a day trip to a farm, lake, or museum
3. A spontaneous picnic or trip to pick strawberries
4. Outings to sporting events, family reunions, or other travels

Family activities at home that build a sense of mastery and groundedness include:

1. Cooking together
2. A family game evening, with board or card games
3. Family movie night—rent a movie and have a dinner of unexpected food like popcorn and cheese
4. Decorate the house or front door for a holiday
5. Craft projects—making necklaces, valentines, or a model train track
6. Planting a children's garden that your child designs
7. Designing a bedroom, or picking out a lamp or bedspread
8. Reading a story or book to the whole family
9. Sharing in religious practices together
10. Figuring out a pleasant surprise for a family member or neighbor

Solitary pursuits are a wonderful way to center, have fun, and build a sense of mastery and competence. Children who play on their own often grow up to be creative, out-of-the-box thinkers.

1. Building a model or sewing a doll's outfit
2. Listening to a tape of a favorite song or story
3. Reading, drawing, or coloring
4. Playing with puzzles or doing crossword puzzles
5. Playing a card game like Solitaire
6. Collecting—stamps, bottle caps, coke bottles, shells—you name it
7. Caring for a pet
8. Playing a musical instrument

Tools for Managing Out-of-Control Behavior

Tool 13. Changing Behavior: Positive Reinforcement, Ignoring, Modeling, and Shaping Behavior

Positive Reinforcement   Positive reinforcement aims at increasing a behavior by rewarding it. For example, Henry is an active second grader who hates homework. He prefers active games like soccer and begs to play on his Game Boy. Writing sentences with his spelling words is boring for him. His parents note that if he starts homework before dinner he works more efficiently than when he starts later at night. They make a rule that there are no computer games or television during the week, but if he finishes all his homework before dinner, he can have 30 minutes of television or Game Boy later in the evening. Henry starts doing his homework before dinner to get this reward.

Chart to Increase and Reward Certain Desired Behaviors
(Circle if the behavior occurred during the day)

Calm down by oneself	S	M	T	W	Th	F	S
Ready for school at 7:30 a.m.	M	T	W	Th	F		
Playing with sister in friendly way	S	M	T	W	Th	F	S
Head on pillow at 8:30 p.m.	S	M	T	W	Th	F	S

Negative Reinforcement   Negative reinforcement aims at increasing a behavior by withdrawing or stopping something that is undesirable. For example, you are in a hurry. You get into the car and start the ignition but your car starts to squeal. You put on your seatbelt and the car is quiet. Stopping the squealing was a negative reinforcement to increase the behavior of putting on your seat belt.

> **Tip:** Both positive reinforcement and negative reinforcement increase behavior.

Ignoring Behavior   When you want a behavior to disappear, you ignore the behavior and do not reinforce it. Often there will be an initial increase in the behavior, but if you stay strong and stick to your plan, the undesirable behavior should go away.

For example, Georgeanne wants you to buy her the new American Girl doll. You explain that it is too expensive and that she just got another doll for her birthday. Georgeanne starts screaming that you are unfair and that she must have this doll. You explain that you are not going to discuss the matter any more. When she starts on this subject you ignore her or leave the room. Georgeanne immediately ups the ante, going into her room and throwing all of her dolls onto the floor. You ignore her. She does not get the doll and gradually stops demanding that you buy it. You have decreased her undesirable behavior.

Shaping Behavior   Often the behaviors that we want our children to acquire are complex. Let's return to Henry and focus for a minute on how we can guide this active, disinterested boy to the point where he is handling his homework on his own. Initially Henry wants his parent to sit with him while he does his work and will only work when this cheerleader is in place. To shape behavior means that you consider the steps involved in a complex skill and reinforce each step successively until gradually you get the whole desired behavior. If the desired goal is doing all one's homework independently, one would reinforce each step in a cumulative manner until the goal is reached. Here is an example of the steps you might ultimately want Henry to master.

- Getting the backpack
- Getting out the assignment book
- Starting on the first assignment independently
- Working to finish the assignment in an efficient, focused manner
- Getting out the second assignment and working to completion
- Putting books and papers into the backpack
- Putting the backpack by the door

Initially you reinforce the most important step, in this case getting started on the first assignment. You might sit with him while he settles in. Gradually, you spend time doing other things, coming back to tell him what a good job he has done to finish the first assignment. You then get him started on the next. Slowly you reduce your presence and your reinforcement, and instead tell him how responsible he is to have completed both assignments independently. Your next step might be to get him to put his materials into the backpack. Then you might want to reinforce sitting down independently, getting the backpack, and reading the assignments independently. Linking several steps together is called chaining. Throughout all of this you reinforce Henry by telling him how mature he is, and possibly also keeping the concrete reward of Game Boy time or television.

> **Tip:** Ignoring behavior and having negative consequences for behavior result in behavior decreasing.

Tool 14. Teaching Consequences and Repair

Children need to know that there are consequences for their actions, but at the same time one wants the child to retain some self-respect and not feel stupid and rejected. When one wants to stop a behavior, and positive reinforcement of the desired behavior has not worked, you may need to impose a consequence on the child. Picking the right consequence needs careful thought. Ideally, natural consequences work best.

1. *What did the child do wrong?* Mat comes home from watching the fireworks and demands chocolate milk. His mother tells him that she does not want him to have chocolate milk so late at night because he may have trouble sleeping. Mat disregards her, grabs the milk from the refrigerator, and immediately spills the milk. Describe in specific behavioral terms what went wrong. In the case of Mat, "There is a problem. The chocolate milk is all over the floor and needs to be cleaned up."

2. *Listen to your child.* Sometimes your child gives you insight into what happened so that you understand the problem in a new way. Maybe Mat really did not hear you. Maybe he was dehydrated and dizzy and needed liquid. Whatever the case, Mat needs to be listened to, even if you then disagree with his view of the facts.

3. *Observe your limits.* Explain why this is a problem for *you.* "This milk needs to be cleaned up because it is sticky. It is late and I don't have a great deal of energy for cleaning up the milk."

4. *Avoid all categorical statements.* Try not to say anything that is a put down. Do not say, "You are acting like a spoiled brat. You are such a temperamental child. You are so immature." Why? Such statements may feel right at that moment, but they rarely help make the child behave better. In fact, when a child hears words such as *inappropriate, lazy, messy, careless, irresponsible, disappointing, drama queen, stupid, hopeless, clueless,* he tends to get embarrassed, dig in and become even more trying. At worst, the child internalizes these words as a judgment on what kind of person he is, which results in a major blow to his self-esteem.

5. *Consequences.* If the behavior has been serious and the parent feels the behavior needs to have a consequence, avoid making a decision when all parties are upset. "We will discuss this in the morning!" can calm the situation and have a sobering effect.

6. *Natural consequences.* Whenever possible, natural consequences work best. If Mat is so wiped out that he could not help clean up the milk at night, then the next day he needs to do some cleaning that would help his parent. "Mat, last night you were so tired that I knew you couldn't clean up the milk. Therefore I helped you by cleaning it up. Today you could help me by washing the dishes."

In determining consequences, it can be helpful to get the child's input. Again one describes the problem in specific behavioral terms and asks what consequence makes sense. Usually you are aiming at a punishment that fits the crime and an action that repairs at least some of the damage. Children can be fair and think up a consequence that they feel addresses the problem they have caused. At other times they will continue to defend themselves and deny responsibility for the event. In either case, the parent is the one who makes the final decision. Here are some examples of natural consequences.

The child did not get dressed on time—*get dressed in the car.*

The child took/broke another child's toy—*return/replace the toy.*

An enraged child pushes a sibling, who then trips and falls—*make breakfast for the sibling and bring it upstairs so the child does not have to climb steps.*

The goal is to be reasonable and listen to your child. However, when your child is clearly off base, you want to teach what is right and gain the child's attention so he can learn. You also want to help him understand that there are consequences for one's actions.

Sometimes natural consequences have no impact on the child who continues to behave badly. It then may be necessary to impose a consequence that you know means something to the child. Again we caution you that this may backfire because aversive consequences have the potential of frustrating and therefore disorganizing the child. We therefore feel that they should be used sparingly. The **Tool Sheet 16, Time-Out** is an example of an aversive consequence. Here are some examples of consequences that have worked with a variety of children:

- Sometimes losing something of importance is powerful; that is, loss of television time, loss of dessert, being unable to go on a family outing.
- Having to go to bed earlier.
- Loss of the privilege of using "screens," that is, computer, computer games, television, etc.
- Loss of the privilege of going on a sleep over.

7. *Doing a repair.* Sometimes the child needs to make a repair, which requires him to do something for the person who has been hurt by his actions. In order to do this, the offending child needs to figure out what the other person would appreciate. This requires thinking about the person in his own terms and trying to empathize with him so that you can learn what is important to him. For many children this is a difficult, but important task.

Tip: It is important for every family to consider what is a right and what is a privilege. For instance, having dinner is a right, but some families consider dessert a privilege. Most families would agree that a parent reading to a child is a right, but some families would consider reading to be a privilege. It is important to be fair and not too harsh when imposing consequences.

Tool 15. Observing Limits

In dealing with hard-to-manage children, it is always difficult to know where to draw the line. The important thing is not *where* you draw the line, but that you actually *draw it*. These intense, reactive children respond intensely to limits, in part because they have so little control of themselves. Yet limits are often what they need in order to feel secure and contained.

We differentiate between "observing" limits and "setting" them. Because hard-to-manage children are easily humiliated, they often react negatively to someone "setting" limits, which they may perceive as arbitrarily telling them what they can and cannot do. When you *set* limits, these intense children may think that you do not trust them or they have done something wrong. What helps is being clear about your own limits. When you *observe* your own limits, you are simply saying what *you* can or cannot do, so that it is more about you and the household functioning effectively. Observing limits means that you are putting a structure in place for the benefit of the whole family. By doing this, you are able to be a more effective parent and provide the order and stability that your children need. The rationale between setting and observing is important. However, the language of the final instructions may be the same.

> **Tip:** Observing limits has been shown to be more effective with acting out children than setting limits.

Steps to Follow in Observing Limits
1. Goal. Figure out what your goal is. What is the issue and what do you want to have happen? What is necessary for one family will not be the same for a different family.
2. Observing limits. Define your limits in specific behavioral terms.
3. Validate the child. Show your child that you know how he feels.
4. Explain limits as a need to observe your own limits. This is about what will work for the family as a whole. We need a plan that works for everyone, including mom and dad.
5. Evaluate. Try this for several weeks and then decide if it is working. If you are continuing to have a problem, you may need to change your goal or introduce consequences to support the limits that you need to have respected.

For example, your child is a procrastinator who starts his homework after dinner and stays up too late. He is sleep deprived.

1. Goal—To get your child to start homework at 4:30 so that he can get much of it done before dinner.
2. Observing limits—"You need to start homework at 4:30," rather than, "You need to be responsible about your homework!"

3. Validate the child—"I know you have been working hard at school and you want to relax rather than start on your homework."
4. Explain limits as a need to observe your limits—"If you work on your difficult math homework in the kitchen while I am cooking, I will be able to help you. After dinner, I need to put your brother to bed and I cannot help you then. I need to be able to get everyone to bed at a reasonable time so that I can get the sleep I need."

Tool 16. Time Out

There are times when a child needs to be removed from a situation in order for him to calm down. These guidelines are intended to help you be effective in teaching your child to observe your limits and learn to calm down when he is upset.

Meeting   The parents call a meeting. To get the child's attention, you might want to make this a somewhat formal event, such as sitting in the living room or going out for breakfast.

1. Describe what the child is doing right in detail: "We are so impressed that you get dressed before you come down stairs."
2. Observe your limits and explain what is not working for the family. This behavior needs to be defined in a concrete, descriptive way. "Biting is a problem. You cannot hurt another child by biting, hitting and name calling. In our family, we do not hurt other people." Be clear about what you want and do not want. Avoid categorical judgments such as "You are selfish and mean," or "You are out of control."

Outlaw Behaviors   Try to be as clear as possible and describe the target behaviors in a way that can be counted. For example, a child is bullying her sister. The outlaw behavior might be: You may not touch your sister. A child repeatedly calls her brother bad names. The outlaw behavior is: You may not use "put downs." A child gets into a temper tantrum. The outlaw behavior is that: You may not scream and throw things. It is important to work with the child until there is a clear operational definition of the behavior that must be stopped. Being more cooperative is too general. Stamping your foot and refusing to come to the table, is clearer. Limit the outlaw behaviors that you are targeting to between one and three.

Now, Steps One, Two, Three, and Four

   One, Warning   The parent needs to give a warning or a signal to tell the child that he is doing the outlaw behavior and should stop. Sometimes it is helpful to say "One" or "Warning," but with some children this is like a red flag to a bull. If this is the case, use an agreed upon signal, such as a simple nod or holding up one finger.

   Two, Calm Yourself Down   This means that the child *must leave the room* and calm down by himself. He can come back when he is not doing the outlaw behavior and he is ready to cooperate. This is the *most important step* because the child needs to get himself back into control *by himself*. Here parental insight is vitally important. What calms your child? Help your child develop a plan of self-calming for step two. Here are some activities to calm down.

- With your child, gather some materials that are calming and put them in a basket or on a shelf: a favorite book, puzzle, toy or drawing materials.
- Figure out a special place to go and calm down. For example, make a private fort behind a sofa or out of a card table covered by a blanket. Pick something special to put in the fort such as a stuffed animal that will be soothing.

- Other children require something more active to regulate themselves, such as running around the yard or going up and down stairs several times.
- For children with sensory integration issues, a trampoline or Dizzy Disc may be helpful in regaining self-control. Often these children calm down best with deep pressure and may climb under a pile of quilts.
- Music is very powerful as a mood changing agent.

Pay Attention! Step two is the most important step because we are helping the child to become aware of when he is out of control and then we are teaching steps for regaining control. This is a long process. Don't expect your child to be able to reboot immediately. However, with time the child will gain a sense of competence as he learns to get himself in control, rather than needing his parents to do it for him.

Three, I Will Help You Get Back in Control   If your child comes back into the room after step two and proceeds to engage in an outlaw behavior, it is your turn to help the child get into control. What happens next depends on the age or developmental level of the child.

- If this is a young child, the parent might want to hold him tightly. If the parent's body is calm, the child will begin to calm down and breathe with the parent.
- With an older child, you may want him to sit in a time out spot such as on the stairs or on a stool. The length of time out is gauged by the age of the child: one minute per year of age.
- Some children simply will not stay put. These children may need to be placed in their rooms. However, time out does not work if the child is pulling on the door inside the room and the parent is pulling on the door outside the room. Therefore, the parent must be prepared to install a lock on the door, usually with a hook and eye catch at the top of the door so that a child cannot reach it. Once the latch is installed, the child should be told that if he does not try to open the door, the latch will not be put on.

Usually this results in the child staying where he is until the parent tells him he may get out. Obviously, you would unlock the door after the time out period is over. Never leave a child locked in a room when you are not close by or at night.

Four, What Did I Learn?   After your child has calmed down, tell him that he has done a great job. "You cannot always prevent getting upset, but I am impressed at how well you got yourself in control." This will most likely be the end of the event because the child has already had a consequence for his actions. You usually don't need to belabor the point of what went wrong. However, if the child's action was truly harmful to another person and your child has the resources to do it, you might want to consider a repair.

Repair   When dealing with intense children, mistakes often happen. Things are messy, things get forgotten, the unexpected happens. The wise parent will not notice many of these short-comings, or will accept an apology and then have a natural consequence. If you haven't picked up, you can all pick up now; if you forgot something, you can do it now.

However, there is another type of mistake which needs a *repair*. This occurs when the mistake is serious and has a big impact on another person. A repair means that you cannot just expect life to go on as it is. You must take ACTION to make the situation better. Repairs come in all shapes and sizes.

The point of a repair is that the child needs to understand the negative consequences of what he has done and take some action to repair the problem. An additional benefit is that when the child is trying to figure out how to make amends, he must consider what the other child would like. Having to take the other person's point of view is hard for many children. That is why it is helpful to practice it.

Tool 17. A Token Economy: Rewarding Positive Behavior

A token system can be helpful when you are teaching a new behavior, such as eating a new food, or trying to increase behaviors, such as getting dressed and ready for school on time.

Parents and child have a meeting:

1. Explain in detail what the child is doing right. Give lots of concrete examples.
2. Explain that there is a problem. Observe your limits. The child is doing many things well, but certain behaviors are not working for the family. For example, imagine the case where a child only eats white foods. The parent might say, "I think that you are doing a good job with so many things in your life. You no longer need to be called five times in the morning. However, I think it would be good for all of us if you could explore a broader range of foods. This would help you get the vitamins that you need and also let you eat more of what the family is eating. It would also simplify meal time for all of us."
3. Try to get a commitment from the child to change. Explore with him the pros and cons of the current situation. The advantages here might be that if he ate more foods, he would be able to go to different places and eat what everyone else is eating. What are the disadvantages of only eating white foods?
4. The parent then explains that getting comfortable with new foods is going to be hard and that it may take a while to master the new skill. To make this more fun, the parent suggests a reward for doing the difficult task. Once the task is mastered, the reward will no longer be given, but the child can then decide what new behavior he wants to work on. For those of you who are against rewarding behavior and consider this bribery, remember that most adults do not go to their jobs unless they are paid.

> **Tip:** Bribery is the term used for doing something illegal or immoral.

5. We want your child to buy into this system. Ask if there are any other behaviors that your child wants to improve on and put on the list. For example, an older child might decide that he wants to be encouraged to practice the piano more. Then practicing the piano gets rewarded as well as the targets that the parents have set.

Rewards   The rewards in a token economy should be things that the child loves, even if they are things that the parent is not wild about. If your child adores television and you are not so keen, you could allow your child to earn television time. If your child hates vegetables and loves noodles and sweets, a reward for eating carrots might be vanilla ice cream. There are several rules to keep in mind about rewards:

1. Although the child may be able to suggest a specific reinforcer, the parent controls what has to happen to get it. The parent controls how many bites constitute a taste, and how much ice cream is a reward.
2. Any reinforcement system must be reexamined every 2 weeks because otherwise the child becomes bored and the system may no longer work. It may require a change such

as adding peas to the target behavior, or it might require a change in the nature of the reinforcer, such as renting a movie.

3. Natural reinforcers are most powerful. Should you get dressed and downstairs at 7:30, there will be time to have waffles for breakfast because Mom has time to make them. If your child can learn to eat a broader range of foods, he could go out to a new restaurant with friends.

4. Sometimes, the reinforcer cannot be given immediately. The child may want to earn a video game or a trip to McDonalds. In this case, one needs a point system to keep track of what the child has done. Poker chips are a handy device, with each child in the family having a different color of chip to avoid appropriating a sibling's chips. When the child earns a point for eating the peas, a poker chip is immediately (if possible) put in the jar for him. This introduces the concept of saving in a concrete, easily understandable form. The parent controls how many chips are necessary to earn the reward of the game or trip.

5. We want children to be committed and buy into this system. Therefore be prepared to negotiate. You think 40 chips are necessary for a video game but the child thinks that is too high. Compromise. Let the child feel that he has been listened to—remember, we want him committed to the system.

6. Keep a sense of humor and do not become legalistic. When in doubt, let the child win.

7. Clear record keeping is important, particularly when using a point system. It usually works best if one parent is in charge of recording points or putting the chips in the jar. Also one parent should make a chart that lays out the rules of the system and what the rewards are. Because these rules will change, these charts should be informal and easily revisable. You could write the rules on a white board or simply a piece of paper scotch taped to the refrigerator.

8. Do *not* take chips away as a punishment. Once the child has earned the chip, it is his. If he has done something naughty, think of another consequence, but don't take away chips.

9. You do not want to include rewards that are rights. For instance, in some families, reading to a child at night is a right not a privilege. Watching baseball with dad may be a right rather than a privilege. A privilege is something that is optional, that is special, that you can earn.

An Example of a Token Economy

Goal: to get dressed by oneself and be ready to go to preschool on time.

Behaviors to be rewarded:

Getting clothes on

Brushing teeth

Combing hair

Being in the kitchen at 7:00 a.m.—draw a picture of a clock.

Have coat on and backpack at 7:45 a.m.—draw a picture of a clock.

Rewards

Grab bag—after completing the desired behavior the child gets a pick out of a grab bag of goodies. The bag might include toys such as a bouncy ball, baseball cards, a gorgeous pencil, or sugarless gum. A grab bag is an immediate reward and therefore very powerful. Decide what works for you but be generous and immediate.

Token economy—one gets one poker chip for each behavior

> 1 chip = 10 minutes of TV
> 5 chips = an ice-cream sandwich
> 15 chips = a trip with dad to McDonalds
> 10 chips = breakfast in bed
> 30 chips = a trip to a water park

Tools for Providing Structure

Tool 18. Food Rules

1. Establish a schedule for mealtimes. If your child doesn't eat a meal, avoid the temptation to try again in another hour. Stay with the schedule. There should be three main meals and two scheduled snacks (in the middle of the morning and afternoon). No extra snacks should be served, even if your child did not eat at one of the meals or snacks. This way your child will start to feel hunger and satiety and understand that when he eats, it satisfies his hunger. When it's time for the next meal, talk about feeling hungry. After eating, talk about being full.

2. Don't worry about how much he eats at mealtime. When it's clear that your child is finished, take away the food and, if your child cannot play unsupervised on the floor, try giving him something to play so you might be able to finish your own meal.

3. Begin with food that your child can eat on his own, such as pieces of banana.

4. Always eat something with your child. This socializes the mealtime and keeps him interested in eating too. Be careful not to diet when your child is in this program. He will get the message that you are avoiding foods to lose weight and will model your behavior.

5. All meals are in the high chair or other appropriate seating. No eating should occur while your child roams the house or is in other places (i.e., bathtub, car seat, etc.).

6. Take plates, food, cups, etc. away if they get thrown. Give one warning, saying clearly "No throwing!" If the throwing continues, end the meal.

7. Let your child self-feed whenever possible. For younger children who cannot spoon feed, you can put out a small dish for baby to use while you feed him. Focus on foods that let your child self-feed and that are easy to manage in the hands or by spoon. For example, sticky foods such as applesauce or pureed bananas are easier than more liquid foods. Finger foods should be julienne strips of

steamed vegetables or pieces of fruit or cheese that can be easily managed in the hand and mouth.

8. Limit mealtime to 30 minutes. Terminate the meal sooner if your child refuses to eat, throws food, plays with food, or engages in other disruptive behavior. If your child is not eating, remove the food after 10 to 15 minutes.

9. Separate mealtime from playtime. Do not allow toys to be available at the high chair or dinner table. Do not entertain or play games during mealtimes. Don't use games to feed and don't use food to play with.

10. Don't praise for eating and chewing. Deal with eating in a neutral manner. It is unnatural to praise someone for chewing and swallowing food.

11. Don't play games with food or sneak food into your child's mouth.

12. Withhold expressions of disapproval and frustration if your child doesn't eat.

13. Offer solid foods first then follow this with liquids. Drinking liquids will fill the stomach so that the child will not be hungry for solids.

14. Hunger is your ally and will motivate your child to eat. Do not offer anything between meals, including bottles of milk or juice. The child may drink water if he is thirsty.

15. Do the "special play time" (child-centered activity) before or after mealtime to give your child attention in positive ways.

16. Emphasize mealtimes as a social, family gathering time. In this way, the focus is on socialization rather than worrying about how much your child is eating. Be sure the television is turned off.

17. All caregivers need to agree to the program or it won't work!

Tool 19. Being Content Alone

Learning to be alone is not easy for some children. However, it is a skill, like many others, that can be taught. Our goal is to help your child be content and self-sufficient, with a growing sense of independence and mastery.

1. Play disappearing games with objects and people.

   Infants and toddlers: Play disappearing games with objects. This is easier than having a favorite person disappear. Start with what is not so emotionally charged for your child. Hide favorite toys under sofa cushions, under tables, around the room threshold, etc. Then encourage your child to find her "Big Bird." You can hide and retrieve objects or make the game more elaborate by hiding the toy, then take your child outside the room for a few seconds with you, then run back to find the toy.

   Preschool and school-aged children: Older children enjoy treasure hunts, a more elaborate version of hide and seek with objects.

2. Play versions of hide and seek and moving into enclosed spaces.

   Infants and toddlers: Play peek-a-boo around corners of rooms, from under blankets, and behind furniture. Also play games that move from one room to another like rolling a ball and chasing it into the next room. (Note: Play these games only for infants 9 months and older who understand that an object is there even when you cannot see it.)

   Preschool and school-aged children: Play hide and seek games and variations of it, such as making a treasure hunt, giving clues along the way to the next hiding place.

3. Practice going places alone.

   Preschool and school-aged children: Older children may be challenged by asking them to go on a short errand in the house. They may be reassured by using a walkie-talkie to communicate with you as they do their job. You can sing to your child or periodically call his name to inquire how he is doing. Some children like their parents to stand in a designated place (for example, at the bottom of the stairs) while they do a short task like go upstairs and brush their teeth. Gradually lengthen the time that he is alone in a part of the house doing these tasks.

4. Practice separation games outside of the house.

Preschool and school-aged children: Your child can go up to the counter and order an ice cream while you stand five to ten feet away. You can engage your child in tasks like "go to the slide over there and go down while I watch you." Use your imagination. You might have your child deliver flyers for a neighborhood picnic while you wait at the curb side.

5. Document greetings and goodbyes and family members doing outings.

Infants and toddlers: Make a "hello," "good-bye," book with pictures of mom, dad, and child; mom waving, mommy coming home, etc. Use the book to read to him. You can give it to him when you leave him at the babysitter's or at day care. Take pictures of the places that you go to when you are away from your child so that he can visualize "work" or other places that you visit without your child.

Older children like taking their own pictures of themselves and family members in different places.

6. Formalize goodbyes.

Infants and toddlers: Many parents slip out the door to avoid goodbyes. This is not a good idea as your child may get worried that you will trick him and leave unexpectedly. Instead, let your child see you get ready to leave. Ritualize the goodbye so that he can predict the routine. When leaving him at the babysitter, take some extra time so that it's not a rushed time. You may want to figure out a special "Good-bye signal," such as a raised thumb that you and your child have for leaving each other. You should be sure to have a reunion when you return, offering a  hug and a kiss or some other gesture to let your child know you are glad to see him. You may practice saying goodbye and leaving for short periods of time while you do a brief chore (e.g., 5 minutes), gradually increasing the time that you are away.

7. Give your child a favorite object to remind him of you when you leave.

Infants and toddlers: Leave a favorite object (stuffed animal, keys, blanket) with him when you leave. You should carry this object with you and your child when going places to attach special meaning to it. It becomes a symbol that you will come back.

Preschool and school aged: Sometimes older children need a keychain with your picture on it or other reminders of you to take with them to school. Find a suitable object that is socially accepted and appropriate for your child to take to school.

When away for several days: For a young child, leave a series of little presents, one a day. The child will open a package a day and on the day of the last package, the parent will be home.

8. Practice nesting.

Sleep is a nesting activity. Let your child find a suitable "nest" to cuddle in like a bean bag chair or submerging his body in a pit of plastic balls. Playing in a pup tent or other enclosure provides a similar sense of safety and nesting.

Tool 20. Strategies for Managing Your Child at Night

Getting Ready for Sleep

1. Develop an appropriate sleep-wake schedule for your child and a bedtime routine that is predictable. Discourage daytime sleeping for more than three consecutive hours for a newborn and for more than one and a half to two hours for toddlers or preschool-aged children. If you have an older child and he goes to bed quite late, move the bedtime back by increments of 10 to 15 minutes every two nights until you reach an appropriate bedtime.

2. Address sensory problems that make your child overly aroused (e.g., high need for movement stimulation, noise or touch sensitivities). Sensory activities should be provided in a scheduled way. Vigorous movement experiences such as running, jumping on a trampoline, or swinging on a swing are useful when provided in the afternoon. Avoid roughhouse or movement experiences after dinner. Only do gentle movement activities such as rocking in a rocking chair in the evening. Remember that movement activities help to burn off energy and satisfy a need for movement stimulation, but that they also increase arousal. Firm, deep pressure activities such as a back rub, lying down and being covered with a mound of pillows, or rolling up tight in a quilt are especially useful in the evening.

3. Dietary factors: find out if milk intolerance is affecting your child's sleep. If your child is breast fed, you need to be sure that you are not drinking or eating milk products that might affect the child's sleep. Check to see if your child has a high caffeine or sugar intake that might affect sleep as well.

4. Put your child in bed awake rather than drowsy or asleep. This should follow a predictable bedtime routine that both you and your child enjoy. A warm bath, stories, songs, hugs, massage, and holding a transitional object are some of the things that most children and parents enjoy in this ritual. You should limit the length of the bedtime routine and not let your child snare you into "just one more story" or "one more game." Bedtime is not a playtime and should be differentiated as such. You should explain to your child what time you have designated as "lights out" and stick to it.

5. Give your child a security object at bedtime to provide him with comfort in the middle of the night should he awaken. Most children like a transitional object that they also use during the daytime hours as well, such as a stuffed animal. Some children like having an object that "smells" like the parents (e.g., mother's perfume). It is often helpful for the mother or father to carry the object with them and the child for a few days wherever they go to acquire importance as a transitional object and to get some of the

scents of the parents. Some parents will sleep with the object for a few nights to give it their scent. Sometimes you have to wash this transitional object. After it is clean, you may want to add a few favorite scents to it, such as a perfume.

6. Use the Ferber method (Ferber, 1985) once your child reaches 6 to 7 months of age to address night wakings, with increments of waiting before going into the bedroom to reassure the child. The program involves instituting a schedule of visiting your child when he wakes and begins a full-blown cry. The first night, you go into your child's bedroom after 5 minutes of crying. Pat your child and reassure him but do not pick him up, rock him, or play with him. After he is settled, leave. The next night, wait until 10 minutes of crying before you go in. Each night the length of time is increased by 5 minutes. This interval may be modified to smaller increments for some children who need a more gradual approach.

7. Think calmly about how you will cope with crying or awakenings in the night. Many parents feel that they are abandoning their child or feel that their child is fearful. Your child needs to sleep but may be overtired or want to play. By letting your child cry, you help him learn that this is a time to rest and that sleep will come naturally. You can't sleep or eat for your child. These are tasks that your child must learn for himself. Try to avoid projecting your own feelings onto the situation, "Oh, you're afraid of the dark, aren't you?"

8. Don't allow your child to fall asleep with a bottle or to have a middle-of-the-night feeding (after 4 months of age). If you must feed your young infant during the night, give 1 to 2 ounces less of formula than you would during the day or nurse on only one side. When children are fed a snack in the middle of the night, it becomes increasingly difficult to eliminate this as the child grows older. Try to avoid giving your child cereal before bedtime in an attempt to induce sleep. Research shows that it doesn't work.

9. For children over 9 months, avoid playing or holding him if he awakens in the night unless he is ill. It is a good idea to leave the child's room door open to help reduce nighttime fears. If your child awakens and is fearful, you may check in on him and reassure him. If your child should become so upset that he spits up, it is best to throw a large towel over it rather than taking your child out of the crib or bed to clean the sheets. This way, you avoid lifting your child out of the crib and giving more attention to the distressed behavior. It is usually a good idea to remain in the room until your child calms down or has gone back to sleep if he has become extremely upset and very fearful.

10. Assure that the bedroom environment supports sleep. Try soothing techniques such as an oscillating fan, white noise, a stuffed toy that "smells" of a parent, and lullabies. When your child is put in bed or the crib, turn on some soft music. The room should be reasonably dark and quiet and the television should be turned off during the bedtime ritual and after your child has gone to sleep.

11. Address separation issues during the daytime with games such as peek-a-boo, hide and seek, or treasure hunts. Look to see if your child can move away from you on his own.

12. Provide opportunities to play about sleep such as nesting into pillows or cubbies during the child-centered play described in **Tool Sheet 13**. Older children often like to play with toy animals or dolls using dollhouses, beds, stables, wagons, or other symbols of containment. Preschoolers enjoy role playing putting their parents to sleep and developing a system of rules for bedtime.

13. Institute a calm and organized bedtime ritual. The time between dinner and through the bedtime ritual should be organized and presented to your child in a relaxed and enjoyable manner. If you feel rushed or irritable because you feel pressured, your child will also feel this way.

14. Get enough rest and relaxation so that you are available for caretaking activities and to feel that you have the reserves to carry out the bedtime program. Research shows that adults need a minimum of seven and a half hours of sleep a night, with the norm ranging from seven and a half to nine hours. How can you get this? One parent may need to be "on" for certain nights while the other parent sleeps in a quiet area. One parent may want to sleep in one weekend morning, while the other parent sleeps in the other weekend morning. If you are a single parent, see if you can get some respite services from relatives, friends, people at your church or synagogue, or school. Sleep is critical in staying calm and balanced with your child.

15. Recognize the strong emotions you will feel when your child doesn't sleep. You may feel very angry at your child, defeated that you are so exhausted, or guilty that you are passing on your own anxieties to your child. Find a trusted person to talk with about these feelings.

16. Discuss a plan for bedtime with all the caregivers and be consistent. It is very important that when there are two or more caregivers, there is agreement on the philosophy of the bedtime program. This avoids the possibility that one caregiver might sabotage the program (e.g., hold the child when he cries, or invite the child into the parents' bed). If you feel strongly about sleeping with your child, it is important to think about why you feel this way. Is it because you don't like to be alone at night? Are you anxious about your child's well-being when you are away from him? Do you have marital issues and your child makes it easy not to look at them? What will make you feel secure that you are doing a good job in putting your child to sleep? Remember that some children are more difficult and need more attention and emotional security at bedtime. What worked for your friends' children may not be the same for your child. Also keep in mind that if you feel anxious or upset, you won't be as able to help your child to feel secure at nighttime. Many children develop anticipatory anxiety at bedtime when parents express strong emotions.

17. Maintain a daily sleep log. Note activities that were done during the daytime (e.g., high intensity movement activities in the afternoon, a nap), the child's mood, and the nighttime sleep schedule to help understand your child's sleep rhythms and what has helped or not helped in the process.

18. Use sedatives at night for your child if other methods described above have not worked. These should be prescribed by your child's pediatrician. Melatonin and Benadryl have been used successfully under the guidance of a physician as a means of treating serious and chronic sleep disorders. Some children also do well drinking chamomile tea before bedtime.

19. Discuss bedwetting with your pediatrician. If your child is a bed wetter, it is often helpful to discourage drinking fluids after dinner. Suggest to your child that he take only a few sips of water or suck on a hard candy if he is thirsty after dinner. He should empty his bladder before bedtime, and then be awakened in the middle of the night to visit the bathroom. In the morning, force fluids and visit the bathroom every 30 to 45 minutes to help your child feel the sensations of a full and empty bladder. Often children with chronic bed wetting problems need a bed alarm. This is a special pad that lies over the

mattress and has an alarm that rings when the child has wet the bed. The bed alarm is available through medical supply stores.

How to Make this Program Work

1. Stay calm and firm. Tell your child what will happen if he awakens in the night, what you will and won't do. You will check on him, you might rub his back for a few minutes, and you might sing a lullaby. You won't give him something to eat, take him out to play with him, or stay in the room indefinitely. You will leave after 10 minutes because you need your sleep too.

2. Reinforce bedtime rules, whatever they might be; for example, only two bedtime stories or only 10 minutes of lying next to your child before leaving the room.

3. Be consistent. Stick with the rules that you have set. This shows your child that you mean business.

4. Use positive reinforcement for going to bed on time and staying in bed. Reinforce your child if his head is on the pillow at a particular time. You may need to shape staying in bed. For example, waking only once in the night gets a sticker. After two weeks, your child gets a sticker only if he does not call out in the night. Let your child know that he can wake up but he needs to put himself back to sleep on his own using the calm-down strategies.

5. Reinforce the morning routine. After you have been successful with the above steps, give your child praise and positive reinforcement for getting up in the morning, getting dressed, and being ready for the day's activities.

6. Weaning your child from sleeping with you (for children older than 18 months):
   a. Plan for weaning to take about 2 to 3 weeks.
   b. *Week 1:* Your child sleeps in his own bed and mom or dad are on a cot next to his bed. Every few days, move the cot a few more inches towards the bedroom door.
   c. *Week 2:* A parent sleeps on a cot in the hallway.
   d. *Week 3:* You will check in on your child before he falls asleep and offer one hug if he wakes in the middle of the night.
   e. Give your child checks, stars, or stickers for moving through the plan. When he wins five checks, he gets a special treat of some sort, like a dessert, a movie, a trip to the dollar store, or whatever reinforces your child.
   f. If your child needs more immediate reinforcement, let him visit the Mommy Treat Bag filled with small items (dollar toys, fruit roll-ups, or Lego pieces that eventually build an entire set). See **Token Economy, Tool Sheet 17**.
   g. If your child awakens and comes into your room, stay firm about the rules. Some children regress and you may need to back up to the plan of a prior week to be successful.

Tool 21. Helping Your Child Feel Less Fearful At Nighttime

1. Demystify "monsters." If your child is old enough to understand the concept, you may encourage your child to "spray" out monsters in the bedroom using a water or perfume spray bottle. Read stories such as *There's a Nightmare in my Closet* by Mercer Mayer to demystify the idea that monsters actually are alive and kicking in the closet.

2. Talk about bad dreams with sensitivity. Make a dream catcher out of yarn, sticks, and sea shells that help to capture bad dreams. When your child talks about his dream, listen calmly and respond in a neutral way with little or no emotion. Many children respond well to the notion that they can rewrite their dream story to have a better ending.

3. Repetitive and rhythmic activities soothe anxiety. Do repetitive counting activities like counting beads to go on a necklace, knitting, etc. People count sheep for a reason. Counting appears to relax the brain.

4. Promote relaxation. Read a "relax your body" script. See **Tool Sheet 9, Systematic Relaxation**.

5. Teach your child how to quiet his mind. Do a mindfulness exercise like the one in **Tool Sheet 8, Mindfulness: Stilling the Mind**. Focus on a quiet body, deep breathing, and other thoughts that quiet the mind.

6. Neutralize the fears. Make up a story about fears that helps your child to be in charge of those fears. First have your child tell you everything about his fear. Then talk about the fear in parts. Rewrite the story of his fear so that he knows the difference between reality and fantasy.

7. Debrief about the day and capture the good parts of the day in a journal. Keep a notebook, "Thoughts of the Day," beside your child's bed. As you relax at night, ask your child what were his favorite moments of the day. Then write these anecdotes into the book. Ideally this will focus on positive events and will help him relax in a happy frame of mind. It also provides a delightful history of the pleasant events in your child's life and emphasizes competence.

Tool 22. Providing Structure to the Day

It is extremely difficult to manage children who can be uneven in temperament and volatile in their behavior. These children need structure more than most children and often struggle with organizational problems. The following ideas will help you to provide a predictable daily routine that will help your child feel settled and competent.

1. The structure of time: specify times for the following during the day.
    a. Getting up.
    b. Being dressed.
    c. Ready to leave the house.
    d. Time to start homework.
    e. Time for dinner.
    f. Time to be in bed, head on pillow.
    g. Time for lights out.
2. The structure of space: simplify your child's spatial world so there are fewer things to organize and manage. Less is more!
    a. Space stations: limit toys, each toy has a space for storage.
    b. A simple system for clothes: bin for dirty clothes, easily opened drawers for clean clothes.
    c. No distractions in the bedroom, such as TV, computer.
    d. Have a designated place near the door for keeping gear when one comes home: backpack, shoes, and coat.
    e. Have a designated place for doing homework.
    f. Have a designated place for school supplies: a tackle box that can be taken room to room. See Chapter 9, The Curious, Clueless, Disorganized Child, for more details.
    g. Help your child pick up and organize his space, with good humor.
3. Homework help.
    a. Space: what is the specific place to do homework? Does he need to be near you?
    b. How to do homework: with music, lying on the floor, sitting at a desk? Talk with your child about what works for him. Background noise helps some children. Some children need the physical support of lying down.
    c. When to do homework. When to start? When must you be finished? Reward starting early. If your child is taking too long, tell him he should spend 20 minutes on

each homework task. Write a note to the teacher explaining that you cut him off after 20 minutes. Consider together an appropriate length of assignment. Can your child catch up on work on the weekend?

    d. Breaks: When? How long? Keep them short—push ups, jumping jacks, going to the bathroom. (Do NOT let your child go online for a short break.)

    e. Figure out the best assignment book and also set up a monthly calendar on the wall so one can record tests, quizzes, written reports and project dates.

    f. Play Beat the Clock to increase focus. First estimate how long a specific assignment will take. Set a timer. If you finish before the timer goes off, you win a token.

4. Helping with materials.

    a. Make sure your child has two special folders for the backpack (ideally plastic in different colors): one for assignments to be done, and the other for all finished work—essays, tests, finished worksheets, etc.

    b. Backpack: Does your child need wheels on the bag? Duplicate books? Homework reminder tag? Check occasionally that mice have not moved in to eat the old sandwiches.

    c. Have a tackle box at home with necessary school supplies.

5. Helping your child study.

    a. Figure out if your child is a visual, auditory, or kinesthetic learner. All of the above?

    b. What is emotionally supportive to your child when he studies? A person near by, supportive comments, having a parent find interesting articles related to what he is learning, having a parent study with him, having a parent read a passage in his book?

    c. Encourage your child to be active rather than passive: fill out study sheet, talk about the essay, build a diorama, see an exhibit, draw a map.

    d. Repetition: build longer cells in the brain by repeated trials. What drill works?

    e. Relate new learning to what the child already knows.

    f. Use metaphors to teach: that is, school is like a bowl of cherries—you have interesting teachers and delicious friends, but having to do homework might be the pits.

    g. Encourage your child to think. Thinking takes time. Write down novel ideas or Creative bursts as they happen, in the book, in a notebook, or on a Post-it note that you put on the page. These are simply interesting ideas—importantly the child's idea.

6. Work with the school.

    a. Encourage communication with teachers.

    b. Stress the need for the teacher to validate the child. What is he doing right?

    c. Some children need more reminders than others.

    d. Give the child a desk next to an organized child.

    e. Encourage children to show what they know in different ways, for example, if writing is a problem, can the child take tests orally?

f. Adjust output demands: fewer math problems, draw a picture rather than write a story, given an oral report rather than a written report.

g. Encourage use of specific learning tools: a computer for writing, a calculator for math.

h. Structured homework time at school.

Tools for Improving Interpersonal Skills

Tool 23. The Ice-Cream Sandwich

Intense children often have trouble navigating their social interactions. Some children gravitate toward saying negative things to others and simply demanding that they get their way. Our goal is to get these children to slow down, be more positive with their friends, and communicate more clearly about what they want. One technique for doing this is the Ice-Cream Sandwich.

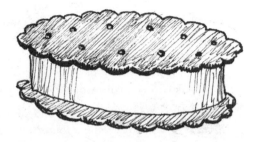

The chocolate layers show that you should say something positive about the other person and the ice cream is saying how you feel and asking for what you want. For example, Hannah is a fourth grader who has a history of turbulent relationships with other children. She gets easily irritated and tends to say mean things to others when they don't do what she wants. She and Courtney are having a fight. Courtney has told Hannah that Hannah does not have any friends and nobody likes her because she is so bossy. An Ice-Cream Sandwich for Hannah to use with Courtney might be the following:

"Courtney, I really like you and I am so glad that you are on my soccer team. When you tell me that no one likes me, it makes me sad. I wish you would not say things like that that hurt my feelings. I really want to be your friend and hope that we can have a play date this week."

Chocolate wafer: something positive—I like you and like playing soccer with you.
Ice cream: how I feel and what I want—you made me sad so please don't say mean things.
Chocolate wafer: something positive—I want to be a friend and have a play date.

Tool 24. Having GREAT FUN Communicating

Here is a structured communication technique to use when you are trying to communicate with someone who may have trouble hearing you. This works well with your school-aged children, your spouse, and the check out clerk at the grocery store.

The acronym tells it all:

G What is your Goal? Where do you want to end up?
R Review what has happened.
E Express how you feel.
A Ask for what you want.
T Think why someone would do what you are asking.

Example: It is a Saturday night and your child wants to stay up until 10:00 to watch a video. You know he will be wiped out tomorrow if he stays up this late.

G Your goal: is to get your child in bed as close to his bedtime of 8:30 as possible, but you also want him to feel that he can do something special because his brother is away on a sleep-over.
R Review what is happening: "It is 7:30 and we are approaching bedtime. You will not have time to see the whole movie. However, we can start it and finish it tomorrow."
E Express how you feel: "I am happy for you to see the movie, but I also know that you need a good night's sleep. If you stay up and watch the whole movie you won't get enough sleep and tomorrow will be hard for all of us."
A Ask for what you want: "I want you to go up stairs at 8:30, and then watch the rest of the movie tomorrow."
T Think why he might do it your way: "If we can figure out how to get to bed at a reasonable hour, I would be happy to rent you another movie next weekend."

How You Do a Great

F Be fair.
U Show understanding.
N Be prepared to negotiate.

In our example, the parent communicates with FUN.

F She is fair to her son and gives him the movie as a treat because his brother got a sleep over.
U She understands that he needs to have a good time as well as sleep.
N She allows him to negotiate a 9:00 pm bedtime. He will still have to finish the movie the next day, but he feels that she heard him and that she is giving him something special.

Tip: When you communicate, try to use a gentle, easy-going style. That way, the other person will be interested in listening to you.

Tool 25. Teaching Responsibility and Cooperation

The following is a list of ideas to think about as you think of activities to increase your child's sense of responsibility and cooperation within the family. Remember to be light. Give your children choices of what they might do. Give them lots of positive reinforcement for their helpfulness.

Tasks for 18 months to 3 years old
  Feed the fish
  Water the flowers
  Pick up toys with parent
  Put recyclables in the recycle bin
  Empty the waste paper baskets
  Wipe the table
  Wash unbreakable dishes
  Set the table with silverware and napkins
  Wash vegetables and fruit
  Put away cans
  Turn off lights while being carried
  Help pull up covers on the bed
  Get own snack or cereal
  Run simple errands around the house
Tasks for 4 to 6 year olds
  Pull up covers on bed
  Put dirty clothes in the hamper
  Straighten up room, perhaps with
    parent's help
  Put away toys
  Write name or other information on
    birthday invitations
  Pick out appropriate presents for
    friends and family members
  Help do the grocery shopping by find-
    ing certain items
  Help to bring in and put away
    groceries
  Help in cooking: making brownies,
    supervised cooking, learning to
    use kitchen tools
  Sort and fold clothes for laundry

Put away clothes
Plant and water own garden
Put dishes in the dishwasher
Measure soap and start the dishwasher
Rake leaves
Walk pets
Have an allowance and save some of that money
Tasks for 7 to 12 year olds
Record homework
Figure out where to study
Figure out what one needs to concentrate
Figure out a method for keeping track of homework sheets and completed assignments
Care for pets
Take responsibility for a household task such as unloading the dishwasher, taking out the trash, sweeping the kitchen floor
Make a dish for a meal on one's own
Run the washing machine and dryer
Cooperate with parents when they need help on a household task, such as painting a fence or running a load of wash
Wash the car
Help younger children
Change sheets on bed
Read to younger siblings or play games with them when they are sick
Look after a parent who is sick in bed
Help a younger sibling learn something that is measurable, such as learning letters, basic math facts, sight words, etc.

A contract may help with school-aged children:

1. Have a family meeting to discuss what they want to do and where you need help.
2. Get a commitment to do specific tasks, specifying what chore they will do, when they will do it, and if appropriate, the amount of time they will work on chores or other responsibilities such as independent reading.
3. Consider whether there is a reward for fulfilling the weekly contract.
4. Give bonus points when the contract is filled without hassle. Don't be punitive!
5. Type up the contract and have everyone sign it.
6. Revise the contract if needed at a family meeting.

Glossary

Adaptive behavior: The ability to respond in a purposeful and organized manner to changing situations and new sensory or cognitive experiences.

Agoraphobia: Fear of open places or of being in places or situations in which it is difficult to escape or where help is not available.

Anxiety: A diffuse feeling of fear or apprehension that creates agitation.

Arousal: A state of awareness that ranges from sleep to wakefulness.

Attachment: The sense of trust and dependability that a child develops with his major caregiver so that he prefers to be in that person's presence and that person calms and centers him.

Attention deficit disorder (ADD): A condition consisting of persistent inattention to tasks and impulsivity. Often appears as "day dreaming." Usually little physical activity.

Attention deficit disorder with hyperactivity (ADHD): A condition consisting of persistent inattention to tasks, hyperactivity, and impulsivity.

Auditory defensiveness: Oversensitivity to certain sounds that elicits a startle response, avoidance, agitation, or a need to flee from the sound.

Autism: A developmental disorder characterized by severe impairment in social relationships, communication, and development.

Autonomic nervous system: The part of the nervous system that controls automatic, unconscious bodily functions, such as breathing, sweating, temperature control, and digestion.

Compulsion: An action that one feels forced to do even though it makes no rational sense, such as hand washing or repeated checking.

Creative burst: The insight, reaction, or creative thought that occurs as you are reading and studying.

Defensive reaction: A response to real or potential danger that causes a self-protective response.

Depersonalization: Feelings of unreality or a sense of lost personal identity.

Discriminative system: The part of the sensory system that allows one to distinguish among sensory stimuli.

Dyspraxia: Difficulty planning and executing novel motor actions or a series of motor actions. Often related to problems with processing movement and touch.

Empathy: The ability to understand how another person feels and understand a different point of view.

Encopresis: Withholding stools for a sustained period leading to serious constipation.

Executive functioning: The ability to organize oneself around time and space in order to complete complex tasks, such as doing homework, writing papers, and doing multistep projects.

Exposure: Repeatedly experiencing what one fears until the event no longer triggers anxiety.

Extinction: Ignoring behavior so that it stops occurring.

Generalized anxiety disorder: A prolonged, intense fear that is chronic and felt in many situations.

Gravitational insecurity: An extreme fear of falling produced by changes in movement or the head position.

GREAT Communication: A communication technique characterized by the following: G – be gentle, R = review what has happened, E = express how you feel, A = ask for what you want, T = think about why the person should do it your way.

Habituation: Doing an action repeatedly until one is comfortable.

Hypersensitivities: Oversensitivity to sensory stimulation characterized by a tendency to be fearful and cautious or to react in extreme ways to avoid the stimulus.

Hyposensitivities: Undersensitivity to sensory stimuli characterized by a tendency to either crave intense stimulation or to not process the stimulus at all, thus becoming passive and unresponsive.

Ice-cream sandwich: A communication technique in which one makes a positive comment, then asks for what one wants, then states another positive comment.

Impulse control: Difficulty restraining one's actions, words, or emotions.

In vivo: Doing something in real life rather than just role playing the action.

Limbic system: The part of the brain that processes information from the senses and is primarily involved in processing emotions and inner drive.

Manic depression: A type of mood disorder that usually involves fluctuations between abnormal and persistent elevated, expansive, or irritable moods and episodes of depression.

Modulation: The brain's regulation of its own activity.

Motor planning: The ability to plan, organize, and sequence complex and unfamiliar body movements in a coordinated manner; also referred to as praxis.

Muscle tone: The degree of tension normally experienced in muscles when in a relaxed state; it enables the body to maintain posture and alignment.

Neurotransmitters: Chemical messengers of the nervous system that transmit information from one nerve to another across synapses or gaps between the cells.

Night terrors: Very bad dreams that lead to waking suddenly in the night screaming in intense fear. Usually the child cannot articulate what happened. This usually occurs between 3 and 5 years.

Observing limits: Understanding one's own limits. What one will and will not do or tolerate to have done to them.

Obsession: A recurrent thought that often is unreasonable or irrational but nevertheless intrudes into one's thinking and is hard to dismiss.

OCD: Obsessive compulsive disorder, characterized by lack of control over recurring thoughts and behaviors.

ODD: Oppositional defiant disorder characterized by a pervasive refusal to follow requests and instructions by those in authority.

Olfactory: Related to the sense of smell.

Oral defensiveness: Aversive responses and intolerance for food textures and certain tastes; a desire to avoid eating certain foods.

Overload: A state of physical exhaustion and nervous system overarousal, which usually results in overstimulation and shut-down of behavioral responses.

PANDAS (Pediatric autoimmune neuropsychiatric disorder associated with streptococci): Antibodies produced to attack strep bacteria end up attacking brain tissue and causing OCD symptoms.

Panic: A sudden surge of acute terror accompanied by severe agitation.

Perception: The meaning that the brain gives to sensory information.

Perseverate: A continuation of activity or behavior when it is no longer appropriate.

Phobia: A disrupting and persistent fear aroused by specific situations, such as heights, certain animals (i.e., dogs, snakes), or objects, that is out of proportion to the possible danger.

Positive self-talk: Phrasing issues in a positive manner that encourages producing behavior.

Praxis: The ability to conceptualize, plan, organize, and carry out a sequence of unfamiliar actions.

Proprioception: The unconscious awareness of sensations coming from one's joints, muscles, and ligaments which aids in the sense of body position in space.

Receptors: Special cells that receive specific sensory messages and send them for processing in the central nervous system.

Reframing: Expressing an idea from another point of view.

Reinforcement: Changing behavior either by encouraging it (positive reinforcement, such as praise) or discouraging it (negative reinforcement, such as whining).

Scrupulosity: A strict adherence to rigid, unreasonable behaviors because one feels a religious obligation to do so.

Selective mutism or elective mutism: The decision of a child who is capable of speech to refuse to speak in certain situations.

Self-regulation: The ability to self-calm, control one's state of alertness and activity level, particularly when distressed, and to self-organize adaptive responses to emotional and sensory experiences.

Sensorimotor: The body's ability to process sensory information and react with a physical or motor response.

Sensory defensiveness: Symptoms of aversion or defensiveness to non-noxious or normally nonirritating stimuli from one or more sensory modalities.

Sensory diet: The optimal sensory input one needs everyday to integrate mind, body, and emotion to feel alert, in control of one's body, and in an optimal organized state for adaptation.

Sensory sensitivity: An over-awareness of a sensation but may not include a defensive response.

Sensory integration: The capacity of the nervous system to take in information from one's body and environment through the senses, to organize this information and use it in planned, adaptive responses to varying challenges for learning, emotional control, and behavioral function.

Sensory integrative dysfunction: Inefficient neurological processing of sensory information that results in learning, motor, developmental, and behavioral problems.

Sensory modulation: The capacity of the nervous system to regulate and organize sensory information and to inhibit or suppress irrelevant sensory information to allow for focus on the most relevant sensory inputs.

Serotonin: A group of chemical neurotransmitters involved in some types of depression and anxiety.

Shaping behavior: Trying to achieve a new behavior by gradually reinforcing the little steps that lead to the new behavior.

Social phobia: A persistent fear of one or more situations in which the person feels scrutinized by others or is embarrassed or ashamed to engage in social interactions.

Stranger anxiety: The ability of a child around 9 months of age to differentiate between familiar and unfamiliar people and their desire to avoid the latter.

SUDS (Subjective Units of Distress Scale): A 0 to 100 scale rating the degree of distress that one is experiencing.

Tactile defensiveness: An aversion or strong emotional response to certain touch sensations, especially to light or unexpected touch.

Tactile sense: The sensory system involved in perception of touch-pressure, vibration, movement of the joints, temperature, and pain through skin and joint receptors; it involves the sense of touch whether self-initiated, other-initiated, or imposed by the environment.

Temperament: Different personality characteristics that are present at birth and affect mood, adaptability, responsiveness, intensity, activity level, distractibility, and attention.

Token economy: A reinforcement system that gives a neutral currency such as poker chips or stars in response to desired behavior. These tokens can then be exchanged for desired privileges or treats.

Transitional object: Valued object such as a blanket or stuffed animal that helps a child make transitions to new, uncomfortable places.

Trauma: An emotionally threatening event that results in long-standing emotional agitation and may lead to pronounced changes of behavior, particularly avoidance.

Validation: Affirming who a person is by recognizing their feelings, their intentions, and their positive actions.

Vestibular sense: The inner ear mechanism that perceives changes in head position and body movement in space.

Visual defensiveness: Oversensitivity to light that may cause visual distractibility or aversive responses.

Visualization: The process of forming mental images of objects, people, or scenes in the mind.

Bibliography

Barkley, R. A. (1997). *ADHD and the nature of self-control*. New York: Guilford Press.

Barkley, R. A., & Benton, C. M. (1998). *Your defiant child*. New York: Guilford Press.

Carey, W. B., & McDevitt, S. C. (1995). *Coping with children's temperament*. New York: Basic Books.

Chatoor, I., Hirsch, R., & Persinger, M. (1997). Facilitating internal regulation of eating: A treatment model for infantile anorexia. *Infants & Young Children*, 9(4), 12–22.

Chess, S., & Thomas, A. (1996). *Temperament: Theory and practice*. New York: Brunner/Mazel.

Cohen, C. (2000) *Raise your child's social IQ*. Silver Spring, MD: Advantage Books.

Daws, D. (1989). *Through the night: Helping parents and sleepless infants*. London: Free Association Books.

DeGangi, G. A., & Greenspan, S. I. (1997). The effectiveness of short-term interventions in treatment of inattention and irritability in toddlers. *Journal of Developmental and Learning Disorders*, 1(2), 277–298.

DeGangi, G. A., Sickel, R. Z., Wiener, A. S., & Kaplan, E. P. (1996). Fussy babies: To treat or not to treat? *British Journal of Occupational Therapy*, 59(10), 457–464.

Ferber, R. (1985). *Solve your child's sleep problem*. New York: Simon & Schuster.

Greene, R. W. (1998). *The explosive child*. New York: Harper Collins.

Greenspan, S. I. (1992). *Infancy and early childhood: The practice of clinical assessment and intervention with emotional and developmental challenges*. Madison, CT: International Universities Press.

Greenspan, S. I. (1997). *Developmentally based psychotherapy*. Madison, CT: International Universities Press.

Greenspan, S. I., & Glovinsky, I. (2002). Bipolar patterns in children: New perspectives on developmental pathways and a comprehensive approach to prevention and treatment. Bethesda, MD: Interdisciplinary Council for Developmental and Learning Disorders.

Greenspan, S. I., & Greenspan, N. T. (1989). *The essential partnership*. New York: Viking.

Koplewicz, H. W. (1996). *It's nobody's fault: New hope and help for difficult children and their parents*. New York: Times Books.

Kovacs, M., & Beck, A. T. (1977). An empirical-clinical approach toward a definition of childhood depression. In J. G. Schulterbrandt & A. Raskin (Eds.), *Depression in childhood: Diagnosis, treatment and conceptual models* (pp. 1–35). New York: Raven Press.

Kranowitz, C. S. (1998). *The out-of-sync child: Recognizing and coping with sensory integrative dysfunction*. New York: Perigee Publishing.

Linehan, M. M. (1993). *Skills training manual for treating borderline personality disorder*. New York: Guildford Press., pp. 70–83.

Muir, E. (1992). Watching, waiting, and wondering: Applying psychoanalytic principals to mother-infant intervention. *Infant Mental Health Journal*, 13(4), 319–328.

Quinn, P. O. (1997). *Attention deficit disorder: Diagnosis and treatment from infancy to adulthood*. New York: Brunner/Mazel.

Rapp, D. (1980). *Allergies and your family*. New York: Sterling Publishing.

Rapp, D. (1986). *The impossible child*. Tacoma, WA: Sciences Press.

Schaeffer, C. E., & Eisen, A. R. (1998). *Helping parents solve their children's behavior problems*. Northvale, NJ: Jason Aronson.

Shure, M. B. (1994). *Raising a thinking child*. New York: Pocket Books.

Turecki, S. (1989). *The difficult child*. New York: Bantam.

Wachtel, E. F. (1994). *Treating troubled children and their families*. New York: Guildford Press.

Webster-Stratton, C., & Herbert, M. (1994). *Troubled families: Problem children*. New York: John Wiley & Sons.

Zull, J. E. (2002). *The art of changing the brain*. Sterling, VA: Stylus Publishing.

Anxiety and Depression

Brenner, A. (1997). *Helping children cope with stress*. New York: John Wiley.

Brooks, B., & Siegel, P. M. (1996). *The scared child: Helping kids overcome traumatic events*. New York: John Wiley.

Chansky, T. E. (2001). *Freeing your child from obsessive-compulsive disorder: A powerful, practical program for parents of children and adolescents*. New York: Three Rivers Press.

Chansky, T. E. (2004). *Freeing your child from anxiety*. New York: Broadway Books.

Dacey, J. S., & Fiore, L. B. (2000). *Your anxious child: How parents and teachers can relieve anxiety in children*. San Francisco: Jossey-Bass.

Greenspan, S. I. (2003). *The secure child: Helping our children feel safe and confident in a changing world*. Cambridge, MA: DeCapo.

Greenspan, S. I., & Glovinsky, I. (2002). *Bipolar patterns in children: New perspectives on developmental pathways and a comprehensive approach to prevention and treatment*. Bethesda, MD: Interdisciplinary Council for Development and Learning Disorders.

Hockey, K. (2003). *Raising depression-free children: A parent's guide to prevention and early intervention*. Surrey: Hazleton Publishing.

Hyman, B. M., & Pedrick, C. (1999). *The OCD workbook: your guide to breaking free from obsessive-compulsive disorder*. Oakland, CA: New Harbinger Publications.

Kovacs, M., & Beck, A. T. (1977). An empirical-clinical approach toward a definition of childhood depression. In G. Schulterbrandt & A. Raskin (Eds.), *Depression in childhood: Diagnosis, treatment and conceptual models* (pp. 1–35). New York: Raven Press.

Penzel, F. (2000). *Obsessive-compulsive disorders: A complete guide to getting well and staying well*. New York: Oxford University Press, 2000.

Rapee, R. M., Spence, S. H., Cobham, V., & Wignall. A. (2000). *Helping your anxious child: A step-by-step guide for parents*. Oakland, CA: New Harbinger, 2000.

Rapoport, J. L. (1989a). *The boy who couldn't stop washing: The experience and treatment of obsessive compulsive disorder*. New York: E. P. Dutton.

Rapoport, J. L. (1989b). *Obsessive compulsive disorder in children and adolescents*. Washington, DC: American Psychiatric Press.

Schwartz, J. M. (1996). *Brain lock: Free yourself from obsessive-compulsive behavior*. New York: Regan Books/HarperCollins.

Wagner, A. P. (2002). *What to do when your child has obsessive-compulsive disorder: Strategies and solutions*. New York: Oxford University Press.

Obsessive Compulsive Disorder

Dornbush, M., & Pruitt, S. (1993). *Teaching the tiger: A handbook for individuals involved in the education of students with attention deficit disorder, Tourette's syndrome or obsessive-compulsive disorder*. Duarte, CA: Hope Press.

Hyman, B. M., & Pedrick, C. (1999). *The OCD workbook, your guide to breaking free from obsessive-compulsive disorder*. Oakland, CA: New Harbinger Publications.

Rapoport, J. L. (1989a). *The boy who couldn't stop washing: The experience and treatment of obsessive compulsive disorder*. New York: E. P. Dutton.

Rapoport, J. L. (1989b). *Obsessive compulsive disorder in children and adolescents*. Washington, DC: American Psychiatric Press.

Asperger Syndrome and Autistic Spectrum Disorders

Hall, K. (2001). *Asperger syndrome, the universe and everything*. London: Jessica Kingsley Publishers.

Ives, M., & Munro, N. (2002). *Caring for a child with autism: A practical guide for parents*. London: Jessica Kingsley Publishers.

Klin, A., Volkmar, F. R., & Sparrow, S. S. (Eds.). (2000). *Asperger syndrome.* New York: Guilford Press.

Leicester City Council and Leicestershire County Council. (2002). *Asperger syndrome—Practical strategies for the classroom: A teacher's guide.* Shawnee Mission, KS: Autism Asperger Publishing Co.

Maurice, C., Green, G., & Luce, S. C. (1996). *Behavioral intervention for young children with autism.* Austin, TX: Pro-Ed.

Moyes, R. A. (2001). *Incorporating social goals in the classroom: A guide for teachers and parents of children with high-functioning autism and Asperger syndrome.* London: Jessica Kingsley Publishers.

Ozonoff, S., Dawson, G., & McPartland, J. (2002). *A parent's guide to Asperger syndrome and high-functioning autism: How to meet the challenges and help your child thrive.* New York: Guilford Press.

Paradiz, V. (2002). *Elijah's cup: A family's journey into the community and culture of high-functioning autism and Asperger's syndrome.* New York: Free Press.

Siegel, B. (1998). *The world of the autistic child: Understanding and treating autistic spectrum disorders.* Reprint. New York: Oxford University Press.

Stewart, K. (2002). *Helping a child with nonverbal learning disorder or Asperger's syndrome: A parent's guide.* Oakland, CA: New Harbinger Publications.

Wiley, L. H. (2001). *Asperger syndrome in the family: Redefining normal.* London: Jessica Kingsley Publishers.

Wing, L. (2001). *The autistic spectrum: A parent's guide to understanding and helping your child.* Berkeley, CA: Ulysses Press.

Attachment Disorders

Brazelton, T. B., & Sparrow, J. D. (2001). *Touchpoints three to six: Your child's emotional and behavioral development.* Cambridge, MA: Perseus Publishers.

Brisch, K. H. (1999). *Treating attachment disorders.* New York: Guilford Press.

Forehand, R., & Long, N. (2002). *Parenting the strong-willed child* (2nd ed.). Lincolnwood, IL: McGraw-Hill/Contemporary Books.

Jernberg, A. M., & Booth, P. B. (1998). *Theraplay: Helping parents and children build better relationships through attachment-based plan.* New York: John Wiley.

Attention Deficit Disorder and Learning Disabilities

Barkley, R. A. (1995). *Taking charge of ADHD.* New York: Guilford Press.

Barkley, R. A. (1997). *Defiant children: a clinician's manual for assessment and parent training.* (2nd ed.). New York: Guilford Press.

Brown, T. E. (2005). *Attention deficit disorder: The unfocused mind in children and adults.* San Antonio, TX: Harcourt.

Garber, S. W. (1997). *Beyond Ritalin: Facts about medication and other strategies for helping children, adolescents, and adults with attention deficit disorders.* New York: Harper Collins.

Hallowell, E. M., & Ratey, J. J. (1995). *Driven to distraction: Recognizing and coping with attention deficit disorder from childhood through adulthood.* New York: Simon & Schuster.

Attention Deficit Disorder

Levine, M. (1992). *All kinds of minds: A young student's book about learning abilities and learning disorders.* Cambridge, MA: Educators Publishing Service.

Levine, M. A. (2003). *One Mind at a Time: America's top learning expert shows how every child can succeed.* New York: Touchstone Books.

Rourke, B. P. (1989). *Nonverbal learning disabilities: The syndrom and the model.* New York: Guilford Press.

Silver, L. B. (1998). *The misunderstood child: Understanding and coping with your child's learning disabilities.* New York: Three Rivers Press.

Silver, L. B. (1999a). *Attention-deficit/hyperactivity disorder: A clinical guide to diagnosis and treatment for health and mental health professionals* (2nd ed.). Washington, DC: American Psychiatric Press.

Silver, L. B. (1999b). *Dr. Larry Silver's advice to parents on ADHD* (2nd ed.). New York: Times Books.

Sommers-Flanagan, R., & Sommers-Flanagan, J. (2002). *Problem child or quirky kid!* Minneapolis: Free Spirit Publishing.

Stein, D. B. (1999). *Ritalin is not the answer: A drug-free, practical program for children diagnosed with ADD or ADHD*. San Francisco: Jossey-Bass.

Thompson, S. (1997). *The source for nonverbal learning disorders*. East Moline, IL: LinguiSystems.

Whitney, R. V. (2002). *Bridging the gap: Raising a child with nonverbal learning disorder*. New York: Perigee.

Learning Theory

Zull, J. E. (2002). *The art of changing the brain*. Sterling, VA: Stylus Publishing.

Behavioral Management

Breen, M. J., & Altepeter, T. S. (1990). *Disruptive behavior disorders in children: Treatment-focused assessment*. New York: Plenum Press.

Carr, T. (2004). *131 Creative strategies for reaching children with anger problems*. Champaign, IL: Research Press.

Kazdin, A. E. (2005). *Parent management training: Treatment for oppositional, aggressive, and antisocial behavior in children and adolescents*. New York: Oxford University Press.

Linehan, M. M. (1993). *Skills training manual for treating borderline personality disorder*. New York: Guilford Press.

Waugh, L. D., & Sweitzer, L. (1999). *Tired of yelling: Teaching our children to resolve conflict*. Atlanta, GA: Longstreet.

Development in Children

Greenspan, S. I. (1992). *Infancy and early childhood: The practice of clinical assessment and intervention with emotional and developmental challenges*. Madison, CT: International Universities Press.

Greenspan, S. I. (1997). *Developmentally based psychotherapy*. Madison, CT: International Universities Press.

Greenspan, S. I., & Greenspan, N. T. (1989). *The essential partnership*. New York: Viking.

Greenspan, S. I., & Greenspan, N. T. (1994). *First feelings: Milestones in the emotional development of your baby and child*. Reprint. New York: Penguin USA.

Greenspan, S. I., & Wieder, S. (with R. Simons). (1998). *The child with special needs: Encouraging intellectual and emotional growth*. Cambridge, MA: Perseus.

Greenspan, S. I., DeGangi, G., & Wieder, S. (2001). The Functional Emotional Assessment Scale (FEAS) for infancy and early childhood. Bethesda, MD: Interdisciplinary Council on Developmental and Learning Disorders.

Healy, J. (1994). *Your child's growing mind*. New York: Doubleday.

Leach, P. (1997). *Your baby and child: From birth to age five*. New York: Knopf.

Moskewitz, M., Monk, C., Kaye, C., & Ellman, S. (Eds.). (1997). *The neurobiological and developmental basis for psychotherapeutic intervention*. Northvale, NJ: Jason Aronson.

Rolf, J., Masten, A. S., Cicchetti, D., Nuechterlein, K. H., & Weintraub, S. (1990). *Risk and protective factors in the development of psychopathology*. New York: Cambridge University Press.

Shure, M. (1994). *Raising a thinking child*. New York: Simon & Schuster.

Siegel, D. (1999). *The developing mind: How relationships and the brain interact to shape who we are*. New York: Guilford Press.

Siegel, D., & Hartzell, M. (2003). *Parenting from the inside out*. New York: Tarcher/Putnam.

Eating Disorders

Abraham, S., & Llewellyn-Jones, D. (2001). *Eating disorders: The facts*. New York: Oxford University Press.

Albers, S. (2003). *Eating mindfully: How to end mindless eating and enjoy a balanced relationship with food*. Oakland, CA: New Harbinger Publications.

Antonello, J. (2006). *Naturally thin kids: How to protect your kids from obesity and eating disorders for life.* Rochester, MN: Heartland Book Co.

Claude-Pierre, P. (1998). *The secret language of eating disorders: How you can understand and work to cure anorexia and bulimia.* New York: Random House.

Garner, D. M., & Garafinkel, P. E. (1997). *Handbook of treatment for eating disorders* (2nd ed.). New York: Guilford Press.

Goodman, L. J., & Villapiano, M. (2001). *Eating disorders: The journey to recovery workbook.* New York: Brunner-Routledge.

Irritability and Mood Problems

Carey, W. B., & McDevitt, S. C. (1995). *Coping with children's difficult temperament.* New York: Basic Books.

Chess, S., & Thomas, A. *Temperament: Theory and practice.* New York: Brunner/Mazel.

DeGangi, G. (2000). *Pediatric disorders of regulation in affect and behavior: A therapist's guide to assessment and treatment.* New York: Academic Press.

Eastman, M. (1994). *Taming the dragon in your child.* New York: John Wiley.

Edwards, C. D. (1999). *How to handle a hard-to-handle kid: A parent's guide to understanding and changing problem behaviors.* Minneapolis: Free Spirit Publishing.

Geller, B., & DelBello, M. P. (2003). *Bipolar disorder in childhood and early adolescence.* New York: Guilford Press.

Greene, R. W. (2001). *The explosive child: A new approach for understanding and parenting easily frustrated, chronically inflexible children* (2nd ed.). New York: HarperCollins.

Greenspan, S. I., & Glovinsky, I. (2002). *Bipolar patterns in children.* Bethesda, MD: Interdisciplinary Council on Developmental and Learning Disorders.

Greenspan, S. I., & Salmon, J. (1996). *The challenging child: Understanding, raising, and enjoying the five "difficult" types of children.* Cambridge, MA: Perseus Publishing.

Kahnstamm, G. A., Bates, J. E., & Rothbart, M. K. (Eds.). (1989). *Temperament in childhood.* New York: Wiley.

Klass, P., & Costello, E. (2003). *Quirky kids: Understanding and helping your child who doesn't fit in—when to worry and when not to worry.* New York: Ballantine Books.

Kurcinka, M. S. (1992). *Raising your spirited child: A guide for parents whose child is more intense, sensitive, perceptive, persistent, energetic.* Reprint. New York: Harper Perennial.

Miklowitz, D. J., & Goldstein, M. J. (1997). *Bipolar disorder: A family-focused treatment approach.* New York: Guilford Press.

Nowicki, S., Jr., & Duke, M. P. (1992). *Helping the child who doesn't fit in.* Atlanta: Peachtree.

Rapp, D. (1986). *The impossible child.* Tacoma, WA: Sciences Press.

Sears, W. (1985). *The fussy baby.* Franklin Park, IL: LeLeche League International.

Thomas, A., Chess, S., & Birch, H. G. (1969). *Temperament and behavior disorders in children.* New York: New York University Press.

Turecki, S. (with L. Tonner). (2000), *The difficult child* (2nd ed.). New York: Bantam.

Wachtel, E. F. (1994). *Treating troubled children and their families.* New York: Guilford Press.

Medication Management

Wilens, T. E. (2002). *Straight talk about psychiatric medications for kids.* New York: Guilford Press.

Meditation

Kabat-Zinn, J. (1990). *Full catastrophe living: Using the wisdom of your body and mind to face stress, pain, and illness.* New York: Delta.

Kabat-Zinn, J. (1994). *Wherever you go there you are: Mindfulness meditation in everyday life.* New York: Hyperion.

Sensory Integration Disorder

Ayres, A. J. (1979). *Sensory integration and the child*. Los Angeles: Western Psychological Services.

Biel, L., & Peske, N. (2005). *Raising a sensory smart child: the definitive handbook for helping your child with sensory integration issues*. New York: Penguin Books.

Bundy, A., Lane, S., & Murray, E. (2002). *Sensory integration theory and practice* (2nd ed.). Philadelphia: F. A. Davis.

DeGangi, G. (2000). *Pediatric disorders of regulation in affect and behavior: A therapist's guide to assessment and treatment*. New York: Academic Press.

Dunn, W. (1999). *Sensory profile*. San Antonio, TX: The Psychological Corporation.

Heller, S. (2003). *Too loud, too bright, too fast, too tight: What to do if you are sensory defensive in an overstimulating world*. New York: HarperCollins.

Kranowitz, C. S. (1998). *The out-of-sync child: Recognizing and coping with sensory integrative dysfunction*. New York: Perigee.

Kranowitz, C. S. (2003). *The out-of-sync child has fun*. New York: Perigee.

Miller, L. J., & Fuller, D. A. (2006). *Sensational kids: Hope and help for children with sensory processing disorder*. New York: Putnam.

Murray-Slutsky, C., & Paris, B. A. (2005). *Is it sensory or is it behavior?* San Antonio, TX: The Psychological Corporation.

Roley, S. S., Blanche, E. I., & Schaaf, R. C. (2001). *Sensory integration with diverse populations*. Austin, TX: Therapy Skill Builders.

Smith, K. A., & Gouze, K. R. *The sensory-sensitive child: Practical solutions for out-of-bounds behavior*. New York: HarperCollins.

Trott, M. (1993). *SenseAbilities: Understanding sensory integration*. Tucson, AZ: Therapy Skill Builders.

Wilbarger, P. & Wilbarger, J. (1991). *Sensory defensiveness in children aged 2–12*. Santa Barbara, CA: Avant: Educational Programs.

Williamson, G. G., & Anzalone, M. E. (2001). *Sensory integration and self-regulation in infants and toddlers: Helping very young children interact with their environment*. Washington, DC: Zero to Three.

Sleep Problems

Cuthbertson, J., & Schevill, S. (1985). *Helping your child sleep through the night*. New York: Doubleday.

Daws, D. (1989). *Through the night: Helping parents and sleepless infants*. London: Free Association Books.

Ferber, R. (2006). *Solve your child's sleep problems*. (Revised ed.). New York: Fireside Books.

Mindell, J., & Owens, J. (2005). *Take charge of your child's sleep: The all-in-one resource for solving sleep problems in kids and teens*. New York: HarperCollins.

Pantley, E. (2005). *The no-cry sleep solution for toddlers and preschoolers*. New York: Contemporary Books, McGraw-Hill.

Weissbluth, M. (2005). *Healthy sleep habits, happy child: A step-by-step program for a good night's sleep*. New York: Ballantine Books.

West, K., & Kenen, J. (2005). *Good night, sleep tight: the sleep lady's gentle guide to helping your child go to sleep, stay asleep, and wake up happy*. New York: CDS Books.

Appendix

Sensorimotor History Questionnaire

Georgia DeGangi, PhD, OTR, FAOTA
Lynn Balzer-Martin, PhD, OTR

Name of Child: _____

Gender: M _____ F

Date Completed: _____ Age:

Birthdate: _____

Completed by: _____

DIRECTIONS: The questionnaire may be administered by a parent, teacher, or therapist familiar with the child's functioning in the areas measured by this questionnaire. Sum the scores for each subscale, then enter the scores in the boxes at the bottom of this page. Children showing suspect performance in any one or more areas involving sensory processing or motor planning should be referred to an occupational therapist for further testing of sensory integration and motor skills. Children showing suspect performance in the general behaviors and emotional areas should be referred to a clinical psychologist or early intervention professional familiar with testing and treating in these areas.

SUBSCALE	NORMAL	AT-RISK
A. Self-regulation Activity level and attention	0–3	4+
B. Sensory processing of touch	0–3	4+
C. Sensory processing of movement		
Under-reactivity	0–3	4+
Over-reactivity	0	1+
D. Emotional maturity	0–3	4+
E. Motor maturity	0–3	4+

A. Self-Regulation (Activity Level and Attention)

Is your child:

1. Frequently irritable?	YES (1)	NO (0)
2. Frequently clingy?	YES (1)	NO (0)
3. Overly active and hard to calm down?	YES (1)	NO (0)

4. Overly excited by sights, sounds, etc   YES (1)   NO (0)

5. Frequently withdrawn and unresponsive?   YES (1)   NO (0)

6. Distracted by sights and sounds?   YES (1)   NO (0)

7. Able to pay attention and play with toys for a reasonable time span for his/her age?   YES (0)   NO (1)

8. Able to listen to and follow verbal directions?   YES (0)   NO (1)

9. Restless and fidgety during times when quiet concentration is required?   YES (1)   NO (0)

Total: _____

B. Sensory Processing of Touch

Does your child:

1. Enjoy being touched or held?   YES (0)   NO (1)

2. Dislike being bathed or having his hands, face, or hair washed?   YES (1)   NO (0)

3. Complain that other people "bump" into him?   YES (1)   NO (0)

4. Dislike textured food (chewy, crunchy) and avoid new food textures?   YES (1)   NO (0)

5. Prefer certain clothing and complain about tags in clothing or that some clothes are too tight or itchy?   YES (1)   NO (0)

6. Dislike being bare foot on grass or sand?   YES (1)   NO (0)

7. Frequently bump and push other children and may play too rough?   YES (1)   NO (0)

8. Prefer as little clothing as possible or prefer long sleeves and pants, even in warm weather?   YES (1)   NO (0)

9. Seem excessively ticklish   YES (1)   NO (0)

10. Over-react or under-react to physically painful experiences? (circle which one)   YES (1)   NO (0)

11. Tend to withdraw from a group or seem irritable in close quarters?   YES (1)   NO (0)

Total: _____

C. Sensory Processing of Movement

The first part of this section pertains to children who are under-reactive to movement stimulation, the second part to children who are very sensitive or intolerant of movement in space.

Does your child:

1. Like to swing very high and/or for long periods of time?   YES (1)   NO (0)

2. Prefer fast-moving carnival or playground rides, spinning equipment, not becoming dizzy or seem less dizzy than others?   YES (1)   NO (0)

3. Frequently ride on the merry-go-round where others run around to keep the platform turning?	YES (1)	NO (0)
4. Especially like movement experiences at home such as bouncing on furniture, using a rocking chair, or being turned in a swivel chair?	YES (1)	NO (0)
5. Enjoy getting into an upside-down position?	YES (1)	NO (0)
6. Like to initiate games where vision is occluded, such as putting a scarf over eyes, bag over head, or just keeping eyes closed for fun?	YES (0)	NO (1)

Total: _____

Does your child:

1. Tend to avoid swings or slides or use them with hesitation?	YES (1)	NO (0)
2. Seem afraid to let his feet leave the ground (getting up on a chair, jumping games) and prefer to be very close to the ground in play?	YES (1)	NO (0)
3. Fall down often and have difficulty with balance (like in stair climbing?)	YES (1)	NO (0)
4. Not like riding a see-saw or going up and down on an escalator?	YES (1)	NO (0)
5. Fearful of heights or climbing?	YES (1)	NO (0)
6. Enjoy movement which she/he initiates but not like to be moved by others, particularly if the movement is unexpected?	YES (1)	NO (0)
7. Dislike trying new movement activities or has difficulty learning them?	YES (1)	NO (0)
8. Tend to get motion sick in a car, airplane, or elevator?	YES (1)	NO (0)

Total: _____

D. Emotional Maturity

Does your child:

1. Play pretend games with dolls, cars, etc. with sequences or plots to the game (e.g. the doll gets up, gets dressed, eats breakfast)?	YES (0)	NO (1)
2. Engage you in games that he makes up or wants to play?	YES (0)	NO (1)
3. Seek you out for affection and play pretend games where he will take care of a doll?	YES (0)	NO (1)
4. Assert himself by asking others to give him things and expressing what he wants?	YES (0)	NO (1)

5. Play pretend games which involve assertiveness, exploration, or aggression (car races, soldiers fighting, or a trip to grandma's house)?	YES (0)	NO (1)
6. Understand rules such as to wait for you to say it is safe when crossing the street?	YES (0)	NO (1)
7. Understand that there are consequences to his behavior (if he behaves nicely, you are pleased; if he is naughty, he will be punished)?	YES (0)	NO (1)
8. Have difficulty getting over a temper tantrum (takes longer than 10 minutes)?	YES (1)	NO (0)
9. Have difficulty playing with his peers?	YES (1)	NO (0)
10. Ask "why" but isn't always interested in the answer?	YES (1)	NO (0)
11. Dislike changes in his routine and prefer things to stay the same everyday?	YES (1)	NO (0)
12. Seem unaware of dangers and take too many risks, often getting hurt?	YES (1)	NO (0)

Total: _____

E. Motor Maturity (Motor Planning and Coordination)

Does your child:

1. Change hands frequently, using neither his left nor right hand as a preferred hand for tasks such as eating, drawing, throwing a ball? (for children 5 and older)	YES (1)	NO (0)
2. Use two hands for tasks that require two hands such as holding down the paper while drawing, holding the cup while pouring?	YES (0)	NO (1)
3. Have difficulty getting dressed?	YES (1)	NO (0)
4. Need help in getting dressed?	YES (1)	NO (0)
5. Avoid trying new play activities and prefer to play games that he is confident at?	YES (1)	NO (0)
6. Have difficulty using his hands in manipulating toys and managing fasteners (stringing beads, buttons, snaps)?	YES (1)	NO (0)
7. Seem clumsy and bump into things easily?	YES (1)	NO (0)
8. Have trouble catching a ball with two hands?	YES (1)	NO (0)
9. Have difficulty with large muscle activities such as riding a tricycle, jumping on two feet?	YES (1)	NO (0)
10. Sit with a slouch or partly on and off the chair?	YES (1)	NO (0)
11. Have difficulty sitting still in a chair and seem to move very quickly (runs instead of walks)?	YES (1)	NO (0)

12. Feel "loose" or "floppy" when you lift him up or move his limbs to help him get dressed?   YES (1)   NO (0)

13. Have difficulty turning knobs or handles which require some pressure?   YES (1)   NO (0)

14. Have a loose grasp on objects such as a pencil, scissors or things that he is carrying?   YES (1)   NO (0)

15. Have a rather tight, tense grasp on objects?   YES (1)   NO (0)

16. Spontaneously engage in active physical games involving running, jumping, and use of large play equipment?   YES (0)   NO (1)

17. Spontaneously seek out activities requiring manipulation of small objects? (Legos, building blocks)?   YES (0)   NO (1)

18. Spontaneously choose to do activities involving use of "tools" such as crayons, markers, scissors?   YES (0)   NO (1)

19. Eat in a sloppy manner?   YES (1)   NO (0)

Total: _____

Index